STUDIES IN IMPERIALISM

general editor John M. MacKenzie

Established in the belief that imperialism as a cultural
phenomenon had as significant an effect on the dominant
as on the subordinate societies, Studies in Imperialism
seeks to develop the new socio-cultural approach which
has emerged through cross-disciplinary work on popular
culture, media studies, art history, the study of education
and religion, sports history and children's literature.
The cultural emphasis embraces studies of migration and
race, while the older political, and constitutional,
economic and military concerns will never be far away.
It will incorporate comparative work on European and
American empire-building, with the chronological focus
primarily, though not exclusively, on the nineteenth and
twentieth centuries, when these cultural exchanges were
most powerfully at work.

STUDIES IN IMPERIALISM

Propaganda and empire
The manipulation of British public opinion,
1880–1960   John M. MacKenzie

Imperialism and popular culture
ed. John M. MacKenzie

Ephemeral vistas
The Expositions Universelles, Great Exhibitions
and World's Fairs, 1851–1939   Paul Greenhalgh

'At duty's call'
A study in obsolete patriotism   W. J. Reader

Images of the army
The military in British art, 1815–1914   J. W. M. Hichberger

The empire of nature
Hunting, conservation and British imperialism
John M. MacKenzie

Imperial medicine and indigenous societies
ed. David Arnold

Imperialism and juvenile literature
ed. Jeffrey Richards

Asia in Western fiction
ed. Robin W. Winks, James R. Rush

Making imperial mentalities
Socialisation and British imperialism   ed. J. A. Mangan

Empire and sexuality
The British experience   Ronald Hyam

Imperialism and the natural world
ed. John M. MacKenzie

Emigrants and empire
British settlement in the dominions
between the wars   ed. Stephen Constantine

Revolution and empire
English politics and the American colonies
in the seventeenth century   Robert M. Bliss

Air power and colonial control
The Royal Air Force 1919–39   David E. Omissi

Acts of supremacy
The British Empire and the stage, 1790–1930
J. S. Bratton et al.

Policing the empire
Government, authority and control, 1830–1940
ed. David Anderson, David Killingray

Policing and decolonisation
Nationalism, politics and the police, 1917–65
ed. David Anderson, David Killingray

Popular imperialism and the military
1850–1950
ed. John M. MacKenzie

Policing and decolonisation

POLITICS, NATIONALISM AND THE POLICE, 1917–65

edited by

David M. Anderson
and David Killingray

MANCHESTER UNIVERSITY PRESS

Manchester and New York

Distributed exclusively in the USA and Canada
by ST. MARTIN'S PRESS

Published by MANCHESTER UNIVERSITY PRESS
OXFORD ROAD, MANCHESTER M13 9PL, UK
and ROOM 400, 175 FIFTH AVENUE, NEW YORK, NY 10010, USA

Distributed exclusively in the USA and Canada
by ST. MARTIN'S PRESS, INC.
175 FIFTH AVENUE, NEW YORK, NY 10010, USA

British Library Cataloguing-in-Publication Data
A catalogue record for this book is available from the British Library

Library of Congress Cataloging-in-Publication Data applied for

ISBN 0 7190 3033 1 *hardback*

Printed in Great Britain
by Bell & Bain Ltd, Glasgow

CONTENTS

MAPS AND TABLES

Maps

Tables

[vi]

CONTRIBUTORS

David M. Anderson, formerly of Birkbeck College, University of London, is now Senior Lecturer in History at the School of Oriental and African Studies, London. He is co-editor of the *Journal of African History* and has edited (with Richard Grove) *Conservation in Africa: people, policies and practice* (Cambridge, 1987) and (with Douglas Johnson) *The Ecology of Survival: case studies from northeast African history* (London, 1988). He is working on a history of crime, prosecution and punishment in British Africa.

David Arnold is Professor in the History of South Asia at the School of Oriental and African Studies, University of London. He is author of *Police Power and Colonial Rule: Madras, 1859–1947* (Delhi, 1986) and *Famine* (London, 1988) and editor of *Imperial Medicine and Indigenous Societies* (1988).

David Killingray is Reader in History at Goldsmiths' College, University of London. He is co-author (with Anthony Clayton) of *Khaki and Blue: military and police in British colonial Africa* (Athens, Ohio, 1989) and has edited (with Richard Rathbone) *Africa and the Second World War* (London, 1986). He is co-editor of *African Affairs* and working on a history of Africa during the First World War.

John McCracken is Senior Lecturer in History at Stirling University, and he has also taught in Africa at the University of Dar es Salaam and at Chancellor College, University of Malawi. He is author of *Politics and Christianity in Malawi, 1875–1940* (Cambridge, 1977) and a contributor to *The Cambridge History of Africa, Volume 7* (Cambridge, 1986). He is currently writing a new modern history of Malawi.

Richard Rathbone is Senior Lecturer in the Contemporary History of Africa at the School of Oriental and African Studies, University of London. He has edited (with Shula Marks) *Industrialisation and Social Change in South Africa* (London, 1982); *Africa and the Second World War* (with David Killingray, London, 1986), and (with John Dunn and Donal Cruise O'Brien) *Contemporary West African States* (second edition, Cambridge, 1989). His current research focuses upon the reception and operation of colonial law in the Gold Coast.

Charles Smith studied as an undergraduate at the University of Keele. His doctorate, on British counter-insurgency in Palestine, was completed in 1990 for Cambridge University, where he was a member of Jesus College. He now works as a media researcher.

CONTRIBUTORS

Anthony Stockwell is Reader in Imperial and Commonwealth History at Royal Holloway and Bedford New Colleges, University of London. Among his recent publications are a two-volume set of documents on decolonisation (with A. N. Porter), *British Imperial Policy and Decolonization, 1938–64* (London, 1987 and 1988). He is currently co-editor of the *Journal of Imperial and Commonwealth History*, and editing the Malayan volume in the British Documents on the End of Empire Project.

David Throup is Lecturer in Politics at the University of Keele. He has published *Economic and Social Origins of Mau Mau 1945–53* (London, Nairobi and Athens, Ohio, 1987), along with many articles on the colonial history of Kenya. He is now researching the African policies of the Kennedy administration in the USA.

Charles Townshend is Professor of Modern History at the University of Keele. He is the author of *The British Campaign in Ireland, 1919–21: the development of political and military policies* (Oxford, 1974); *Political violence in Ireland: government and resistance since 1848* (Oxford, 1983), and *Britain's Civil Wars: counterinsurgency in the twentieth century* (1986).

GENERAL EDITOR'S INTRODUCTION

'Law and order', the perennial cry of the politician, is far from being the elegant symbiosis it is often made out to be. From the point of view of the police it represents two very distinct functions, with drastically different implications for relations with their political masters on the one hand and the public on the other. In administering the law, the police's function is clearer and the chances of consent greater. In maintaining order, the police are likely to find themselves inhabiting a grey area between law and government policy. In the first, the police can more readily depict themselves as dealing with that which is evil in itself (like robbery or murder): in the second they are caught up in that which is evil because prohibited by state authority (aspects of labour disputes or political resistance).

These problems are acute enough in societies with elected governments. In colonial territories they are magnified by the alien and autocratic nature of the state. The character of policing in many territories of the British empire can be shown to follow a historical sequence involving three or more periods. The first is generally a time of intense coercion associated with the establishment of imperial authority when 'order' as defined by the new rulers is the prime objective. The second sees the building up of statute and case law, when police forces become more concerned with crime and with reflecting the differences between urban and rural provision (for example in the creation of native authority police in Africa). The third is characterised by a mounting breakdown in order, attendant upon the strains induced by economic crisis, war and the development of indigenous trade union and nationalist consciousness. This period can generally be divided up into a phase of adjustment and incipient insurrection, followed by reform, reorganisation and recruitment to meet the phase of open revolt.

This volume is primarily concerned with the third period (in both its phases), the breakdown in order associated with the transition from imperial to nationalist systems. Faced with renewed violence, police forces became more paramilitary in character, developed more centralised command systems, established special branches, and usually grew dramatically in size. They often had to negotiate a new relationship with the military, with metropolitan authorities more concerned with central appraisal and control, and with both international fears (alleged global communist conspiracy, for example) and highly localised circumstances. In coping with this complex of problems, they drew upon the personnel, practices and ideas of supposedly comparable revolts. The Irish, Palestinian and Malayan disturbances all contributed to the bank of more or less relevant experience drawn upon in the last years of imperial rule.

Although the literature on decolonisation is now vast, consideration of the vital role of the police in these processes has been notably absent. This volume goes a long way to remedy this defect of current historiography. A group of well-known scholars surveys the role of the police in the emergence of new states in Ireland, India, Palestine, Ghana, Malaya, Kenya, Nyasaland and Cyprus. This companion volume to the earlier *Policing the Empire* is an intriguing survey of similarities and differences in policing policy, offering insights into the role of the police in the new decolonised states as much as in the imperial system.

John M. MacKenzie

ACKNOWLEDGEMENTS

Most of the papers in this volume were initially prepared for a conference on the topic 'Policing the Empire', held at Birkbeck College, University of London in May 1988. Of the twenty-seven papers delivered at that conference, six are published here, along with a further two chapters by Townshend and Anderson, and nine others which are published in a companion volume, *Policing the Empire: Government, authority and control, 1830–1940*. The editors are grateful to all those who attended the conference and contributed their ideas and comments to the discussion. Particular thanks must go to those who chaired panels – David Arnold, Clive Emsley, John Lonsdale, Andrew Porter, Peter Robb, Jim Sturgis and Richard Rathbone – and to Ann Mylcs for invaluable secretarial and administrative assistance.

D.M.A.
D.K.

CHAPTER ONE

An orderly retreat? Policing the end of empire

David Killingray and David M. Anderson

Sometime not long after 3 p.m. on Saturday 20 February 1948, a procession of ex-servicemen and others sympathetic to their grievances advanced upon Christiansborg Castle, Accra, the seat of the governor of the Gold Coast. The marchers were halted by a police cordon on the road approaching the governor's residence, and were ordered to disperse. The crowd refused and stones and missiles were thrown. The police used tear gas, but the wind was in the wrong direction and this proved fruitless: a baton charge was out of the question as the police detachment was outflanked. The European officer in charge of the police detachment warned that his men would open fire, but according to the official report on the incident and its aftermath (the Watson Commission), his order appeared not to have been heard by the constables. The commanding officer then seized a rifle from one of his constables and fired six shots at the crowd.[1] Thus did Police Superintendent Imray write himself into the history of the decolonisation of Africa.

It is ironic that Imray should emerge as one of the very few policemen to be credited with a distinctive role in the history of British decolonisation. As nationalism enveloped the British in each colony, the colonialists struggled to secure their immediate and longer-term interests. Managing an orderly retreat from empire was, in almost every case, an essential part of the political strategy developed by the British. The role of the colonial police in this process was absolutely crucial. In the specific 'events' of decolonisation – such as Imray's actions at the crossroads below Christiansborg Castle – the police were placed in closer proximity to the forces of nationalist politics and anti-colonial protest than any other arm of government, while in the final arrangements for the transfer of powers, the transition of the police from their role as the principal agency of colonial control to becoming an institution at the service of a new independent government was the most sensitive and important of political issues. The colonial police were therefore a ubiquitous

[1]

presence in the story of decolonisation, yet so far they have played a strangely anonymous part in its retelling.

The essays in this volume examine the role and functions of the colonial police forces during the process of British decolonisation and the transfer of powers in eight colonial territories. State structures within the colonial empire varied, as did the nature and extent of the political challenge offered by emergent nationalisms and the timing of decolonisation. In some territories the transfer of powers was a relatively peaceful process: in others it was accompanied by long periods of opposition to colonial rule, by inter-communal conflicts, by rural and urban disorder, and by armed insurrection. But whatever the social or political circumstances of particular territories, the colonial police forces played a major and increasing role in the attempts to maintain the authority of the colonial state and in upholding law and order during the process of disengaging and transferring power to the new rulers. The maintenance of law and order was a vital element in the political economy of all colonial territories, and the nature, level and intensity of policing said much about official perceptions of political security and stability. When the legitimacy of colonial rule was barely questioned, policing was modest: as legitimacy was increasingly challenged and political instability grew, so the operational role and intensity of policing was extended.

In this process, colonial policing also changed from a local to a metropolitan concern: politicians and officials in London drew upon the experience of policing in one colony to inform the practice in another. Policing, security and the gathering of political intelligence became closely interwoven activities that were directed from London to an unprecedented extent. Despite all of this, much of it implicitly acknowledged in the many text books and surveys of decolonisation now available, historians have been slow to train their sights upon the police themselves.[2] These essays are amongst the first examples of historical research focused specifically upon the decisive part played by the police in the final days of British rule in the colonies of Africa, Asia and Europe.[3]

The cases gathered here each provide a detailed account of policing in a specific territory. They focus upon several related themes – the impact of nationalist politics, the difficulties of policing communal conflicts, the militarisation of police forces and their use in counter-insurgency measures, political intelligence-gathering and its uses, and the reform, development and shifting ideologies of policing: and they cover a chronological span of nearly half a century, from the First World War to the mid-1960s. Yet in only one of our cases, Ireland, did decolonisation take place before 1945: for the remaining cases the 1940s and the 1950s were the critical years. There are those who might question the

[2]

inclusion of Ireland as an example of the process of decolonisation, if for no other reason than its independence struggle took place in an earlier and quite different era. However, there can be no doubt, as Charles Townshend (chapter 2) emphasises, that the British adopted a 'colonial' solution to their problems in policing insurgency in Ireland.[4] Nor should there be any doubt as to the importance of the Irish example for later decolonisation. Both the methods of policing used in Ireland, and the personnel involved, spread their influence to other parts of the empire from the 1920s to the 1950s. For the military especially, as the recent study by Thomas Mockaitis has shown, Ireland marked the beginnings of a new learning curve in the handling of insurgency:[5] with regard to Emergency Powers, to military–civil relations in the organisation of counter-insurgency, and to the nature and extent of the problems confronting the police in a political situation of this sort, the Irish example has a pertinence for later colonial experience that is now glaringly apparent with hindsight, but that was also consciously drawn upon at the time. There are therefore powerful reasons for taking Ireland as the first benchmark in any discussion of the policing of decolonisation.

All our other cases – India, Palestine, Ghana, Malaya, Kenya, Malawi and Cyprus – are closely grouped chronologically, each gaining their independence from Britain over a period of less than twenty years after 1945. But here, India also stands somewhat apart from the rest. The decolonisation of South Asia was a protracted business, in which the various arms of government had considerable time to take stock of the changing political horizon after 1918. There may have been more time to prepare the ground, yet in the final phase, decolonisation was as rushed in India as anywhere else, and the problems that the acceleration of the political timetable for the transfer of powers brought for the Indian Police, described here by David Arnold (chapter 3), were not so very different from our other colonial examples. In India, as in Ghana and Malawi, the police had to deal with considerable unrest and disorder leading up to the transfer of powers, but not with armed nationalist insurgency. In Ireland, Palestine, Malaya, Kenya and Cyprus armed rebels led the assault upon the authority of the colonial state, and in these territories the impact upon the routines and functions of police duties were more profound. There were some broad similarities along with many specific differences from colony to colony in the experience of the police, but in all cases the process of decolonisation marked a distinct, novel and important phase in the evolution of policing. For all colonial police forces it was an unfamiliar and often uncomfortable experience, and one that bears careful analysis if we are to better understand the history of the end of empire.

[3]

Reaction and reform

Each colonial territory had its own police force. They varied greatly in size, structure and organisation. Many were very small while some, the Indian Police for example, were substantial bodies with an important role at central and provincial government level. Everywhere, as empire drew to a close, the police service was expanded. In India during the period 1938 to 1943 the police grew from just over 190,000 to 300,000, with an increasing proportion of the force carrying arms: in the Gold Coast from 1945 to 1956 police numbers increased from 2,500 to 5,360: over the same period in Nigeria central government police forces doubled in size to 10,500: and in Ireland the increased police presence after the Easter Rising of 1917 was described as 'an army of occupation'. Most forces were armed and performed an internal security role. Ultimate authority for the police lay in the hands of the executive, usually the governor himself. Colonial policing had initially developed in an *ad hoc* way, each colony cutting its coat from local cloth. From the later 1930s, in the wake of the Fisher Committee recommendations, a Colonial Police Service was established to co-ordinate and regulate policing throughout the dependent empire, and London took an increased role in dictating the methods and standards adopted in colonial policing and in monitoring the performance of individual police forces.[6]

Most colonial police forces were centrally organised and controlled. In some territories provincial police forces also existed, along with specialist police for railways, ports and customs, frontiers, mines and so on, but these also generally came under central control. Against this pattern there were the Native Authority Police Forces, found all over British Africa and also in Aden and Fiji. A product of the practice of indirect rule, these forces were established during the inter-war years mainly for the purpose of rural policing. With this development the policing of the countryside became the province of the native authorities and the local district administration. A similar system of local police under local control existed in India, although here it had much deeper historical roots.[7] 'Native' police forces varied greatly in size and effectiveness: too often they were little more than 'Chiefs' Messengers', the agents of an arbitrary 'traditional' rule. In general they were strongly disliked by the populations they policed.[8] In much of the empire, then, it was assumed that the 'professional' centrally-controlled Colonial Police and Indian Police took care of serious crime, security matters and the ordering of urban society, while locally-controlled 'native' police coped with the trivia of day-to-day affairs in the countryside. The army also had a role to play, and whether in Ireland, India, Palestine or Africa,

[4]

there existed an ill-concealed rivalry between the army and the police over questions of security. The army was reluctant to perform the civil duties of policing, while police officers increasingly saw their function as markedly different from that of soldiers. These tensions, first and perhaps most vividly exposed in Ireland, were especially evident when Emergency Powers and other special orders threw police and army into each other's arms in combined operations. The experience of Palestine in the 1930s and 1940s graphically demonstrates this point (Smith, chapter 4).

In all cases where nationalist politics challenged the authority of the colonial state, from India to Aden, colonial police forces invariably had an awkward dual role to perform: the police were expected to continue to perform their general civil duties, involving the prevention and detection of crime and the regulation of society through the enforcement of the law, yet they also took on an increased security function in dealing with unrest and insurrection prompted by anti-colonial politics. Most colonial police forces were already armed, but to meet these new challenges they were re-equipped and reorganised. Transport and communications systems were greatly improved, armoured vehicles – from water-cannon to gun-carriers – were put at the disposal of the police, and new units were created to perform 'special duties'. These units ranged from highly-trained riot squads and special operations teams to untrained men recruited for guard and escort duties. Among such units were the 'Black and Tans' in Ireland, the Police Mobile Force in Nyasaland, the General Service Unit in Kenya, the Mobile Police Reserve in Cyprus, and auxiliaries and Special Constables almost everywhere. At the same time the gathering of political intelligence became a central aspect of police work, and where the British were confronted by armed rebellion, police Special Branches often worked closely with military intelligence. Ireland here taught the British many lessons, some learned at considerable cost, that would be applied in the methods and organisation of intelligence gathering in later colonial emergencies. By the mid-1950s colonial intelligence-gathering, prompted by the Cold War and anxieties over communism, was becoming a more sophisticated operation (see Rathbone, chapter 5, and Stockwell, chapter 6).

The rapidly changing political conditions of the 1940s and 1950s, coupled with the emergence of metropolitan interests in creating a more efficient and modern police service in the colonies, placed colonial policing under the reforming gaze of London. In 1948 an Inspectorate General of Colonial Police was established within the Colonial Office, the first appointee being W. C. Johnson. He was served by a small office of police advisers who scrutinised details of policing from all parts of

[5]

the colonial empire. The office also drew upon the advice of the Home Office, frequently appointing senior officers from British constabularies to serve upon commissions of inquiry and appointment boards for the colonies.[9] This reflected a broad intention to inculcate in the colonial police services the methods and standards of policing in Britain.

The establishment of the Inspectorate resulted in the regular monitoring of police forces and their activities. Each colony had a tour of inspection from the Inspector General, or his deputy, at least once every three years, and Commissions of Inquiry were regularly appointed to investigate specific and often technical matters of police recruitment, training and performance. Colonial administrations did not always welcome the critical comments of Police Commissioners who took a dim view of the low priority sometimes given to expenditure on policing. Closer scrutiny of colonial police forces certainly revealed that many were weak, ill-organised and poorly funded, unsuited to effective civilian policing or to combat potential threats to internal security. Reports on the Jamaica Police for 1951, for example, revealed that the force lacked a proper headquarters, and that ill-disciplined policemen in each parish operated as independent units each with a different set of orders.[10] The weakness and unreliability of the police in British Guiana in 1953, according to a colonial official, 'was one of the main reasons why we had to send United Kingdom troops to the colony', and the police in Bathurst could not be relied upon in event of a riot because 'every policeman is bound to have some friends or relatives in any crowd causing trouble'.[11] The condition of the Cyprus Police in 1956 was particularly damned: it was by then confronted by the terrorism of EOKA, but for twenty years had

> been neglected, under-paid in gazetted as well as lower ranks, ill-equipped and subject to poor conditions of service; with the result that it had neither the confidence of the public nor proper pride of service; was found lacking in leadership, resolution and efficiency, and without material means to deal with the situation which faced it.[12]

In the same year the Aden Armed Police received similarly sharp criticism, especially with regard to the poor qualities of leadership in the senior ranks and the generally low morale of the force.[13]

Regular inspection by and accountability to senior representatives from the metropole shook up colonial police forces, removing officers unable or unwilling to change and those who had been content to preside over moribund bodies. This all increased central control and direction. Native Authority Police Forces in Africa were reorganised in the mid-1950s, being gradually incorporated into national police forces. But this development was a matter of controversy. It made perfect sense to police commanders as part of a progressive process of improvement and modernisation: to colonial field administrators it was more commonly deplored as a premature disruption of the local political order, removing the informed and politically sensitive role of the district administration from the policing domain. In London, the Colonial Office was cautious about rapid centralisation, as it was feared that centrally-controlled police forces were in danger of becoming more political than official as constitutional change proceeded: at the same time it was recognised that centrally-organised forces were essential for dealing with the array of tasks by then confronting the police.[14] For example, in the Gold Coast the Coussey Committee on constitutional reform had recommended in 1949 that the Native Authority Police Forces should be replaced by central forces, a view reaffirmed by an official report on the Gold Coast Police in 1952.[15] The major issues in Sierra Leone were the size and distribution of the police in the Protectorate, an area unpoliced yet subject to increased illicit diamond mining and smuggling, and also whether the police or the administration should have direct responsibility for the maintenance of law and order. Local standing committees in each district and province were suggested, similar to those established for the emergencies in Malaya, Kenya and Cyprus, a 'sort of combined authority jointly responsible for local action to secure peace and good order'. The unwillingness of the administration to sacrifice its sole jurisdiction effectively delayed the extension of police authority.[16] In Kenya the principle of extending centralised police authority had been accepted in 1943, but limited resources meant that its implementation was very slow (Throup, chapter 7). In Northern Rhodesia, by contrast, the Cartmel-Robinson report recommended against a change of this nature.[17]

By September 1956 a Colonial Office submission to the Secretary of State argued strongly that in Northern Rhodesia, but also in every other colony, the police force 'by virtue of its responsibility for law and order, under the government, should not be excluded from any part of the territory but should permeate the whole area'.[18] In these debates a developing notion of the professionalisation of policing was confronting an older – and by the 1950s less credible – set of values about the means and purpose of colonial rule. Paradoxical though it may seem, the colonial police were often more prepared for reform than were other colonial officials. Of course, this yen for 'progress' was fuelled by the knowledge that reform inevitably meant a greater role for an expanded and improved police service.

The professionalisation of colonial policing really took shape in the 1950s, but its origins can be traced back to the Irish disturbances between 1917 and 1921. Here were the beginnings of serious British reflection on the style and functioning of colonial policing, but of more immediate significance, here also were the beginnings of the learning process for the police themselves. When Ireland became independent as a Dominion in 1921, a steady stream of former officers of the Royal Irish Constabulary (RIC) moved into the Indian and Colonial Police forces. They were valued for their experience in the difficult circumstances of Ireland, for their training (which was usually of longer duration and higher quality than that available to ordinary recruits), and for their reputation for stern discipline. RIC men 'stiffened' the ranks of many colonial forces during the 1920s, but their most notable (although perhaps also notorious) contribution, as Charles Smith documents (chapter 4), was made in Palestine. With the independence of India and the relinquishing of the Palestine mandate in 1947–8, a second wave of 'migratory' police officers found their way from these territories to Malaya, Nyasaland and to West Africa, where Stockwell (chapter 6), McCracken (chapter 8) and Rathbone (chapter 5) note their contribution to counter-subversion and anti-terrorist operations.[19] By the mid-1950s, Police Commissioners in trouble spots like Kenya and Cyprus inevitably sought to recruit officers with experience of other colonial counter-insurgency operations (see Throup, chapter 7, and Anderson, chapter 9). It is not suggested that the same individual officers followed a chain of transfers from Ireland to Cyprus, but it is clear that individuals and ideas passed along the line on a significant scale. In this respect the movement of individual officers, even of junior rank, may have had more direct influence upon policing practice than any accumulated process of learning achieved by senior commanders and applied to colonial policing as a matter of policy.[20]

Alongside European officers with experience of counter-insurgency stood the rank and file of local recruits. In many parts of the empire, notably in India and in West Africa, patterns of recruitment to the police had favoured the supposed 'martial races', often from the more peripheral regions of the colony. The colonial policeman was seldom the familiar local who knew his beat well and who could use that knowledge to act with discretion, but was rather the feared alien, a man who could be relied upon to carry out the instructions of his colonial masters.[21] As the reforming zeal of the Inspector General began to take a grip in the 1950s, and attempts were made to improve the educational standards and training of the colonial police forces, patterns of recruitment began to change. The rise of nationalist politics also made senior police commanders more sensitive to the questions of ethnicity and who was policing whom. But in many colonies it was difficult to combine a regard for educational standards in recruits with the desire to broaden the base of recruitment.

Compromises had to be made as independence approached and the necessity for the rapid indigenisation of the higher ranks became more urgent.

Whatever the standards set for recruits, finding them in adequate numbers was no easy task. The image of the colonial police did not encourage people to join up. All too often, Inspector General Muller noted of British Guiana in 1953, police time was taken up with 'petty crimes ... which show the police to a large section of the community as interfering oppressors'.[22] As nationalist sentiment and rhetoric charged popular and communal feelings, the police were the easy butt of popular hostility, seen as agents of the colonial state and thus as opponents of local representation. In Cyprus (Anderson, chapter 9) and Malaya (Stockwell, chapter 6) especially, the origins and ethnic backgrounds of serving policemen came to determine the effectiveness with which they were able to carry out their duties, and set limits upon their reliability as agents of colonial control. Whether supervising traffic or controlling crowds at a political rally, once nationalist politics were in the air life for every locally-recruited colonial policeman became more complicated. Like others who served the colonial state, the police were caught in a predicament of loyalties. Local policemen were often socially and economically, as well as politically, vulnerable. They had the authority and power of their uniform, stigmatised though it might be, yet they commonly suffered from low pay, poor housing and a lack of social prestige. When anti-colonial politics confronted the police, sometimes deliberately victimising them to exploit their vulnerability, it is not surprising that police morale plummeted and that their efficiency declined. Throughout the process of decolonisation, the British had to make calculations as to how far local police could be trusted: where they could not, they resorted to the military, but in doing so the British were all too well aware that the legitimacy of colonial rule suffered irreparable damage.

Reform within the colonial police services, first conceived as necessary in the late 1930s and in the midst of implementation in the 1940s and early 1950s, was therefore seriously disrupted by the politics of nationalism. Paradoxically, yet hardly surprisingly, new political challenges worked to accelerate reform by bringing more resources to policing. But in these circumstances it was seldom possible to implement reforms as they had been intended. In Cyprus, for example, Governor Harding continued to express his desire to see a 'British model' of policing on the island when it was apparent that the Emergency had transformed his police into a quasi-military force, fundamentally unable to carry out the normal duties of civil policing (Anderson, chapter 9). Reform was therefore not always smoothly implemented, and the police forces which effected the transfer of powers were seldom in the condition that their own Police Commissioner or the Inspectorate General would have wished: in practice, reform was more often reactive than proactive. Nationalists accelerated the pace of political change and greatly fore-shortened the time-scale upon which the British were working: the police, along with every other arm of government, made compromises to cope with the new priorities. Ultimately, debates over the style or form of colonial policing became irrelevant. In the final phase of de-colonisation in Ireland between 1919 and 1921, in India and Palestine in the 1940s, and elsewhere in the 1950s and 1960s, the police were responding to events. In these circumstances, only rarely could the police determine their own role or retain all of the principles and standards which they had set for themselves.

Politics and nationalism

Decolonisation marked an uneasy political transition for the colonial police. Officers and constables who one month carried out the surveil-lance of nationalist leaders and anti-colonial protesters, in the next month found these same 'suspects' transformed into their paymasters and political overlords. It is therefore not difficult to appreciate why the history of policing in the transfer of powers remains a matter of some political sensitivity and one upon which documentary sources are still commonly withheld from public scrutiny.

The political dilemmas of reorganising policing in the midst of emergent nationalism was first exposed in relation to the handling of labour disputes. Labour unrest had always been seen as a challenge to the authority of the colonial state. The state was itself often the single largest employer of waged labour in a colony, and its interests (and revenues) were closely linked to the smooth functioning of the economy. As 'state servants', the Indian Police intervened to put down strikes and other forms of labour unrest on plantations and in the factories and docks, with increasing intensity from the 1920s onwards.[23] In the Caribbean a similar role was played out, and especially in the disturbances of the 1930s the police were placed in direct confrontation with organised labour in Trinidad and Jamaica, as well as on other islands.[24] In Africa, too, the strikes on the Copperbelt in 1935 had been violently suppressed by the police, and further confrontations occurred during rail and dockworkers' strikes in East and West Africa during the later 1930s and throughout the 1940s.[25]

By the 1940s it was common for trade union activists to also be in-volved in nationalist politics, and the line between the two was not always perceived by the police or by others in colonial authority. This was especially true as the atmosphere of the Cold War permeated the colonial world, and trade union actions were seen as an expression of radicalism that should be vigorously suppressed. In some instances, such as the shootings of striking miners at Enugu Colliery in Nigeria during 1949, the ineptitude of the colonial police in handling such matters was only matched by the ferocity of their actions.[26] On the Copperbelt the threat of radical unionism, involving both black and white workers, became a prime concern in the Colonial Office during the 1950s, prompting the expansion of the police force in Northern Rhodesia, the installation of improved police communications systems in the towns of the industrial zone, and a significant increase in the size and scope of Special Branch to monitor the activities of the unions and their leaders.[27] In other colonies, too, anxieties about the potential combustability of the blend of union with nationalist politics led to the redeployment of police resources to protect railways, mines, diamond workings and other economic enclaves,[28] and to the establishment of private security forces (some of which worked closely with the colonial police).[29] Once nationalist politicians held portfolios in interim governments, the resolution of labour disputes became treacherous terrain for police and politicians alike.

The rise of trade unionism presented many colonial police forces with their first taste of overtly political policing, at a time when, with the post-1945 expansion of the infrastructure and functions of the colonial state, the police had already been expected to assume a greater responsibility in the civil domain. But civil policing was very different from policing political disorder, and the police were soon confronted by an array of essentially political tasks for which they were poorly prepared. At a general level, the creation of the new institutions of self-government placed considerable tensions upon colonial police forces. Colonial governments wanted a stable transfer of power at both central and local levels. For the police this was difficult to achieve. It involved transforming police forces that were seen to be alien bodies serving the narrow political interests of the colonial regime, into bodies that would remain an effective arm of government but would become politically neutral. The speed with which this had to be accomplished was one problem – the structure of most colonial police forces another.

Most obviously, the prospect of the transfer of powers raised serious questions about operational and administrative control of the police. The India experience in the post-1919 dyarchy years, as described by Arnold (chapter 3), was that control of the police was kept subject to reserve powers and deliberately withheld from provincial ministers. But as independence loomed and the provincial governments assumed more responsibilities, this became more difficult to enforce: control of the police was, after all, an essential element in 'good government', and lack of control of the police placed any government in jeopardy. Elsewhere in the empire the political control of the police was generally withheld from local transitional governments with greater rigour than had operated in India. The political sensitivities here were evidently well understood by the British by the end of the 1940s, and perhaps the Indian experience provided lessons. In discussions in late 1949 on the draft constitution of the Gold Coast, Governor Charles Arden-Clarke commented that:

> defence cannot be divorced from internal security and one of the principal instruments in the maintenance of internal security is the police. There will be some opposition locally to the police being under an ex-officio member and not an elected minister but I regard it as essential that at this stage defence, internal security and police should remain in the Chief Secretary's portfolio.[30]

This position was reaffirmed in the pre-independence constitutions of many other colonies, often in the face of much opposition from nationalist leaders.[31] In Nigeria during the constitutional conference of 1953, it was agreed that full control of the police within each region would be vested in the Regional Commissioner solely responsible to regional governors and ultimately responsible to the Governor-General. The British purpose in doing this was to secure reserved powers and also to block any attempt to place the regional police under local political control.[32] Equally contentious was the organisation of the police in the Central African Federation. The Southern Rhodesian representatives argued for a nationalised police force, centrally directed from the new federal capital at Salisbury. The Colonial Office view, advanced by Sir Charles Jeffries, was for three decentralised forces but with unified standards to be maintained by a shared inspectorate – a policy endorsed by the Douglas Committee, which also kept the CIDs and Special Branches separate in each of the three territories.[33] McCracken's account of policing and decolonisation in Malawi (chapter 8) shows that this decision came to have great significance as the Federation broke up after 1959.

Protecting the integrity of the police force during the transfer of powers and also thereafter was a matter that greatly concerned British colonial officials. The immediate aim was to avoid the possibility of political interference by transitional governments. But could the impartiality of the police, itself a novel concept in the colonial context, be protected in the transfer of powers? In the many discussions of how to deal with this problem, the favoured solutions to emerge were that the governor should remain as the recognised police authority, or that a Police or

Public Service Commission be set up with safeguards written in to constitutional instruments. In August 1953 the Colonial Office issued a recommendation to all colonies that they set up separate Public Service Commissions, 'because a corrupt and complacent police force is the readiest instrument of tyranny, and the need to protect senior appointments from political influence is greater in the case of the police than any other public service'.[34] By early 1954 several colonies had already complied with this directive. However, the attempt to transform the colonial police into a politically neutral body that would be a loyal and impartial servant of the successor state had a poor base from which to build: more than ever in the transitional period, colonial police forces remained unequivocally the agents of the colonial state.

The impartiality of the police was also often compromised by ethnic patterns of recruitment that had created and maintained forces unrepresentative of the population they policed. Nationalism, especially its more radical kind, tended to accentuate these difficulties. Anderson (chapter 9) illustrates how the recruitment of Turkish Cypriot policemen to maintain public order against Greek Cypriot insurgents worsened the political situation confronting the British and ultimately compromised the constitutional settlement for the transfer of powers. In Kenya too, as Throup (chapter 7) shows us, the ethnic nature of the Mau Mau rising halted recruitment of Kikuyu into the police force during the Emergency, worsening an already uneven ethnic balance which could not be put right before independence despite efforts to change recruitment patterns. In Hong Kong, Fiji, Guiana, Malaya, and elsewhere also, the ethnic bias of police forces limited their utility and planted the seeds of unreliability within the very body that was charged with an increasing political security role. The lack of promotion of local recruits in many colonial forces added a further dimension to this problem. As the European officers of the Colonial Police were withdrawn at the transfer of power, police forces had to be 'indigenised', often at a much faster rate than had been planned or was thought wise given the demands of training and experience. To do this in a manner that reflected the ethnic composition of the wider population was a goal that could seldom be achieved.

The colonial police were therefore not well suited to dealing with political protest, least of all with nationalist politics with which many of their own local recruits undoubtedly sympathised. European officers, especially, were used to dealing with opposition to government with a firm hand, yet as the politics of decolonisation began to unfold a more cautious approach was called for: not all police found it easy to adapt. In Palestine, for example, British police and troops of all ranks displayed strong racial prejudice in their treatment of both Arab and Jewish populations (Smith, chapter 4). Racism was also certainly present among European Police Inspectors serving in Africa throughout the colonial period.[35] On the other hand, the close proximity of the police to the politics of opposition, the increased powers they were granted when crises erupted, and their importance to the political stability of the emergent independent states, all gave the police service enhanced political status and influence. To this extent, the transfer of powers itself empowered the police: this was a fact of which senior police officers and nationalist politicians were each well aware, and one that had some consequence in the former colonies after decolonisation was complete.

An orderly retreat?

How far, then, were the British successful in policing an orderly retreat from empire? To answer this we have to see colonial policing in relation to the wider concerns of British security and strategy after 1945. The final stages of Indian emancipation, the escalating violence in Palestine, the development of the Cold War, communist insurrection in Malaya and political unrest in the Gold Coast had all, by 1950, raised the cost of the security forces; this was at a time when Britain faced both a financial crisis and a military manpower shortage, and when colonies themselves were anxious to devote scarce revenue to economic development and social welfare schemes.[36] The increased cost of military and police for internal security exercised all colonial governments. Sir John Hall, governor of Uganda, stated in 1949 that 'the Defence contribution proposed [by the CO] is more than three-quarters of the cost of the civil administration of the country, while the total expenditure proposed on internal security, including Police, is nearly one-and-a-third times that cost. These proportions are quite inappropriate to the circumstances of Uganda.'[37] The Chief Secretary for Nigeria argued in 1956 that the Federation was seriously under-policed: excluding Native Authority Police, the Nigerian Police had a ratio to population of 1 : 3,300, whereas in the Gold Coast the ratio was 1 : 915. The Inspector General had recommended an expansion of the force, but the formidable costs of this had to be balanced against the needs of the Nigerian economic development programme.[38]

London was anxious that each colony should meet the costs of its own internal security and not make demands for imperial grants-in-aid, but when the political temperature overheated this proved to be beyond the meagre budgets at the disposal of most dependencies. Expenditure on the Cyprus Police, for example, climbed from £600,000 in 1954 to £1,600,000 in 1956, while in 1956 the impoverished government of Somaliland was compelled to seek a grant-in-aid of £56,151 to meet some 90 per cent of the costs of recommended improvements in the police force.[39] The percentage of revenue spent by each colony on the police force in 1952 ranged from nearly 11 per cent in Singapore to only 2 per cent in Sierra Leone, with most colonies spending between 4 and 8 per cent. For most colonies this percentage steadily climbed throughout the 1950s, and the financial demands made upon London increased dramatically,[40] most notably in the case of Nyasaland as a result of the crisis of 1959–60 (McCracken, chapter 8).

That money was found for internal security in the colonies was at least partly to do with British perceptions of the need to reorientate, expand and improve its intelligence services as the Cold War set in. At the same time as the Inspectorate of Colonial Police was established in 1948, separate desks were created in the Colonial Office to co-ordinate matters of defence, security and intelligence. Officials dealing with the police and with security and intelligence worked closely with those responsible for defence and legal affairs. Where advice was needed, the Home Office and MI5 were consulted. The requirements of Military Intelligence, and staff seconded directly from MI5, undoubtedly played a significant role in the setting-up and running of Special Branches in many colonies during the 1940s and 1950s. The details of this process, the activities of the individual officers involved, and the effectiveness of intelligence-gathering in general are matters which are difficult to gauge because relevant papers have either been destroyed or are still withheld from public scrutiny. The shafts of light which occasional surviving documents throw upon these matters are, however, highly illuminating, as Rathbone's analysis (chapter 5) of Special Branch intelligence reports on political activitists in the Gold Coast vividly demonstrates.[41] Many Special Branch officers were evidently obsessed with the supposed threat of communist activities and spent much of their time collecting information, often of a personal nature, on the interests, actions and contacts of nationalist politicians.

That the colonial state was busy watching such people there is no doubt: but it is difficult to know how efficient Special Branches were in gathering real intelligence and how much note was taken of such intelligence in political decision-making. Throup (chapter 7) suggests that officials in Kenya ignored the findings of Special Branch during the crucial period prior to the Mau Mau emergency, while Anderson (chapter 9) describes the slow 'rehabilitation' of the Special Branch in Cyprus after the EOKA terrorist campaign had effectively destroyed its ability to function. Even within the Colonial Office, officials disputed the efficiency of the Special Branches.[42] In a number of colonies during the mid-1940s Special Branches still only consisted of a few poorly-trained officers who assembled information that was readily available from public sources, more often than not concerning people and institutions that offered no conceivable threat to colonial order. Even as better training and clearer awareness of security needs improved the performance of Special Branch intelligence gathering, there were still serious short-comings: in Cyprus the Special Branch was hampered by the lack of reliable Greek-speaking officers, while in South East Asia plans to penetrate Chinese political organisations were set back by the shortage of Chinese-speaking officers (see Stockwell, chapter 6). Military Intelligence officers were undoubtedly frustrated by the failings of Special Branch in some colonies, not least in Cyprus, where security and intelligence matters had perhaps a higher importance for the British military than any other colony: yet the political and financial imperatives of keeping military involvement in the policing of colonial societies to a minimum, even where violent insurgency had erupted, dictated that the gathering of intelligence should remain essentially a police task.

The need for better intelligence-gathering was a major impetus behind London's efforts to foster closer liaison between the various colonial police forces in the 1950s, the Colonial Office being particularly concerned that all forces should know what was now expected of them. In April 1950 James Griffiths, as Secretary of State for the Colonies, suggested that there be a conference of senior colonial police officers 'to discuss the function and responsibilities of Police Forces in the Colonies in relation to normal police work, to 'cold war' conditions and in the event of a major war'.[43] The first such meeting was held at the Police College at Ryton-on-Dunsmore in April 1951. The agenda provides an indication of the concerns that exercised the Inspector General of Colonial Police and his staff of advisers. Senior representatives from sixteen colonies, including those from Malaya and the Gold Coast, were first addressed by Sir Percy Sillitoe and Mr G. D. White of the Security Services on Soviet subversion, the role of the British Communist Party, the functions of security liaison officers, and counter-subversion strategies. Riot procedures and the role of Native Authority Police Forces were then discussed. This preoccupation with security and intelligence matters also dominated the second conference three years later, in July 1954. Much emphasis was placed upon the experience gained from operations in Malaya and Kenya, with discussion of how the systems developed in those colonies could be adapted for use elsewhere: but there was also time given over to consider police organisation and the role of policemen as 'guardians of the peace' rather than merely enforcers of the law. By June 1957 the Commissioners assembled for the third conference were again focusing their attention upon security and riot control, but questions of constitutional safeguards for the police and the creation of Police Service Commissions were also then prominent on the agenda.[44]

In their day-to-day work, the police were profoundly affected by the increased emphasis given to matters of intelligence-gathering and internal security. Commissioners of Police were not always happy to see senior army officers and liaison officers from the colonial administration being given a direct role in the discussion of policing priorities. This was invariably the position once Emergency Powers had been declared by the governor, and the military were formally acting in aid of the civil power. Liaison between police and military had presented its problems in Ireland, and some of the same difficulties arose elsewhere. Whilst Emergency Powers gave the police greater freedom of action, any such measures inevitably meant that policing operations were being conducted in a hostile and therefore more difficult environment. Although Commissioners of Police enjoyed a higher political profile in these circumstances, their executive authority was to some extent watered down by the need to liaise with other arms of government more closely than before.

This was especially evident in the case of intelligence-gathering and the work of Special Branch. While Special Branch commanders held a rank below that of the Commissioner of Police, and were in theory directly responsible to the Commissioner, the structure of Intelligence Committees tended to cut Special Branch adrift from the main body of the police. In practice, Special Branch often became more directly accountable to the head of Intelligence for the colony or region – often a senior officer seconded from the Security Services in London (MI5) or from the army – than to the Commissioner of Police. In these circumstances, as Rathbone suggests (chapter 5), it was not always easy to know who was determining the actions of Special Branch, nor for what precise purpose particular actions were being conducted. The delicate matter of Special Branch accountability had to be handled with care in negotiating the constitutional position during the transfer of powers. It was in the interests of British security to maintain the maximum flow of information up to the latest possible moment during decolonisation. On the other hand, nationalist politicians were acutely aware of the importance of Special Branch and were keen to place it under their own direction at the earliest opportunity. The work of the intelligence community in the colonial world during the 1950s is certainly a topic deserving of further serious research.

The refinements of intelligence-gathering should not disguise the fact that the policing of decolonisation was frequently a violent business. There is some evidence – from Ireland, Cyprus, and Palestine especially (Smith, chapter 4) – that a significant rump of colonial police officers

[17]

relished the 'Emergency' conditions that political disturbances brought. The additional powers, the militarisation of policing, and the increased surveillance and oppression of suspect groups gave the police an enhanced authority that some individual officers exploited to the full and even abused. But there is also substantial evidence that many more officers loathed such conditions, considering that the crumbling of civil order was a mark of failure against the police and against colonial rule: some later expressed this as a sense of self-doubt and personal loss; others more prosaically reflected that the job had 'gone wrong'.[45] Whatever their views, few policemen could have enjoyed their position as the targets of anti-colonial demonstrations, assault and even assassination. At the command level, throughout the colonies and also in London, it is clear that senior police officers were exceedingly worried about the ability of ordinary policemen to cope with these pressures: the average colonial policeman was simply not trained to operate under Emergency Powers, the demands of which inevitably stretched the capacity of many officers and constables.

The colonial police were not well prepared for the role they were called upon to play in the final act of empire. Whilst many forces were in the midst of reforms when the cannon of political nationalism exploded in their faces, the reforms they were embarking upon were not those designed to cope with conditions of political dissent, disorder and insurrection. Nationalism challenged the expectations of the police and substantially changed their remit. In seeking to keep order in the retreat from empire, British colonial officials were only partially successful. As one colony followed another along the road to decolonisation, the British accumulated experience in how to handle emergent nationalism and how to organise the police for that purpose, and were thereby better able to contain the forces that confronted them. But in the final analysis it is perhaps surprising to note how little of what was learned from each example of decolonisation could be directly applied to the next. Certainly, some basic principles were established for the police by the mid-1950s, especially in regard to their operations under Emergency Powers, yet it is evident that the wheel had to be redesigned – if not reinvented – to meet the differing institutional, political, strategic, economic or ethnic conditions confronting the police in each colony.

The essays collected here indicate the extent to which the policing of decolonisation was a common colonial experience: they also emphasise the extent to which it turned upon the fulcrum of local factors. In the eight cases which follow we hope that the veil of anonymity that has shrouded the colonial police may be removed, to reveal their central role in the histories of the end of an empire and the birth of new independent nations.

Notes

1 *Report of the Commission of Enquiry into Disturbances in the Gold Coast 1948* (Watson Commission), Colonial No. 231.
2 The literature on decolonisation is expanding remarkably with the availability of archive materials for the 1950s, and now the early 1960s. For the most important recent general studies, see R. F. Holland, *European Decolonization 1918–81: an introductory survey* (London, 1985); J. D. Hargreaves, *Decolonization in Africa* (Harlow, 1988); J. Darwin, *The End of the British Empire: the historical debate* (Oxford, 1991); and A. N. Porter and A. J. Stockwell, *British Imperial Policy and Decolonization 1938–64, Volume 1, 1938–51* (London, 1987), *Volume 2, 1951–61* (London, 1989), which, although a collection of documents, includes a very fine and stimulating set of introductory essays.
3 But see D. Arnold, *Police Power and Colonial Rule: Madras, 1859–1947* (Delhi, 1986); D. Arnold, 'The armed police and colonial rule in South India, 1914–47', *Modern Asian Studies*, II (1977), pp. 101–25; J. McCracken, 'Coercion and control in Nyasaland: aspects of the history of a colonial police force', *Journal of African History*, 27 (1986), pp. 127–47; and D. Killingray, 'The maintenance of law and order in British colonial Africa', *African Affairs*, 85 (1986), pp. 411–37. For fuller comments on the literature available on the history of colonial policing, see our companion collection, David M. Anderson and David Killingray (eds.), *Policing the Empire: government, authority and control, 1830–1940* (Manchester, 1991), especially the introduction.
4 See also Charles Townshend, *The British Campaign in Ireland, 1919–21: the development of political and military policies* (London, 1975)
5 Thomas R. Mockaitis, *British Counterinsurgency, 1919–60* (London, 1990). See also, Charles Townshend, *Britain's Civil Wars: counterinsurgency in the twentieth century* (London, 1986), and Julian Paget, *Counter-Insurgency Campaigning* (London, 1967).
6 Sir Charles Jeffries, *The Colonial Police* (London, 1952) remains the only general history for this period.
7 Peter Robb, 'The ordering of rural India: the policing of nineteenth-century Bengal and Bihar', in Anderson and Killingray, *Policing the Empire*, ch. 8.
8 Killingray, 'Maintenance of law and order', pp. 416–19. Little has been written on Native Authority police; see Walter Rodney, 'Policing the countryside in colonial Tangayika', Proceedings of Annual Social Sciences Conference of the East African University, 1973, and E. O. Rotimi, 'A history of Native Administration police forces in Nigeria, 1900–1970', Ph.D. thesis, University of Ife, 1990. For developments elsewhere in Africa in the 1950s see 'Native Authority police forces – Northern Rhodesia, 1954–6', PRO CO 1037/28, and 'Reorganization Somali Police Force, 1955–6', PRO CO 1037/32.
9 Jeffries, *Colonial Police*, ch. 6. For the organisation and personnel of the Police Department at its inauguration, see *The Colonial Office List, 1948* (London, 1949).
10 *Report of the Commission of Enquiry into the Jamaica Police Force* (Kingston, 1951), PRO CO 1031/106. See also, W. A. Muller, Inspector General Colonial Police, 'Report on Jamaica Police Force', January 1953, PRO CO 1031/107.
11 Minute by N. L. Mayle, 25 January 1955, on Inspector General Colonial Police Report on British Guiana Police Force, PRO CO 1031/103; and R. J. Vile, 'Minutes concerning Police Forces in West Africa', 16–22 March 1955, PRO CO 1037/45.
12 Minute by K. P. Witney, 8 May 1956, on Report of Cyprus Police Commission, PRO CO 1037/10. For the report itself, see PRO CO 1037/11, and for a fuller analysis, see Anderson, chapter 9 below.
13 See papers in the following files, all dealing with the Aden Police Force for 1956: PRO CO 1037/22, CO 1037/23, CO 1037/24 and CO 1037/27.
14 *Record of the Conference of Colonial Commissioners of Police at the Police College, Ryton-on-Dunsmore, April 1951.* Conclusion No. 2. Printed Misc. no. 517, PRO CO 855/119.
15 *Report to His Excellency the Governor by the Committee on Constitutional Reform 1949, Gold Coast* (Coussey Committee), para. 173 (London, 1949); *Statement of the Gold Coast Government on the Report upon the Gold Coast Police by Col. A. E. Young* (Accra, 1952).

16 MacDonald (Chief Secretary, Sierra Leone) to R. S. Vile, 22 April 1955, secret, PRO CO 1037/50; 'Organisation of Police Force in Sierra Leone, April 1955–July 1956', PRO CO 1037/49; *The Introduction of Police Forces into the Protectorate*, Sessional Paper no. 4 of 1954, Sierra Leone (Freetown, 1954).

17 'Policing rural areas in Northern Rhodesia, 1954–7', secret, PRO CO 1037/28.

18 Colonial Office submission to the Secretary of State, 'Northern Rhodesia. Police and organisation of intelligence in rural areas', September 1956, PRO CO 1037/28.

19 See also McCracken, 'Coercion and control', pp. 138, 140, for Palestine recruits to Nyasaland.

20 This observation is made by Mockaitis, *British Counterinsurgency*, pp. 180–9.

21 Anderson and Killingray, *Policing and Empire*, introduction.

22 W. A. Muller, Inspector General of Colonial Police, 'Report on British Guiana Police Force', 24 March 1953, PRO CO 1031/103.

23 Raj Chandavarkar, 'Labour disputes and the police in Bombay', paper to the conference on 'Policing the Empire', London, May 1988.

24 *Report of the West Indies Royal Commission (Moyne Report), December 1939*, Cmd. 6607 (London, 1945).

25 *Report of the Commission Appointed to Enquire into Disturbances on the Copperbelt, Northern Rhodesia, 1934–35*, Cmd. 5009 (1935); Frederick Cooper, *On the African Waterfront: urban disorder and the transformation of work in colonial Mombasa* (New Haven and London, 1987), esp. pp. 247–73.

26 Agwu Akpala, 'The background of the Enugu Colliery shooting incident in 1949'. *Journal of the Historical Society of Nigeria*, 3 (1965), pp. 335–64.

27 Minute by D. Williams, 'Security in Northern Rhodesia', 14 December 1951, PRO CO 968/273; Anthony Clayton and David Killingray, *Khaki and Blue: military and police in British colonial Africa* (Athens, Ohio, 1989), p. 54.

28 For example, the 36-strong Nyasaland Railway Watch-ward Force, ex-KAR men enrolled as Special Constables in 1954. 'Nyasaland Police Force', PRO CO 1037/30.

29 The Sierra Leone Selection Trust Ltd. formed a Diamond Protection Force in 1935: by 1950 it numbered eighty-five men, by 1957 662, in addition to Auxiliary Police paid for by the company. See Peter Greenhalgh, *West African Diamonds 1919–83: an economic history* (Manchester, 1985), pp. 171–2.

30 Arden-Clarke, quoted by Gorsuch to Wheeler, secret, 10 January 1950. PRO CO 96/821/6 and DEFE 7/422.

31 'Constitutional developments in Gold Coast and Nigeria', Memo. by Secretary for Cabinet, Secret, 13 May 1953, PRO PREM 11/1367.

32 *Report by the Conference on the Nigerian Constitution, July–August 1953*, Cmd. 8934, p. 8, PRO PREM 11/1367; 'Nigerian Police Force: establishment and strength, 1956', PRO CO 1037/48; T. N. Tamuno, *The Police in Modern Nigeria* (Ibadan, 1970), ch. 6.

33 Minute by Sir Charles Jeffries, 18 December 1952, on 'Functions of the Federal Police Service, Central African Federation, 1952–53', PRO CO 1015/224; *Southern Rhodesia, Northern Rhodesia and Nyasaland. Draft Federal Scheme: Report of the Civil Service Preparatory Commission*, Cmd. 8673 (1952).

34 Colonial Office Circular Despatch, August 1953, 'Police Service Commission, Nigeria 1956–7', PRO CO 1037/9. See also *Record of the Third Conference of Police Commissioners, Ryton-on-Dunsmore, June 1957*: Constitutional Questions, Appendix vi, 'Constitutional safeguards for the police', PRO CO 885/133.

35 See, for example, David M. Anderson, 'Policing the settler state: colonial hegemony in Kenya, 1900–52', in Dagmar Engels and Shula Marks (eds.), *Contesting Colonial Hegemony: state and society in Africa and Asia, 1858 until independence* (in press).

36 A special meeting of ministers (Prime Minister, Foreign Secretary, Treasury, Defence, Colonial Office and War Office), 10 December 1948, agreed that colonial governments should be expected to bear the costs of maintaining internal security. This only changed when military forces were called upon to assume a major role in internal security, especially where emergency powers were declared. 'African Forces Conference, 1949', PRO PREM 8/1340.

37 Hall to Creech Jones, 17 September 1949, and 'Colonial Office Annex I & II to African Colonies', from Creech Jones, 20 August 1949, PRO DEFE 10/1.
38 'Nigerian Police Force: establishment and strength, 1956', memo. by Chief Secretary, Nigeria, secret, 14 September 1956, PRO CO 1037/48.
39 'Report of the Cyprus Police Commission, 1956', PRO CO 1037/10; 'Reorganisation of Somali Police Force', Treasury to Colonial Office, 24 April 1956, PRO CO 1037/32.
40 The figures for colonial police forces in 1952 are to be found in PRO CO 1037/49.
41 See, for example, 'Coordination of the report of the Inspector General of Colonial Police, 31 December 1951: intelligence and security', PRO CO 968/278; also, 'Political intelligence reports: West Africa, 1949–', PRO CO 537/4728.
42 Minutes by R. J. Vile, concerning police forces in West Africa, 16–22 March 1955, and minutes by Stourton, 16 March 1955, both in PRO CO 1037/45.
43 *Record of the Conference of Colonial Commissioners of Police at the Police College, Ryton-on-Dunsmore, April 1951.* Printed Misc. no. 517, PRO CO 885/119.
44 For records of the second and third conferences, see PRO CO 885/124 and PRO CO 885/133, respectively.
45 See the reminiscences of former colonial police held in the Oxford Development Records Project, Rhodes House, Oxford, and surveyed in Clayton and Killingray, *Khaki and Blue*, Part 1.

B

CHAPTER TWO

Policing insurgency in Ireland, 1914–23

Charles Townshend

> Live with the people or be torn to pieces.
> Maria Edgeworth

The end of British rule

Between 1911, when the third Home Rule Bill entered the political arena, and 1923, when the irreconcilable Irish Republican Army (IRA) gave up their open fight against the Irish Free State, Britain conceded the political independence of Ireland. Whether this 'Irish revolution' was as much illusory as real is an issue which vexes modern scholars.[1] Put in simple terms, the exercise of political power was transferred from London to Dublin and Belfast. British administration, influenced but uncontrolled by Irish representation at Westminster, was replaced by representative government. How far this outcome differed from the notion of 'Home Rule' adopted by Gladstone in the 1880s was impossible to say, since Home Rule had always been a fatally vague conception. In the view of the signatories of the Anglo-Irish Treaty in December 1921, it was a marked advance on the old proposal – an advance desired by the Irish and resisted by the British. In the view of the anti-Treaty republicans, 'Dominion status' was no improvement on Home Rule, since both compromised Irish independence by requiring loyalty to the British crown.

This conflict of views remains a matter of life and death in Ireland today. There is plainly no resolution of it; all that can be said is that the concessions wrested from the British government by Sinn Féin between 1916 and 1921 were wrested by force. The degree of force was insignificant alongside the global war of 1914–18, but was high by British domestic standards. The government tried to ride it out for several years, in part because of an abstract repudiation of political violence, but in greater part because of a concrete dislike of Sinn Féin's demands.

Sinn Féin began as a movement of non-violent civil resistance aiming to secure a dual monarchy on the Hungarian model, and ended as a guerrilla movement fighting for the independent republic which it declared in January 1919. The evolution of its peculiarly effective mixture of politics and violence was fairly slow, beginning with the unionist reaction to the third Home Rule Bill. The Ulster Volunteer Force (UVF) inspired its nationalist counterpart in the Irish Volunteers, much of which was under the control of the old revolutionary organisation the Irish Republican Brotherhood (IRB). Even before 1916, when the IRB staged its dramatic insurrection, the Irish Volunteers were often called 'Sinn Féin Volunteers', and the osmotic process quickened when the Sinn Féin organisation was enlarged after the rising.[2] Its organisational culmination came with the threat of conscription in spring 1918, which drove even the parliamentarians into withdrawal from Westminster, and brought mainstream nationalists into a broad alignment with Sinn Féin.

When Sinn Féin swept the nationalist constituencies in the general election of 1918 it was able to place the government in an acute dilemma. Up to this point, Britain had assumed that a measure of Home Rule would secure Irish consent and delegitimise 'extremist' violence. From now on, the attempt to distinguish between moderates and extremists became much more difficult, and ultimately impossible. Government was thrown back on the use of force to secure a 'return to constitutionalism' and, more desperately still, the 'restoration of order'. This application of force was the final test of the political will and the administrative capacity of the British regime in Ireland. In practice, this meant the final test of the Irish police.

Government policy in this crisis was extraordinarily ill-defined. Ian Macpherson, Chief Secretary for Ireland in 1919, was at a loss to understand it. Lloyd George's coalition was plainly divided over Ireland, and before the arrival of Hamar Greenwood as Chief Secretary in March 1920 the main influence on the shaping of policy was probably Walter Long, who chaired the Cabinet Irish Situation Committee. Long had a traditional Tory view of the Irish, a sort of orientalism in geographical reverse, and though he had the capacity to formulate the problem clearly – earlier than most, in December 1918, he recognised 'It is a fair and square fight between the Irish Government and Sinn Féin as to who is going to govern the country'[3] – he was not effective in formulating concrete measures beyond the fourth Home Rule Bill, which became the Government of Ireland Act in December 1920.

Nationality and policing

Policing, as has often been remarked, is a function of consensus. The capacity of a police force to operate successfully within a legal system constructed around principles such as *habeas corpus* and trial by jury is dependent on the free co-operation of the general public, as informants, witnesses, or jurors. In other words, the police are a sensitive barometer of the political climate, registering in their success or failure the relative cohesion of the social and ideological order. They are perhaps the most effective yet vulnerable arm of the modern state; almost magically effective when giving force to dominant assumptions, bafflingly ineffective when acting against the grain. The study of public attitudes should, of course, be a constant preoccupation of democratic governments, though these are often, paradoxically, more careless and mechanical in their methods than are so-called 'police states'. In any case, the measurement of ideological climates is a dauntingly complex process, so that even if the simple assertions with which this paragraph opened were the whole truth, the assessment of policing would still present formidable difficulties.

In fact, the social function of police forces is considerably more complicated. Policing is dependent on public co-operation, but it also requires appropriate techniques, organisations, strengths, and legal powers. Many of these technical dimensions are, at least indirectly, aspects of the general public culture, but they can only be evaluated or understood in special terms. 'Appropriateness', or lack of it, in these dimensions is often easier to discern after the event than before, a hazard to which policing is more spectacularly vulnerable than any other executive branch of government. Evidently, however, it has proved possible for well-organised police forces, in certain circumstances, to exercise credible police functions in the face of substantial popular indifference, or even disaffection or hostility. Insurgency, or systematic political violence, imposes the severest strain on any police force, but it cannot be a foregone conclusion that an insurgent movement, once established, will undermine and overcome the civil police, or necessarily force it into a militarisation that will subvert its normal function.

In what circumstances is a successful police response to insurgency possible? This question may usefully be raised in the case of Ireland during 'The last days of Dublin Castle', a period which in retrospect can be clearly perceived as a crucial (if incomplete) instance of decolonisation. At the outset this was not so clear. In Ireland, the special problem of colonial police forces confronted with systematic resistance conducted by fellow-nationals against the imperial power did not initially exist in any straightforward form. In 1914 the main police force in Ireland, the

[24]

Royal Irish Constabulary (RIC), was, as it had been in the previous political generation, the instrument of a government committed to 'Home Rule' or national autonomy for Ireland. As in 1886, it was opposed at least as violently by loyalists intend on maintaining British rule as by nationalists intent on terminating it. Home Rule itself was seen as a solution which would somehow reconcile Irish national identity with the British imperial framework. It was the policy endorsed by the vast majority of the Irish public through the Nationalist Party in Parliament. There was no necessary disharmony between such constitutional nationalism and the English notion of 'law and order' which was the *raison d'être* of the RIC. Quite the contrary: constitutionalism had become synonymous with the English way in politics. Mainstream nationalism would underpin, rather than threaten, social order and ideological cohesion.[4]

This fairytale ending was to be rudely chewed up and spat out by less moderate Irish nationalists over the decade between 1911 and 1921. The ideological reconstruction was under way by 1913, when the Irish Volunteer organisation was founded under the aegis of the revived Irish Republican Brotherhood, but few people, whether unionist or nationalist, could have perceived this. The impact of total war forced the pace, and the police found themselves – without appearing to move – steadily becoming more anti-national and thus exposed to increasing nationalist assault. At first this assault was psychological, but eventually it was physical. Sustained denunciation of 'British spies', 'the eyes and ears of Dublin Castle', 'the army of occupation', 'England's Janissaries' was supplemented in 1918 by a social and economic boycott, and in 1919–20 by guerrilla attacks targeting individual policemen, patrols and barracks.

This challenge certainly confronted the RIC with a conflict of loyalties. The force was overwhelmingly 'Irish', in both the generalised sense which even unionists were happy to recognise, and the particular sense ('Gaelic', i.e. Catholic) focused upon by the cultural nationalist movement since the turn of the century. The Sinn Féin/IRA insurgents were fellow-nationals, and their charges of treason against British Crown state servants carried some weight with public opinion. How far they did so within the RIC is harder to judge. Many, if not most, RIC men refused to see their livelihood as unpatriotic. It can, at least, be plausibly argued that the police survived this crisis of loyalty, and that there was no substantial collapse either of morale or of recruitment before 1921. Against the subversive propaganda of the republicans, the RIC largely preserved its professional self-image as a civic institution.[5]

The subsequent fate of the Palestine police raises a somewhat different and rather interesting question, namely whether the government assumed (with or without evidence) that the crisis of loyalty would be too much for the Irish police, and acted accordingly. The decision to recruit outside Ireland after 1919, and the tacking-on of 'Black and Tan' components, could certainly be interpreted in this way. The authorities, in fact, chose to terminate the ethnic homogeneity of the RIC and introduce a 'stiffening' element which implied that the reliability of the main body of the force was on a par with other colonial police forces. In this case, however, the error seems to have stemmed not from ethnic devaluation of the Irish constable, but from more abstract notions about the respective roles of police and military forces in the maintenance of order. As will be seen, militarisation of the police was accepted as a necessary price for the avoidance of overt military rule.

The failure of the Irish police

Although it is possible to be impressed by the resilience of the RIC, and to see its survival (more or less intact) as being, in the circumstances, no mean achievement, there can be no doubt that the record of the force in the twentieth century was one of failure. The RIC failed to enforce the law, it failed to preserve the peace or to guarantee the security of life and property, and it failed to secure the information needed to prevent the growth of subversive organisations; ultimately, in a kind of synthesis of all these failures, it failed to hold Ireland for Britain. This last, transcendent task was never formally stated, but was universally understood. It was, no doubt, understood in somewhat different ways by those of different political persuasions: for unionists, 'holding Ireland' meant defeating Irish nationalism by force if necessary; for liberals, it meant preserving the arena of peaceful constitutional debate for a moderate Home Rule settlement. From whatever perspective, the task amounted to representing the British state and maintaining its legitimacy. Though much of the basis of this legitimacy lay outside the RIC's control, the police themselves formed a crucial segment of it.

How to hold Ireland therefore resolved itself into a question of policing style, which was fundamentally a projection of political aims. The task of the RIC by 1914 had become a kind of palimpsest, with the accretions of successive instructions from former administrations still partly visible amidst the present set. The welter of duties and powers laid out in the *Irish Constable's Guide* compiled by the Inspector General at the end of the nineteenth century provided a vivid illustration of this formless growth. To say that the policeman's lot was a confusing one would hardly be adequate, since at root it was contradictory. The origins of the constabulary as a semi-military force designed as a primary defence against insurrection were only too plainly visible in its twentieth-century successor. The military (its critics said pseudo-military) ambience of police training and organisation, most unmistakably the carrying of service rifles (accompanied by a rather modest course of weapon training) and the concentration of the force in special posts (called barracks), set evident limits to its capacity to evolve into a 'normal' civil police on the English model.[6] The experience of several generations of agrarian terrorism had added a further twist in the detachment of police from the community – the system of preventing constables from serving in their native counties in order to minimise the intimidation of their families. All of this 'semi-militarism' was still required by the unionist version of how to hold Ireland. By contrast, the liberal version plainly required 'normalisation'. Yet any shift of emphasis towards the detection of crime – of which there was, by general consent, remarkably little in Ireland – would have involved the wholesale reconstruction (and probably substantial diminution) of the constabulary. Sporadic moves in this direction were indeed made: recruitment was practically suspended during the Chief Secretaryships of Gerald Balfour and George Wyndham; some of the more egregiously useless military accoutrements, such as the officer's sabre, were abolished. Still the carbine remained, slung heavily round the broad caped shoulder of the local Peeler as he marched off to make enquiries about crop yields or compile a housing register.

Inappropriateness of role and nature must thus be considered as a possible explanation for the cumulative failure of the police. Technical incompetence, still more often cited by critics, had its effect largely within limits that were set from outside the force. Numerical weakness was usually in the same category, as, perhaps most important of all, was the suitability or otherwise of available legal powers. Analysis of successive crises of policing, which will be attempted in the following pages, needs to keep these explanatory elements in broad political focus.

The Ulster crisis

The Liberal government's attempt to legislate Irish devolution between 1911 and 1914 triggered a severe political crisis. The threat of armed resistance by Ulster Unionists, as it developed in 1912–13, never looked like being contained by the police. The abject failure to prevent large-scale gun-runnings in the following year exceeded any in the force's history, and undoubtedly left an enduring impression of weakness and demoralisation. Despite a decade and more of neglect and financial parsimony, however, there is little evidence that the RIC was too weak, physically, to carry out its functions. A verdict of incompetence was certainly returned by General Nevil Macready, who might, if the crisis had developed further, have become military governor of Belfast with authority over both troops and police.[7] Macready's jaundiced retrospective judgement is probably accurate as a general assessment, though its conventional lament for the (perhaps imaginary) lost glories of the Victorian Force is not wholly convincing. What is particularly relevant is that his strictures fell mainly on the failure of nerve which he observed at the higher levels of command. This must have been in part the result of the long subjugation of the RIC to the dead hand of bureaucracy and the enervating exaltation of seniority.

But the paralysing dilemma of Deputy Inspector General T. J. Smith in 1914 was in much greater part produced by the attitude of government. The most significant decision of the Liberal administration, from the Irish policing standpoint, was a negative one: the decision to allow the Arms Act to lapse in 1906, taken against the advice of the Inspector General of the RIC and almost all the Irish Resident Magistrates. As the major crisis came on in 1913, the government law officers laboured vainly to demonstrate that importation of arms for seditious purposes remained illegal, as did military drilling (then becoming a craze with the Ulster Volunteer Force) whether or not approved by a pair of sympathetic magistrates.[8] The RIC believed itself powerless to interfere with the UVF or the Irish Volunteers, and though Macready might attribute this to pusillanimity, the unfortunate affair of Assistant Commissioner Harrel of the Dublin Metropolitan Police (DMP) in July 1914 surely demonstrated that the police view was quite rational.

Harrel called out troops to support his attempt to seize the rifles landed at Howth by the Irish Volunteers. His operation was in itself undoubtedly a failure, since he was cheated of the guns, and the thwarted soldiers marching back into the city became involved in a lethal affray with civilian assailants in Bachelor's Walk. What counted for his fellow policemen, however, was not Harrel's failure, from which operational lessons could have been learnt, but the reaction of the government. Harrel was summarily suspended from duty, and he eventually quit the force. The mild Chief Secretary was visibly enraged by the rude eruption of police stupidity into a tense political scene. The government took a complacent view of the crisis, believing that threats or predictions of civil war were greatly exaggerated. The merits of the case have never been conclusively decided. Harrel and his superior, Sir John Ross of Bladensburg, believed that his action had been authorised by the Castle; the Under-Secretary (perhaps understandably) maintained that he had not been consulted. Ross took the commonsensical view that, whether or not technically authorised, Harrel's action was abundantly justified – indeed demanded – by the facts of the case: 'a body of more than 1,000 men armed with rifles marching on Dublin ... constitute an unlawful assembly of a peculiarly audacious character.'[9] He concluded that the government's reaction could only be taken as showing that illegal activity was to be tolerated for political reasons, and when he could not get Harrel restored to service, he himself resigned. A (recently retired) senior officer of the RIC remarked without much exaggeration that the outcome of this incident 'thoroughly disheartened every police official in Ireland.'[10]

The Easter rebellion

The RIC's reputation was less bruised by the 1916 rebellion than it had been by the less substantial Fenian rising of 1867. In fact, it emerged from Easter week with some credit, though it is not altogether easy to see why. The principal reason was of course that the outbreak was concentrated in Dublin, outside the RIC's bailiwick. There the rebel activity was so intense that the unarmed Dublin Metropolitan Police could play no part, and full-scale military action was immediately presumed to be the only possible recourse. In the provinces, rebel activity was sporadic and for the most part ineffective. The outstanding exception, the action of Thomas Ashe and Richard Mulcahy in Co. Dublin, produced a prophetic disaster for the RIC, when County Inspector Gray and seven of his men were killed, and fifteen wounded, in the attempted relief of Ashbourne barrack. Inexperienced as the rebel leaders were, their instinctive guerrilla skills demonstrated the futility of the RIC's traditional military training. Had more Irish Volunteer companies tried the same thing, it is most likely that the RIC would have faced a catastrophe. For the sake of this ineffectuality, one is driven to reflect, the capacity of the force to evolve into a normal police service had been almost irretrievably compromised.

Probably the last chance of radical alteration or 'normalisation' came in 1916. Some changes were made. The failure of police intelligence to monitor the rebel preparations was disturbing, and at least as damaging was the failure to provide accurate lists for the mass arrests carried out by General Maxwell and the army in the week after the rising. The charming and intelligent, but easy-going Inspector General, Sir Neville Chamberlain, was the first to go in expiation of these failures. He was also practically the last. His successor, General Joseph Byrne, once installed, came out on the side of conservatism. Though he plainly recognised the need to regenerate the intelligence service, he had no special expertise in this area. The recommendations of the Home Office specialist who reviewed Irish intelligence in late 1916 were thwarted by a combination of Treasury parsimony and military suspicion. For instance, the £30 required to provide the Crimes Special Branch with a simple card index system was withheld until the RIC could produce an equivalent saving in cash elsewhere; Byrne's urgent call for widespread provision of telephones in RIC stations remained, astoundingly, unanswered for two years.[11] The notion of a single intelligence co-ordinator was unattractive to the army because it implied dependence on the police.

Overall, the reform of the police under Byrne was cosmetic. In 1917 he testified to the National Convention that there was no need for radical change: the semi-military organisation and role of the RIC would be maintained. And, on the whole, it can be said that through 1917 and 1918 the old system continued to work. Discontent with pay and conditions was by all accounts widespread, but never crystallised into anything like the English police strikes of 1918–19. Recruitment did not wholly meet wastage, but resignations did not pose any serious problem. Except in a few disaffected areas, the boycott promoted by republicans had not yet seriously undermined relations between the force and the community. However, the price of this inertia was to be paid in 1919, when local Irish Volunteer groups reconstituted themselves as the Irish Republican Army after the Declaration of Independence by Dáil Éireann, and began military operations against the police. In the circumstances it was all but inevitable that the government would push the semi-military police into an increasingly military role. General Byrne's conservatism had its last outing against Lord French's decision to reinforce the RIC with British army veterans, and it fell at the first fence.

Guerrilla insurgency: the first phase

The shift from psychological to physical assault on the RIC was quite sudden and fairly shocking. Through 1918 the Irish executive under a new Viceroy, Lord French, had taken the initiative against 'unconstitutional' opposition. The whole Sinn Féin movement, which was committed to a policy of abstention from Westminster politics, was targeted by French, though he was unable to overcome British scruples about the banning of political parties or the imposition of military government. His attempts to streamline decision-making in the Castle were also hobbled.[12] Nonetheless an energetic pursuit of 'extremists' was initiated with the 'German plot' arrests of May 1918, and through the summer a sequence of Special Military Areas were designated under the provisions of the 1887 Crimes Act. Military aid to the civil power facilitated tight controls on movement, imposition of curfews, closure of fairs and markets as collective punishments in disturbed districts, and so on. A system of passport controls, unprecedented within the United Kingdom, was instituted. The Irish Volunteers were rebuilding their local organisation, and confined their response to occasional raids for arms. Most of the energy of the Sinn Féin movement went into political activity. The end of the world war brought major changes.

The powers wielded under the Defence of the Realm Act (DORA) did not immediately lapse, but were exercised much more cautiously. Passport controls, in particular, were abandoned. The general election produced an overwhelming Sinn Féin victory which was shortly followed by the unilateral declaration of independence by the newly-constituted Dáil Éireann on 21 January 1919.

On the same day, the first lethal attack on RIC men was carried out by the IRA in Tipperary. From the republican point of view, this double event transformed the situation irrevocably into one of war, but for several months the insurgents' organisational capacity lagged behind their intentions. The government continued to take an ambivalent view of the threat posed by Sinn Féin, even after the violent rescue of Sean Hogan at Knocklong in May and the daylight assassination of an RIC officer in Thurles in June. Not until September did the intensification of IRA activity trigger a substantive political response, when Dáil Éireann and Sinn Féin were banned. Still, no new special powers were provided, and the RIC were already being forced onto the defensive. County by county, through the early autumn, police barracks were fortified and small posts withdrawn. The process of concentration accelerated through the winter as IRA activity intensified. The constabulary was nearly 1,000 men under its nominal strength of 10,166 and had been hopelessly overstretched in its old distribution across 1,332 barracks and 'huts'.

This concentration, inevitably as it seemed, had far-reaching and irreversible implications for the policing of Ireland. Up to this point, in spite of the long-standing problems caused by its semi-military nature, in spite of its worsening record of detection and prosecution, and in spite of the nationalist boycott, the RIC had preserved the grudging recognition which its sheer ubiquity had secured for it throughout the country. The delicate fabric of legitimacy still sustained it. But ubiquity was the key: when it was removed, the fabric disintegrated. When, eventually, the IRA burned out nearly 300 abandoned police posts to celebrate Easter week 1920 (altogether 424 were burned), they merely set the seal on a transaction that was already complete. The authority of the state extended only as far as the carbines of the police patrols and the rifles of the military raiding parties which were steadily replacing them. When, in 1920, the police carbines were at last replaced by service rifles, this means of lengthening the arm of the law was symptomatic of the progress of policing in Ireland.

Militarisation was the adaptive response indicated, if not dictated, by the RIC's nature. Normal policing was an experiment that was unlikely to be risked when the physical destruction of the police was an apparent aim of the insurgent movement. This is not to say that a decision to militarise the police was ever taken at any level either of government

[31]

or of the police administration. Rather the contrary: the process was a sequence of minor provisions intended to preserve the viability or the mere survival of the force in the teeth of violent opposition. The aim was simply to keep the RIC in the field. The whole drift of the government's assessment of the Sinn Féin challenge was to play down or disguise the element of open military hostility in the guerrilla campaign. Those, like Lord French, who had identified the situation as early as 1918 as one of 'veiled insurrection', and who drew alarming comparisons with the situation in South Africa in 1900–2, were politely (or not so politely) ignored. Probably the most characteristic statement of the government view was provided by Winston Churchill in September 1920: 'I can see no reason why, with patience and firmness, we may not wear the trouble down in the course of a few years and secure the re-establishment of order together with the acceptance by the Irish people of the responsibilities of their own internal government.'[13] Even at the time it was composed, this view must have looked a trifle sanguine. In retrospect its deluded complacency is little short of astonishing.

It was this kind of reasoning that underlay the stiffening of the RIC to make it capable of wearing down the republicans. It is no coincidence that the man chosen to direct the process was Churchill's nominee, Major-General Hugh Tudor. Tudor's arrival in Ireland in May 1920 was the culminating point of the incremental decision that began with Walter Long's suggestion to Lord French in May 1919 'to employ some discharged soldiers in the RIC'.[14] Whilst this suggestion was not quite unprecedented in the RIC's history, since an auxiliary force of over 400 ex-soldiers had been enrolled during the Land War of the 1880s, the Inspector General was alert to its destabilising implications.

Byrne's position was, however, rapidly eroding in 1919. He was engaged in a year-long tussle with the military authorities over the correct deployment of troops to aid the police: French convicted him of 'giving umbrage' to the commander-in-chief. Most critically, he was disenchanted with French's belief in the desirability (and feasibility) of the wholesale suppression of Sinn Féin. The viceroy attacked Byrne's 'spirit of inertia', accusing him of being at worst 'personally hostile to the efforts which have been made' to restore order, or at best defeatist: 'he views with a feeling of despair any drastic action which the Government may have decided to take against what – in his own words – he calls "the clear will of the people".'[15] French studiously refrained from alluding to the fact that Byrne was a Catholic, but it is unlikely that this played no part in his diagnosis. Byrne's most formidable supporter, Warren Fisher, identified him as one of the few 'in high places in Ireland ... who realised the full implications of "proclaiming", that is proscribing in its entirety, a political creed'.[16]

When Byrne resisted the idea of recruiting non-Irish ex-soldiers into the RIC, Shaw proposed a special auxiliary force of five battalions to be furnished by the army but paid and commanded by the police. Byrne responded by pointing out that police discipline, whose sanctions depended on the overriding importance of pension rights to the long-term career constable, would be powerless to control temporary recruits, especially of this kind. Over the next month the pressure against Byrne mounted, and on 10 November 1919 French ordered him to 'have some rest' from the strain of his arduous duties, and take a month's leave. Byrne took the leave but refused to take the hint, and had no intention of resigning. He returned a month later to find that his deputy had effectively taken over, and that on 11 November an order had been issued by the Constabulary Office authorising the recruitment of non-Irishmen into the RIC.

The elbowing out of General Byrne might have seemed of little moment at the time. The inability of his deputy, T. J. Smith, to increase his stature (Byrne was never, technically, replaced as Inspector General), followed by the appointment of a new police chief, produced more obviously momentous changes. In the spring of 1920, Dublin Castle was given a facelift by the importation of a handful of picked officials from Whitehall. Part of this selective transformation was the provision of a Police Adviser to the Irish executive. This turned out to be a man with no police experience, but plenty of combat expertise from the western front. Major-General H. M. Tudor saw his task as strengthening the RIC in every possible way, and 'backing up' all police actions, even those of dubious legality. This task was justified by the widespread fear that the morale of the force was on the point of final collapse, a fear which looks to have been exaggerated.[17] Organisation was tightened up, the hidebound County Inspectorate being grouped (as it had once been in the nineteenth century) under Divisional Commissioners.

Strengthening could only mean, in the circumstances, acceleration of external recruitment and of militarisation, in the shape of rifles and machine gun, motor transport and armoured vehicles. Tudor countered the bureaucratic paralysis of the county Inspectorate by recreating the superordinate rank of Divisional Commissioner: the new Divisions, all but inevitably in the circumstances, were placed – as one Dublin Castle official put it – under 'disbanded military officers who carried the life and death attitude of the fighting man of the 1914–18 war into the day-to-day relations of the police with the civil population'.[18] Tudor fostered the spread of the 'Black and Tans' (so called because the speed of expansion outran traditional rifle-green uniform supplies, which had to be supplemented with military khaki) across the regular RIC, bringing the strength of the force up from under 10,000 to nearly 13,000 by the end of 1920. Most distinctively, he created a separate Auxiliary Division conceived as a spearhead anti-guerrilla force. The triumphs and disasters of the 'Auxies' may stand as an epigraph for the British policing of Ireland.

The crisis of British law

The Auxiliary Division was formed with unusual speed. Tudor told the Cabinet on 23 July that he had obtained 500 ex-officers to serve as 'Temporary Cadets', and the new body was formed on the 27th. Five companies of about 100 each became operational in August, under the administrative (but not operational) command of Brigadier Frank Crozier. Recruits received a short police training course in Dublin before being despatched to work under the direction of the RIC Divisional Commissioners. Each company was fully mobile, independently quartered, and intended to work in co-operation with the army. But at no level was a set of tasks or roles defined; the Auxies were left to work out their own salvation (and that of the union) by trial and error. In practice they often operated quite independently, and the results of placing such a powerful force in conditions of daily frustration, and provocation, without the restraint of military discipline, was on occasion to be explosive.

The Auxiliaries arrived in Ireland at a time when profound changes were occurring in the balance between the state and its opponents. During the late winter and spring of 1920 the implications of the police retreat had been concealed, first by the more extensive use of military forces, and second by the conciliatory atmosphere created by the Castle reforms. The new Chief Secretary reined back the Crown Forces and sought a moderate majority to support the fourth Home Rule Bill, due to become law in December. Sinn Féin hunger-strikers were released. Optimism prevailed until the absence of convictions, indeed the near-absence of cases, at the summer Assizes revealed the full extent of police ineffectiveness. Greenwood suddenly hustled the Cabinet into accepting a tough special powers law, the Restoration of Order in Ireland Act, which was rammed through parliament at breakneck speed in the first week of August. Creating many new offences triable by court martial, this was patently a war measure modelled on DORA, and the government was still most reluctant to countenance it 'in time of peace'. But it proved that peace had ended, even if war had not been declared ('You do not declare war on rebels,' as Lloyd George scolded French), and it foreshadowed a sequence of emergency powers acts under various names which would create, in various territories, forms of 'statutory martial law'.[19]

The illusion of civil authority was preserved, but such functions as the police could exercise were from then on dependent on military power.

Relations between the forces were never very cordial, despite repeated efforts to improve them. A barely-concealed military contempt for the police underlay General Macready's refusal of the joint command in March 1920, when he became C-in-C Ireland, and resurfaced at frequent intervals thereafter. Yet for all their failings, the police remained vital to the military counter-insurgency campaign, especially in the service of intelligence. Despite the battering to which the DMP and RIC special branches were subjected by the IRA intelligence organisation under Michael Collins, the police still constituted a formidable information network. The army was not yet in a position to build up its own, and the appointment alongside Tudor of a new police intelligence co-ordinator, Colonel Ormonde Winter, could have led to a dramatic regeneration of the service and an early shift in the military balance. Winter's personal idiosyncracies may have played a major part in the ensuing failure, but the outcome was a spectacular setback at the hands of the IRA on 'Bloody Sunday', 21 November 1920. Several undercover intelligence officers were among the twelve men assassinated in their beds that morning.[20]

Bloody Sunday was a dramatic juncture in the underground intelligence struggle, but its sanguinary drama was compounded by the action of the Auxiliary company that sallied forth from Dublin Castle that afternoon to conduct a search of Croke Park Football stadium for IRA suspects. The 'Croke Park Massacre', widely seen as a reprisal for the morning's assassinations, threw into sharp relief another dimension of the intelligence question. 'Reprisals' of one kind or another, sometimes admitted, sometimes denied by the authorities, had been occurring since at latest the Cork No 1 Brigade IRA's attack at Fermoy in September 1919.[21] As the label indicates, they largely went in tandem with the pace of the IRA campaign: the bigger the rebel attacks, and the more elusive the rebel forces became, the more provoked and frustrated were the targets/pursuers. The reprisal that first shocked British public awareness was carried out by RIC in Balbriggan, Co. Dublin, after the assassination of a Head Constable on 20 September. Several unidentified police broke into, looted and burned four public houses, killed two alleged Sinn Féiners, and burned or damaged fifty other buildings. Next day, in Co. Clare, an ambush at Rineen in which police casualties had allegedly been mutilated by the IRA was avenged by the destruction of twenty-six buildings in nearby towns and the killing of four people.

This intensification of police violence brought down on the government's head the wrath of the press, and even that of the hawkish Chief of the Imperial General Staff), Sir Henry Wilson, who professed himself 'horrified' that the police had 'marked down certain SFs as in their opinion the actual murderers or instigators and then coolly went and shot them without question or trial'. Revealingly, Wilson found that

Churchill 'saw very little harm in this'.[22] Greenwood refused to accept that the violence had been cold-blooded, and insisted that the 'extreme tension of feeling which now prevails among all ranks' of the RIC required 'very delicate and sympathetic handling'. What this meant became clear as the sequence of reprisals went on later in the year. Men who 'saw red' when their comrades were killed in 'cowardly' attacks would inevitably break the (frail) bonds of discipline and strike out, since the public would not assist them in pursuing and identifying the attackers. Because these circumstances were brought about by the rebels and their sympathisers, not by the police, the police could not be held responsible for their own violence. Underlying this posture of enlightened tolerance was a darker notion that police violence, however distasteful, might be the quickest – perhaps the only – means of neutralising IRA terrorism.[23]

This is not to say that a full-blown campaign of counter-terrorism was planned or even countenanced. As with earlier steps in the militarisation process, the government reacted to piecemeal developments. Republican allegations of deliberate and systematic reprisals are hard to sustain, though the police provided ample evidence to make them effective propaganda. What occurred was, however, quite as bad from a liberal point of view. The confession that only official lawlessness could deal with insurgent violence was itself immensely damaging, and was founded on a diagnosis of Irish resistance as being the work of a small 'murder gang' intimidating the moderate majority. Even if the diagnosis were correct, the policy was a fearsomely double-edged weapon requiring considerable skill in use.

What actually happened is by no means easy to determine. There was extensive contemporary agreement that by the late autumn of 1920 the RIC was incapable of exercising any normal law enforcement functions. The Dublin Castle law adviser, William Wylie, told the Cabinet in late July that in his opinion the RIC would soon be little better than a mob: the policeman now 'either saw white or he saw red'. Early in August a military intelligence officer observed that: 'Anyone passing by a police barrack with its locked doors and seeing the constables looking out through barred windows will at once realize that no body of men could preserve its morale under such conditions.'[24] By September Macready was persistently critical, not only of spectacular manifestations of police indiscipline such as reprisals, but also of a day-to-day laxness and casual brutality (the incompetence shown, for instance, at Dillons Cross, Macroom, or Castleconnell, or the accidental shooting of a mother and child in Galway). Altogether such criticisms amount to formidable evidence of general breakdown, and several modern writers have echoed or even amplified this verdict.

Yet there is some evidence that, overall, the regular RIC (including its 'Black and Tan' component) held together unexpectedly well, and that control was gradually tightened up during the winter of 1920–1.[25] The Auxiliary Division's performance remained patchy, but incidents like Castleconnell, albeit indicative of a dangerous instability, were isolated. While military complaints about the independence of the RIC went on, during the spring of 1921 the police played a substantial part in the more generally successful operations of the Crown Forces. In this sense they more or less met the brief set out for them by the political authorities in the previous summer.

The survival of the RIC was not, however, enough to give the British state the capacity to shape a political settlement on its own terms. The terms of the Truce and the Anglo-Irish Treaty negotiated between July and December 1921 did not appear to any contemporaries as amounting to a British success. In 1922 Britain withdrew its administration and army from the twenty-six counties and handed over authority to the Provisional Government of the Irish Free State. Yet it is precisely the capacity of the British state to project its central political values into the public culture of its successor which has impressed recent Irish historians. Policing provides a perfect instance of this transmission process. The RIC ceased to exist – more completely, indeed, than the Dublin Castle bureaucracy or the Irish judiciary. Yet it was strikingly reincarnated, Phoenix-like, in the Civic Guard (Garda Siochana) created by the Free State. The precise details of the process remain obscure: the only substantial history of the new force did not discover any evidence of the policy discussions which produced the Civic Guard Bill introduced in Dáil Éireann by Kevin O'Higgins in 1923, and copies of the report of the organising committee have not survived.[26] What is quite clear is that the new force was in essentials a direct replica of the RIC. Conor Brady has suggested that a major reason for this was the 'intense admiration' of Michael Collins for 'the efficiency and tenacity' of the RIC; and also that 'since none of his immediate advisors had any experience of any different policing systems, it was natural that the construction of the new Civic Guard should be heavily influenced by the model of its predecessor'.[27] This combination of positive and negative factors is plausible.

It is still not easy to discern the reasoning behind the most remarkable and significant departure from the RIC model, the decision taken in 1923 that the Garda Siochana should be unarmed. It seems that on this crucial issue the power of the 'real' British model transcended that of its Irish variant. There was evidently some dissension on the matter – hardly surprising in the midst of civil war – and the standard pattern of RIC weapons training was continued in the first year of the new force's life.[28] But the strong lawyerly sense of civil supremacy derived from the

[37]

British system by Cosgrave and O'Higgins, and indeed reinforced rather than diminished by the Free State's battle against the 'militarist' IRA, prepared the way for the eventual decision.

By contrast, in Northern Ireland the RIC apparently survived intact, with only a slight shift of nomenclature. Yet the 'Ulster' constabulary was different in spirit from its predecessor. Even without its new appendages of 'A' and 'B' Specials, which were in effect a unionist militia, the Royal Ulster Constabulary rapidly became a Protestant police of 'a Protestant state for a Protestant people'. From the start it was thus inescapably political, and its armament, like the special legal powers with which it was backed, had an ominous appearance as long as the 'nationalist' minority was viewed as a threat to the state.

Conclusion

The Irish republican movement exploited more expertly than ever before the vulnerability of the British legal structure to violence and intimidation. It is likely that the British system had never found in Ireland the cultural underpinnings which gave it its domestic ruggedness. For this reason Irish policing had never been able to approximate to English methods. The republicans thus had marked advantages in their efforts to mobilise Irish opinion – through devices such as the boycott – against the armed RIC. The cards were stacked against the RIC further by events beyond its control, largely in the sphere of government policy. Its history militated against any transition into normal civil policing, though such a process might have been possible if Home Rule had gone through smoothly in 1886 or 1912. By 1916 it was almost certainly too late for any substantial transformation. The pace of militarisation thereafter was dictated by the tempo of the republican guerrilla campaign, but the basic direction was determined elsewhere.

A less monolithic police force, if securely installed before the intensification of political violence, might conceivably have been able to preserve a meaningful civil function while developing appropriate quasi-military units to deal with limited violence. As against this, it has to be recollected that the attitude of the RIC to what would now be called community relations was from the outset distorted. Its sense of distinctness from the community (in this respect, at least, the modern RUC is its lineal offspring) was rooted in a low expectation – rationalised into a low valuation – of public assistance. If it became integrated into Irish public culture, this was a kind of imbrication caused by propinquity over several generations, rather than an organic fusion or synergy. Disarmament might have been beneficial to its work at many times in many areas, but in the last analysis armament was forced upon it by the enduring capacity of nationalist rebels to use deadly force against it. Only a political settlement could have reduced or removed that capacity.

Finally, there must always be limits to the level of violence with which police *qua* police can deal. In Ireland, those limits were being exceeded by the IRA in 1919. The only appropriate response to sustained guerrilla action is the deployment of military force, either in aid of the civil power or, if necessary, under martial law. The former is obviously preferable, but the appropriate forms of military intervention, and still more importantly the harmonising of military and police elements, are delicate and complex matters. The British experience in Ireland indicated that a co-ordinated counter-insurgency campaign was unlikely to emerge spontaneously. A coherent and comprehensible government strategy is the only way of minimising the frictions, confusions and errors inevitable in any civil war. At the heart of such a strategy must be accurate assessment of the conflict: not indeed a declaration of war, but some declaration of emergency which recognises the necessity of abnormal executive action. British resistance to such a declaration was the cause of dangerous obfuscation. Lloyd George's insistence on police primacy was quite rational politically, but was vitiated in practice by a persistent failure to define objectives, powers and roles. The Cabinet's acceptance, in July 1920, of General Tudor's contention that the RIC might be finished as a civil police, but 'might have a great effect as a military body', could only have resulted from an unwillingness to think through the wider issues involved. Short-term political convenience eventually exacted a heavy price, paid in part by the Cabinet itself, but in much larger part by the police and by the people of both Britain and Ireland in the degradation of public standards.

Notes

1 The pathbreaking work of revision was D. Fitzpatrick, *Politics and Irish Life: provincial experience of war and revolution 1913–21* (Dublin, 1977); the issue has recently been surveyed in D. G. Boyce (ed.), *The Revolution in Ireland, 1878–1923* (London, 1988).
2 There is still no monographic study of Sinn Féin or modern replacement for R. M. Henry, *The Evolution of Sinn Fein* (Dublin, 1920). The nearest approach is R. Davis, *Arthur Griffith and Non-violent Sinn Féin* (Dublin, 1974). See also M. Laffan, 'The unification of Sinn Féin in 1917', *Irish Historical Studies*, xvii (1971), pp. 353–79.
3 Cabinet Memorandum by Secretary of State for the Colonies, 31 December 1918. Public Record Office, Kew [PRO], CAB 24 72/1, GT 6574.
4 C. Townshend, 'British policy in Ireland, 1906–1921', in Boyce, *Revolution in Ireland*, p. 174.
5 In the absence of a major scholarly account of the RIC, evaluation of its performance remains difficult. Most of the extant accounts are either nationalist attacks or police memoirs and *pièces justificatives*, the shortest and best of which is 'The Irish Police', by the Special Resident Magistrate (Divisional Commissioner) H. A. Blake, in *The Nineteenth Century*, lvii (1881), pp. 385–96. A rare hybrid can be found in J. A. Gaughan

(ed.), *The Memoirs of Constable Jeremiah Mee, RIC* (Dublin, 1975). The origins and nature of the force are usefully detailed in S.H. Palmer's monumental *Police and Protest in England and Ireland 1780–1850* (Cambridge, 1988), which helps to restore an archipelago perspective. The best modern essay on the final period is R. Hawkins, 'Dublin Castle and the Royal Irish Constabulary (1916–1922)', in T.D. Williams (ed.), *The Irish Struggle 1916–1926* (London, 1966), pp. 167–81.

6 C. Townshend, *Political Violence in Ireland: government and resistance since 1848* (Oxford, 1983), pp. 67–84.

7 C. Townshend, ' "One man whom you can hang if necessary": the discreet charm of Nevil Macready', in J.B. Hattendorf and M.H. Murfett (eds.), *The Limits of Military Power* (forthcoming).

8 Memorandum by Attorney General, 'Illegalities in Ulster', PRO CAB 37 117, f. 82.

9 Chief Commissioner, DMP, to Under Secretary, 27 July 1914. Copy in Ross file, Balfour MSS, British Library Add. MS 49821, ff. 71–86.

10 Memoir by Asst. Commissioner S. Waters, RIC, typescript in author's possession, p. 85.

11 E. O'Halpin, *The Decline of the Union: British government in Ireland 1892–1920* (Dublin, 1987), pp. 130–3.

12 R. Holmes, *The Little Field-Marshal: Sir John French* (London, 1981), pp. 338–43; for a terse reassessment see O'Halpin, *Decline of the Union*, pp. 157–79.

13 Secretary of State for War to Chief of the Imperial General Staff [CIGS], 18 September 1920, PRO WO 32 9537.

14 Lord Lieutenant to Chief Secretary for Ireland, 24 May 1919. Bodleian Library, Oxford, Strathcarron MSS. For the 1880s precedent (of which no formal account seems to have been taken in 1919–20) see the memorandum prepared for the Lord Lieutenant by Sir John Ross of Bladensburg, State Paper Office, Dublin, CSO RP 1883/2214, edited by R. Hawkins as 'An army on police work', *Irish Sword*, xi (1973), pp. 75–117.

15 Memorandum by Lord Lieutenant, 13 January 1920, French MSS 75/46/12; O'Halpin, *Decline of the Union*, p. 195.

16 Fisher to Austen Chamberlain, 18 November 1921, Birmingham University Library, Austen Chamberlain MSS 23/2/16; O'Halpin, *Decline of the Union*, p. 190.

17 C. Townshend, *The British Campaign in Ireland 1919–1921: the development of political and military policies* (Oxford, 1975), p. 42.

18 G.C. Duggan, 'The Royal Irish Constabulary. Forgotten force in a troubled land', in O. Dudley Edwards and F. Pyle (eds.), *1916: The Easter Rising* (London, 1968), p. 93. On the militarisation process see Townshend, *British Campaign*, pp. 40–6. Establishment statistics, and semi-official survey of the force up to the autumn of 1920 can be found in 'I.O.' (C.J.C. Street), *The Administration of Ireland 1920* (London, 1921), ch. X, pp. 269–98.

19 Townshend, *British Campaign*, pp. 103–5, on ROIA; also C. Townshend, *Britain's Civil Wars: counterinsurgency in the twentieth century* (London, 1986), *passim*, on emergency powers.

20 C. Townshend, 'The Irish Republican Army and the development of guerrilla warfare, 1916–21', *English Historical Review*, xciv (1979), p. 327.

21 Townshend, *British Campaign*, pp. 95–7.

22 Diary of Sir Henry Wilson, 23 September 1920, Imperial War Museum, Wilson MSS; Townshend, *British Campaign*, p. 116.

23 General Officer Commanding-in-Chief [C-in-C] Ireland to CIGS, 28 September 1920, Anderson MSS, PRO CO 904 188/1; Townshend, *British Campaign*, p. 120.

24 Lt. Col. Toppin to Under Secretary, 6 August 1920, Anderson MSS, PRO CO 904 188/1.

25 Townshend, *British Campaign*, pp. 160–8.

26 C. Brady: 'Police and government in the Irish Free State, 1922–1933' (University College, Dublin, MA thesis, 1967); *Guardians of the Peace* (Dublin, 1974), pp. 45, 104. The early major studies of the Free State government by Leo Kohn and Nicholas Mansergh contain only passing references to the Garda, and evidently did not regard it as significant (see, e.g., Mansergh, *The Irish Free State: its government and politics* (London, 1934), p. 303). Remarkably little attention has been paid to it by recent historians of independent Ireland, even in specialist accounts of the state-building

process (e.g. J. Prager, *Building Democracy in Ireland: political order and cultural integration in a newly independent nation* (Cambridge, 1986), which likewise contains only passing references, and also contrives to mis-spell its title). F. S. L. Lyons, *Ireland Since the Famine* (London, 1971), is as usual the most reliable commentator, but on this point his account is uncharacteristically vague, merely observing that the decision to create an unarmed police force was 'a remarkable gesture of confidence in the future' (p. 475).

27 Brady, 'Police and government', pp. 43–5.
28 Brady, 'Police and government', p. 46.

CHAPTER THREE

Police power and the demise of British rule in India, 1930–47

David Arnold

The literature on the demise of imperial rule in India is now vast, its bibliography alone running to several pages.[1] In addition to dozens of published memoirs and the twelve volumes of the official *Transfer of Power* documents, numerous monographs and articles have been published about the political manoeuvres and negotiations that resulted in Britain's departure in August 1947. Yet in all this very extensive literature there has been hardly any discussion of the police. The few works on India's police that have so far appeared have added little to our understanding of their role in the imperial end-game or of the conflicts and tensions to which they were subject in the transition from colonial rule to Indian self-government.[2]

Several explanations could be offered for this. It may be that such an omission is by no means rare or exclusive to India and that police and policing generally have been a neglected aspect of imperial history. Seldom the subject of high-level imperial debates and exchanges, the police have frequently been passed over in silence by historians as well, or at best relegated to occasional footnotes and minor asides. By comparison with the more eloquent representatives of the colonial civil service and army, police officers have tended to belong to a 'silent service' and so have done little to rescue themselves from historical obscurity.[3] It would seem, too, that while historians have found high drama in the history of the Indian Army, and much of wider imperial significance in its composition and deployment, they have seen little that was not squalid and routine in the second-rate saga of the Indian Police.

As this chapter will try to demonstrate, the role of the police during the years leading up to August 1947 was far more influential and illuminating than the existing 'transfer of power' literature has recognised. This was partly because the police held such a multiplicity of roles and functions in late-colonial India. As an agency of state coercion and intelligence-gathering, the police were vital to Britain's attempts to hold on to power in India. But in addition to being in the front line of measures to suppress the nationalist movement, ministerial control over the police was also offered as bait with which to woo Indians away from civil disobedience and into constitutional participation. The police were thus caught up in a lengthy tug-of-war between the British and the Indian National Congress for effective authority over them, and though the British for a while successfully held on, the erosion of police loyalty and reliability by the mid-1940s was an important index of Britain's waning power and a significant factor in the decision to quit India.

The police were of no less importance to the colonial state's nationalist opponents and successors. They were a powerful and highly visible element of that state power which the emerging forces of the Congress sought first to contest and then to capture and subordinate to their own control. Nationalist attitudes towards the police illustrated the contradiction between the party of anti-colonial opposition, drawn into protracted and often bitter conflict with the police, and the incipient party of government, anxious to preserve and develop the inherited apparatus of state power in furtherance of its own ends.

I

The importance of India's police has been well attested. 'The Police department in India,' wrote Sir Edmund Cox shortly before the First World War, 'is the very essence of our administration. There is no other which so much concerns the life of the people. To the ordinary villager the ... constable ... is the visible representative of the Sirkar, or Government'.[4] This view was echoed two decades later by J. C. Curry when he remarked that 'The Indian policeman is the ubiquitous embodiment of the government', and went on to claim that millions of villagers who had never seen a squad of soldiers or encountered a British administrator had nevertheless had frequent contact with the police.[5]

Of course such sentiments need to be treated with some caution. Cox and Curry saw the colonial police as the successful embodiment of the English 'genius for establishing law and order';[6] but there were many dissenting voices, even within the colonial administration, which expressed great dissatisfaction with the police and took a far more negative view of their character and attainments. Many present-day scholars would also argue that the colonial constabulary was too thinly spread and too poorly resourced to have much impact upon India's vast and populous society. Certainly, there is no doubting that the police, far from being ubiquitous, were only selectively (and not always particularly effectively)

[43]

deployed against specific targets.[7] But it is pertinent to note that the critics and heirs of empire were as much convinced of the importance of the police as were its advocates and apologists. Thus, for M.K. Gandhi, the police were one of the principal expressions of that 'concentrated and organised' violence which, in his view, the state characteristically represented.[8] Jawaharlal Nehru, who had much cause during the long years of his involvement in the nationalist movement to reflect on the nature of colonial police power, remarked shortly after Independence, in words almost indentical with those Cox had used, that the police came 'more in contact with the day-to-day working of the common people than any other service' and stood for 'the power of the State ... in the most obvious form'. 'Those who have power,' he continued, perhaps thinking aloud as much about the temptations of autocracy as the trials of colonialism, 'have to be very careful of [about?] using that power.'[9]

The political potency of the police was most clearly and forcefully demonstrated by their systematic use against the Indian National Congress during the agitational movements of the 1920s and 1930s. Because of the relative openness of Congress activity and the reliance, under Gandhi's leadership, on non-violent protest and individual or mass civil disobedience rather than armed resistance, the police appeared to the British to be the most effective and least provocative means of countering nationalist agitation. The police played a particularly conspicuous part in defeating the Civil Disobedience Movement of 1930–3. Although this reliance upon police power was not without its hazards for the British administration, especially the outcry against 'police excesses' and the condemnation of British rule as a 'police raj', it was thought preferable to the bloodier forms of military intervention which had led to the Jallianwala Bagh massacre in Amritsar in April 1919, when nearly 400 people were killed attending a banned political meeting. The use of the police was considered doubly successful, for not only was agitation effectively checked and the Congress, by 1934, driven off the streets and back into the constitutional arenas, but the loyalty of the great majority of the Indian policemen was never seriously undermined by nationalist taunts and propaganda.[10]

The suppression of civil disobedience in the early 1930s marked a high point of police action in the service of the colonial state. It showed the extent to which the survival of the colonial regime in India depended upon police arms and intelligence, largely unaided by the military. It epitomised the primary responsibility of the police for combating all but the most violent manifestations of anti-colonial resistance. Such was the priority attached to the maintenance of 'law and order' in its various forms that it was at times elevated into a rationale for the establishment and indefinite continuation of colonial rule itself.[11] Political prominence of this order provided a favourable climate for the growth of police professionalism. Long a cinderella service, bossed about by the Indian Civil Service (ICS) and despised by the army, the Indian Police (IP) had acquired by the 1930s an unprecedented degree of authority within the colonial administration. Never before had the opinions of India's police chiefs carried so much weight or received such appreciative consideration in the inner councils of government as during and immediately after the civil disobedience campaign. Indeed, a spokesman for the Indian Police Association in London in 1931 went so far as to claim that the IP was the most professional body of police in the entire empire.[12] It was equally indicative of this new-found confidence and status that the Simon Commission in its report in 1930 spoke of the ICS and the IP jointly as the 'security services' and urged the retention of the privileged terms of service bestowed upon them both by the Lee Commission six years earlier.[13]

And yet, at the very moment when police power seemed to have reached its apogee, the future of the force was under critical scrutiny in anticipation of a fresh round of constitutional reforms. Under the system of split government, or Dyarchy, created by the Government of India Act of 1919, the police had remained in the hands of official and nominated executive councillors on the 'reserved' side of the provincial government and not entrusted to the elected ministers on the 'transferred' side, though in a few provinces (including Madras and the United Provinces) an Indian executive councillor held the police portfolio for part of the period. But the remoteness of the police from ministerial control, combined with strident public criticism of the police across a wide range of issues from 'law and order' enforcement to recruitment policy and expenditure, made them more than ever a target for condemnation and abuse, and left them with few defenders, even among ministers. Although the running of the provincial police departments was never seriously jeopardised by hostile questions and resolutions in the legislative councils, or even by occasional budget cuts, this barrage of criticism annoyed senior police officers and was alleged to be damaging to subordinates' morale.[14] The provincial Inspectors-General took this as an ominous sign of what would happen if, under a new constitution, the police were transferred to elected ministers. R.J.S. Dodd, the Inspector-General of Police for the United Provinces, told the Simon Commission in December 1928 that:

> a minister responsible to the legislature and not responsible to the Government as at present constituted would find it extremely difficult, and almost impossible, to administer the department as it ought to be administered if law and order are to be maintained. He would find it extremely difficult

to resist the demands made by his constituents and others to interfere with the administration of the police and the department itself.[15]

However, when the Simon Commission made its report it took a significantly different line. It argued that Dyarchy had failed precisely because responsibility had been so divided, and the solution accordingly lay in 'making men responsible for their own actions'. Underlying the proposed transference of the police to ministerial control was a conviction that no government, whatever its political complexion, could dispense with the police or fail to recognise the importance of their efficient operation, while making the erstwhile critics responsible for 'law and order' would have a sobering influence on them and might usefully (from the British perspective) drive a wedge between the more moderate and practically-minded politicians and their more idealistic and extremist fellow-travellers.[16] The British hoped to divert the attention of Indian politicians (especially Congressmen) away from a quest for power at the all-India level by ensnaring them in administrative routine and responsibility in the provinces. Substantial concessions were thus to be made provincially the better to maintain and consolidate British power at the centre.[17] There was also a more immediate and practical consideration in view. As the Simon Commission pointed out, the police could not be hived off from other branches of provincial administration and alone kept as a 'reserved' department beyond ministerial control. Since their inception in the mid-nineteenth century, India's police forces had always been organised on provincial lines. The country was too vast and varied for policing to be other than an essentially provincial affair, and it would have been administratively impractical as well as politically unacceptable suddenly to centralise the entire police administration. Unless the police were included, it would be impossible to convince the Indian public that a genuine measure of provincial self-government was on offer, and there would be no sufficiently inviting bait to tempt the Congress away from civil disobedience and into constructive participation in government. It was a high-risk strategy, but as Sir Harry Haig, the Governor of the United Provinces confided to the Viceroy in December 1937, the British were 'playing for high stakes and ... must take certain risks'.[18]

First formally articulated by the Simon Commission in 1930, these objectives became the cornerstone of British policy towards the Indian Police for the next fifteen years. With some reservations they were endorsed by the provincial government in the early 1930s and in London by the Round Table Conferences of 1930–2 and the Parliamentary Joint Committee on constitutional reforms in 1933–4. Senior police officers, however, protested at being used as a kind of constitutional cat's paw, and anticipated that in a majority of provinces ministries would be formed that were 'hostile to the police and ready to acquiesce in attacks on the morale of the force'.[19] It was some indication of their new-found status (as well as an appreciation of the need for safeguards against any possible abuse of ministerial powers) that their objections were given serious consideration. Among various schemes drafted by police officers to protect them from ministerial meddling, one of the most favoured was to make each province's Inspector-General a secretary to the government, entitled to appeal directly to the governor if any disagreement arose between the Inspector-General and the ministry.

In the pursuit of wider political goals, these service objections were overruled as being contrary to the spirit of the new constitution, but the police did receive some practical reassurances. Under the system of provincial autonomy created by the Government of India Act of 1935, the governor was entrusted with special powers to uphold 'law and order' in cases where his ministers proved unable (or unwilling) to do so. The IP, like the ICS, remained an imperial service immune to ministerial interference as far as its conditions of service were concerned; public service commissions were established (previously only Madras and the central government had had them) in order to minimise political and communal interference in recruitment and promotion. In a significant departure from earlier practice, some aspects of police intelligence work were brought under the direct control of the Government of India's Intelligence Bureau so as to open a channel for confidential communication between the provincial police and the central government.[20] There was the further safeguard that the army, while not a favoured instrument of domestic policing, remained independent of the provinces and could be used as a second line of control if the police should fail in their 'law and order' responsibilities.

The Government of India Act of 1935 was not meant, then, to concede more than a limited devolution of power to the provinces. It was not intended to signal an imminent retreat from empire. But, as far as the police were concerned, the Act (and more specifically the accession of the Congress to ministerial office in seven of British India's eleven provinces in 1937) opened the way for an unprecedented degree of Indian political influence, and marked the beginning of a significant erosion of British control over the colonial police.

II

The years 1937 to 1947 witnessed a series of developments which profoundly affected the position of the police as dependable agents of colonial control. Taken as a whole, these developments contributed to Britain's declining capacity to rule India and to maintain the kind of containing strategy laid out in the Simon Commission's report and embodied in the 1935 Government of India Act. This is not to claim that what happened to the police was alone responsible for persuading the British to leave India in August 1947. We have learnt, if nothing else, that the factors behind Britain's departure were extremely complex and not attributable to any one single cause. But what was happening to the police was not only symptomatic of a more general crisis of colonial confidence and control, but also represented in itself a development of particular significance in view of the previous reliance on the police to contain nationalist opposition and uphold British authority. The changes set in motion by the advent of provincial autonomy under the 1935 Act, and accelerated by wartime events, could not easily be reversed or even halted. Cumulatively they helped to make Britain's position in India administratively and politically untenable.

Although circumscribed by the provisions of the 1935 Act, the Congress ministries which held office between July 1937 and October 1939 and again from April 1946 were nonetheless able to exercise a significant influence over the running of the police departments in their charge. To some extent, certainly, the conduct of the Congress ministries duly fulfilled British expectations. Police power was deployed with what was seen to be commendable (indeed at times excessive) vigour against such customary targets as communists, socialists, striking workers and communal rioters, even though this drew strong protests from the party's left wing and caused much apprehension to those, like Gandhi, who found such ready recourse to state coercion unpalatable.[21] In some provinces mutual antipathy to communism and industrial violence provided a convenient basis for co-operation between European police chiefs and Indian ministers. As early as August 1937 the attitude of the Madras Premier, C. Rajagopalachari, towards 'law and order' and the services was felt to give 'particular cause for congratulation'; and, after a rocky start, G.B. Pant in the United Provinces was soon addressing police parades, visiting police training schools and generally 'beginning to show a better appreciation of the dangers of weakening the police'.[22]

But, for all this, there was deep concern among governors and senior police officers alike that the public abuse of the police by ministers and their supporters, the formation of local Congress committees to intervene between the police and the public, and the pursuit of vendettas against individual policemen who had been conspicuously active during the Civil Disobedience Movement, would have a disastrous effect on the work and morale of the force. Although after a few months in office there was, from the British viewpoint, a reassuring moderation in ministerial attitudes, the underlying fear of police demoralisation remained throughout the two-year period of the Congress ministries. In May 1938 the governor of Bombay told the Viceroy that 'One of the most anxious questions of the times is the morale of the Services and particularly of the subordinate ranks of the Police force'. A few months later, in December, Haig reported that in the United Provinces the police 'have probably suffered more than any other part of the [administrative] machine' from a 'loss of authority'.[23]

General attitudes apart, there were specific examples of ministerial intervention and influence. In Madras, Rajagopalachari strenuously opposed the appointment of a Central Intelligence Officer who could report to the government of India on events in the province without prior reference to his ministry. The Premier was eventually placated, but not before the original appointee had been replaced by one who was more acceptable to him.[24] He, like other ministers, began to exercise an influence over the internal management of the force by, for example, obliging a district superintendent to rescind an order that contradicted Congress policy, or transferring to an unpopular posting an officer who failed to follow ministerial directives.[25] Congress ministers had an even greater impact on the middle and lower echelons of the force, reducing pay where it was thought to be excessive and modifying existing recruitment practices. The Madras ministry began phasing out the employment of Europeans and Anglo-Indians as police sergeants, while favouring other communities, such as the untouchables, hitherto largely excluded from police service. It was not only Europeans, therefore, who were affected by changes in policy. For all its unpopularity, the police force was an important source of employment for many communities, particularly those with a tradition of administrative or military service, and the British had tried (not always with the degree of success they would have wished) to select from communities that were thought to be particularly suited for police work or loyal to themselves. The Congress, with loyalties and priorities of its own in mind, began to change the character of recruitment policy. In the United Provinces, for example, the predominantly Hindu Congress started to squeeze out the Muslims, who had formerly been recruited to the police in numbers far in excess of their proportion of the population, and the communal composition of the police was to become an even more vital and divisive issue in the period immediately preceding and following Partition.[26] But even in the brief period of its first term in office the Congress had given notice of its determination to bring the police department to heel and not simply accept an impotent overlordship.

However, in October 1939 the Congress ministries resigned in protest against India's involuntary involvement in the Second World War and all but one of these provinces returned, under section 93 of the constitution, to bureaucratic control. In July 1942 when the provincial governors were asked about the morale of the police – a matter of urgent concern in view of the threatened resumption of mass civil disobedience by the Congress – the general opinion was that their loyalty had not been irrevocably weakened by Congress rule. After all, it was said, the party had done nothing while in office 'to deserve the sympathy of the police force'. As long as the government publicly defended the police, protected them from 'victimisation', and attended to their material needs, most governors were sanguine about police reliability in the event of any fresh confrontation with the Congress. Some, however, sounded a prescient note of caution, the governor of Bihar warning that the morale of the police in his province had been 'undoubtedly shaken' by continual criticism of the force.[27] When the Quit India movement erupted in August 1942, British confidence in the police seemed largely justified, but there were (from the government's viewpoint) some alarming exceptions, especially in Bihar where police morale all but collapsed in the face of the nationalist onslaught. Mindful of police vulnerability, the government of India firmly resisted demands for an inquiry into action taken during the suppression of the 1942 rebellion.[28]

Congress ascendency over the police was resumed with even greater vigour and effect once the party returned to office following elections in the winter of 1945–6. By the spring of 1946 there was a powerful anticipation that Britain's departure from India was imminent and a corresponding reluctance on the part of the governors and senior police officers to resist political pressure and face a possible constitutional showdown over who had the right to run the police. In the United Provinces in October 1946 the Inspector General, Sir Philip Measures, discovered that Vallabhbhai Patel, Home Minister in the Interim Government in Delhi, was corresponding directly with provincial police officers instead of communicating through him. When Measures protested against this circumvention of his authority, there was an outcry from Patel and from Pant, again installed as provincial premier. The governor, Sir Francis Wylie, persuaded Measures not to resign and promised to use his special powers to override the ministers, but when they in turn threatened to resign, the Secretary of State forced Wylie to give way and Measures promptly departed into retirement.[29] In neighbouring Bihar events followed a similar course. The Congress Prime Minister, S. Krishna Sinha, refused to listen to advice from the European Inspector General, Creed, and issued orders directly to Indian police officers with, the governor complained, 'deplorable results' for police discipline. Krishna Sinha also wanted to pass over a senior European in order to appoint a more junior Indian officer as a deputy Inspector General. A major row ensued, but in the end Creed, like Measures in the United Provinces, took early retirement and left in January 1947 to be replaced by an Indian officer.[30] E.H. Colebrook in Madras summed up the feelings of many senior European police officers when he complained in April 1947 that there had recently been 'some bad examples of discrimination against Europeans' with 'Indians promoted merely for their black skins'.[31] Thus, even before independence the politicians' takeover of the police was already far advanced.

The exercise of ministerial office and influence was, however, only one of the ways in which India's nationalist party sought mastery over the police during the later stages of colonial rule. The Congress also brought to bear the strength of its popular support and the appeal (or threat) of nationalist sentiment. Public antipathy to the police was longstanding and deep-seated, as much a product of their brutality and venality as their status as frontline servants of the Raj. It had been one of the basic ingredients in nationalist protests and demonstrations since at least 1920, and in all the Gandhian civil disobedience campaigns attacks on the police, epitomised by the incident at Chauri Chaura in January 1922 when twenty-two policemen were murdered or burnt to death, was a recurrent theme. The repeated condemnation of police conduct in the press, in the legislatures, and from nationalist platforms further intensified hostility to the police, gave it political legitimacy and fed expectations that the Congress, once in power, would curb such abuses and humble or punish those responsible.[32] The British in turn sought to protect the police and ensure their continuing loyalty by isolating them as far as possible from public criticism and promising them virtual immunity from prosecution. During the Civil Disobedience Movement in the early 1930s, the government went to great lengths to maintain police morale and to fend off nationalist attacks. It attempted to do the same in 1942, but by that date pressure on the police was mounting while promises of continuing immunity from 'victimisation' seemed less convincing as Britain's hold over India weakened and an early resumption of Congress rule appeared inevitable.

The Quit India movement of August 1942 unleashed a new wave of police hatred, in part spontaneous, in part politically contrived. In many areas the police bore the full brunt of the rebellion, with more than 200 police stations burnt down or partially destroyed and sixty-three policemen killed, twenty-six of them in Bihar alone.[33] In the Central Provinces some policemen 'were humiliated by having their uniforms burnt and being compelled to wear Gandhi caps and carry Congress flags in procession'. A 'Free India' bulletin issued in the name of the Congress included among its directives: 'Make the policeman look as one of you; that is relieve him of his uniform and disarm him. This is a noble service for the nation; for in this way you convert a slave into a freeman.'[34] Not for the first time the police found themselves in the front line of confrontation between the Congress and the Raj, but the defeat of Quit India did not bring an end to their discomfort and uncertainty. As the war ended and fresh elections were announced for the provincial legislatures there was a concerted campaign for the punishment of police officers responsible for 'atrocities' committed during the 1942 movement. At one stage in 1945–6 this campaign threatened to overwhelm the services, especially the police, with its bitter vituperation, and it seemed to presage a final showdown with a now demoralised and directionless administration. The immediate crisis was averted, however, and the Congress leadership moderated its demands once it became clear that the British were in earnest about leaving India as soon as a constitutional settlement could be reached and once the Congress, back in office, saw it in its own interests to prevent any further collapse of service morale and efficiency.[35]

Quit India and its aftermath showed, perhaps even more clearly than the period of the first Congress ministries, the nationalist party's own dilemmas and internal contradictions. As a mass-based political party and as the principal vehicle for popular anti-colonialism, the Congress used (or was at times borne along by) the unpopularity of government and especially of the police. As an oppositional movement it toyed with the possibility of replacing constables with its own volunteers, bypassing or superseding the colonial police machine entirely. Certainly this was the Gandhian ideal.[36] But, once in office and with the machinery of government largely at its command, the Congress leadership, encouraged by the expectations of the businessmen, industrialists and landholders who were increasingly important as financial and political backers for the party, preferred the sure rewards of inheritance to the uncertain spoils of usurpation. It sought to take over and strengthen the existing machinery of government, the better to consolidate its own position, reward its supporters and discomfort its adversaries. For all Gandhi's antipathy to state power, many Congress leaders, like Rajagopalachari as Premier of Madras and Vallabhbhai Patel as Home Minister in the Interim Government of 1946–7, had a strong sense of their obligation to uphold 'law and order' and thus found themselves as reliant as their British predecessors had been on the assistance of the established police. 'Atrocities' made good propaganda in opposition and drew a ready public response, but such allegations were quietly dropped once the Congress leadership again held the reins of police power in its own hands.[37]

The kind of psychological and political pressure applied during and following the Quit India movement, coupled with the realisation that the days of British rule were numbered and a Congress Raj was imminent, had a profound effect upon all levels of the police. In November 1945 the Viceroy, Lord Wavell, revealed that European members of the IP and ICS were 'dispirited and discontended', their Indian counterparts were 'uneasy about the future and under strong political and social pressure', and the Indian subordinates 'on whom the administration so largely depends' were 'naturally reluctant to make enemies of the future masters of India'.[38] Whether from a belief that they could at last display their true sentiments, or from more pragmatic and professional motives ('eleventh-hour patriotism' it was sometimes dubbed), Indian Police officers began, often quite openly, to identify themselves with the Congress (or the Muslim League). Many Europeans remained in the service in order to secure the best possible severance pay and pension, but were frankly confused and bewildered by what was going on around them.[39]

III

In an article published in 1973 David Potter suggested that the demise of British rule in India may have been caused by a 'manpower shortage' in the ICS. A dwindling number of suitable European candidates sought entry into the service after the First World War, he argued, partly from uncertainty about career prospects and the future of British rule in India. The erosion of European manpower was then further and fatally accelerated by the cessation of British recruitment during the Second World War and an inability to resume it once the war was over.[40] Given the importance attached to the Indian Police as a 'security service' alongside the ICS and the similarity of its recruitment procedures, it might be argued that a comparable 'manpower shortage' affected the senior ranks of the police and that this too helped to hasten Britain's departure from India.

The figures given in Table 3.1[41] certainly show a declining European presence in the IP during the 1930s, accentuated by the war years and their aftermath. But at no stage before mid-1947 did the European

Table 3.1: European membership of the Indian Police, 1933–47

Date	Europeans	Total IP	% Europeans
Jan. 1933	505	665	75·94
Jan. 1936	437	602	72·59
Jan. 1939	428	609	70·28
Jan. 1940	429	616	69·16
Jan. 1944	361	577	62·56
Jan. 1945	344	559	61·54
June 1947	323	516	62·60

c

element of the IP fall below 60 per cent, though it shrank rapidly thereafter, and this figure was still above the target of parity of numbers between Europeans and Indians laid down by the Lee Commission in 1924 for attainment by 1949. Between 1925 and 1940, 217 Europeans were recruited as against 135 Indians, and it was belatedly realised in 1940 that, because of the way in which recruitment procedures for Indians had been followed since 1925, even the 50 : 50 ratio would be unattainable unless there was an increase in the Indian intake. Successive Secretaries of State and Viceroys were concerned about the difficulty of finding enough suitable Indian as well as European candidates during the 1920s and 1930s, and the problem was greatly exacerbated by the outbreak of the war in 1939 and the cessation of European recruitment the following year. Despite escalating police commitments during the war, the IP's official strength was allowed to contract with posts held open for 'war-service' candidates who were to be recruited once the war was over. The resumption of European recruitment was discussed, albeit with an air of unreality, in 1946, but was soon abandoned, while ageing and war-weary European officers in India anxiously sought leave or retirement.[42]

Against this evidence of dwindling European manpower, however, has to be set the fact that white officers continued to occupy many of the most senior positions in the police hierarchy until early or mid-1947 and in some cases until Independence Day itself. Bihar had an Indian Inspector General as early as 1939, but most provinces had to wait until Britain's departure in 1947; a few European officers stayed on by invitation for months, even years, after Independence. The important post of Director of the Intelligence Bureau was also not entrusted to an Indian before independence.[43] There was an erosion of senior European personnel, but it came relatively late on in the police. Moreover, as we have seen, it was as much the result of pressure from Indian ministers as the outcome of any serious shortfall in European recruitment.

There is a further and weightier objection to the 'manpower shortage' thesis as it might be applied to the police. What may have been critical during the closing years of British rule was not the numbers of Europeans in the ICS or IP (in practice always extremely small relative to the size of the force) or even the strategic importance of the positions they occupied. Of equal, possibly greater, moment was the attitude of the many thousands of Indians in the middle and lower levels of the force, from the sub-inspectors down to the constables, on whose loyalty and obedience the colonial state had come to depend, but whose reliability was increasingly in doubt. External pressure was an important part of this. In addition to the efforts of Congress to gain a hold over the police, whether through abusive propaganda or through the exercise of ministerial office, the force was also by 1945–6 coming under intense pressure from other quarters – from the socialists and the Muslim League in particular – at the very time when the insulation of the police from external influences was difficult to maintain. But it was not only outside influences that were at work. Among the lower ranks of the police there was widespread discontent (as there had been to a lesser degree at the end of the previous war) over low wages and poor conditions at a time of high prices and severe shortages. There was uncertainty about future employment prospects, especially among the large numbers of policemen recruited (with only minimal training) during the war; unease about possible retribution from returning Congress ministries; and an inescapable awareness of the great political and communal ferment that was overtaking India, especially the strife-torn provinces of Bengal, Bihar and Punjab. While official reports were quick to blame outside agitators for fomenting unrest in an otherwise loyal and contented force, there is sufficient evidence to suggest that this was not just externally-contrived discontent. It also reflected and fed upon grievances strongly felt by police subordinates themselves, and it formed a part of that wider 'revolt from below' which helped to paralyse the colonial administration and drive the British out of India.[44]

Police unrest manifested itself in several parts of India between late 1945 and the middle months of 1947. In March and April 1946 there were police demonstrations and protest marches in New Delhi, and on 16 April that year a company of the Malabar Special Police, the Madras government's crack paramilitary force, went on strike over pay and conditions of service. The strike, which the government partly ascribed to communist influence, was defeated after eight days: nearly a thousand men were dismissed and four companies disbanded.[45] But the most dramatic indications of an impending collapse in police morale and discipline came in Bihar.

Discontent among the Bihar police went back several years. During the course of the Quit India movement in August 1942, 205 policemen went over to the Congress, 140 new recruits deserted from a training centre, and 120 constables at Jamshedpur struck for higher wages. The strike's leaders were arrested and thirty-three of the constables were prosecuted: the rest returned to work unconditionally. Although it hastily sanctioned a pay increase to forestall further unrest, the government claimed the strike had been instigated by Ramanand Tewari, a head-constable with 'Congress sympathies'.[46] By late 1945, with the Congress leadership apparently preparing itself for a renewed civil disobedience campaign and vociferously demanding an inquiry into police repression, there was mounting alarm among the subordinate police as among their superiors. In October of that year allegations in the press and on Congress platforms about police 'atrocities' were said to be having 'a very serious effect on morale, particularly in the lower ranks of the police who fear that they will have no protection against victimization'.[47] Just at the time when Bihar Congressmen were returning to office there was a new strike, again led by Tewari, who had recently been released from prison. But the incoming ministry took no serious action against him partly because he was backed by influential Congress and Congress Socialist elements. The latter included Jayaprakash Narayan, who saw in police discontent an opportunity to secure a revolutionary as well as rapid end to British rule in India. According to Bihar's governor, Narayan had been 'suborning the police' and there were now 'no loyal or disciplined police' left in the province.[48] On 24 March 1947, barely a month after the mutiny of Royal Indian Navy ratings in Bombay had sent ripples of excitement through Indian subordinates in all branches of the colonial service, a third police strike erupted in Bihar. Beginning with armed constables in Gaya, it spread rapidly to Patna and Mongyr, and was only quashed with the help of British and Gurkha troops: two policemen were killed and five wounded. This time the Bihar ministry responded with vigour, arresting Tewari and 400 policemen. Speaking in the provincial legislature on 28 March, Bihar's Prime Minister, Krishna Sinha, deplored the strike and warned that no government could 'tolerate disorder ... in a body whose duty is to maintain order', especially 'when power to rule over the country' was 'passing into Indian hands'.[49]

Although this and other manifestations of police discontent were stifled before they could develop into a more widespread and co-ordinated mutiny, they were a telling indication of how unreliable the police (especially the armed police on which the British had depended so heavily since 1918)[50] had now become. And, given the weakness or ineffectiveness of other agencies and instruments of colonial control by the mid-1940s,[51] this crumbling of police power was a significant factor in impelling Britain's early departure from India.

IV

One of the paradoxes of late-colonial India was that state power was rapidly expanding at the very time that the pressure for decolonisation was reaching its height. In response to the escalating crisis of political control, India's police forces mushroomed during the Second World War and acquired an armed strength of formidable and unprecedented proportions. In 1932 there were 215,004 policemen in India (for a population in excess of 300 million) of whom 32,596 (15·16 per cent) were armed. By the end of 1938 the figure had fallen slightly to 193,118, with 28,703 men (14·86 per cent) under arms. But in December 1943, as the political and administrative responsibilities of the police grew, the total reached 300,656 (an increase of over 60 per cent since the outbreak of the war) with 137,222 policemen (45·64 per cent of the total) under arms.[52]

In some respects Quit India – the supreme crisis of Britain's wartime control over India – was an exceptional episode in the policing of the Indian nationalist movement. Marked, on the one side, by an unparalleled degree of mass violence and destructiveness, it was met, on the other, by a state response that included a greater and more protracted use of military force against civilians than at any time at least since Jallianwala Bagh in 1919, and possibly since the Mutiny and Rebellion of 1857–8. Nevertheless, the role of the police remained critical – in meeting the first shock-waves of the revolt, in the raids and reprisals that led to the suppression of the movement, and in rapidly replacing troops in areas like Bihar and the eastern United Provinces where the uprising raged most fiercely.[53] As the war drew to a close, the colonial administration began to realise that, once British troops were withdrawn from critical provinces like Bihar, it would be left without a substantial military backup, despite a political and communal situation that was increasingly difficult to control.[54] This meant that the burden of maintaining 'internal security' as well as 'law and order' fell even more heavily than before on the police, a force whose loyalty and efficiency was seriously in doubt. This was a matter of grave concern to the provincial governors and to the Viceroy, Lord Wavell, and it was one of the factors that forced the government of India in 1945–6 to recognise the need for a speedy solution to the constitutional impasse and a rapid (but, if possible, orderly) withdrawal from a situation that could no longer be effectively policed.[55]

Alongside these developments lay another factor – the changing character and expectations of state power in India. In pursuit of their twin priorities – the maintenance of 'law and order' and the extraction of land revenue, objectives that were not far removed from those of the Mughals before them – the British in India used the police to combat the most obvious manifestations of crime, to quell disorder and facilitate the running of the colonial economy.[56] But during the interwar years, and increasingly by the 1940s, this limited concept of governmental responsibilities appeared outmoded and was being replaced by an ideal of state power reoriented to the service of a national economy and national welfare. *Laissez-faire*, long the linchpin of colonial economic policy, was discarded under the pressure of wartime food shortages in favour of the regulation of essential supplies through rural procurement, urban rationing and statutory price controls. The police were given added responsibility for enforcing these new measures and for combating the smuggling and blackmarketeering that flourished in their wake.[57]

There was talk, as in Britain, of 'post-war reconstruction' while Nehru and the Congress left wing, as well as Indian businessmen and industrialists, anticipated a future in which the state would be more actively and constructively involved than hitherto in economic affairs.[58] Rather ironically in view of Gandhi's own aversion to state power, the Congress ministers who took office in 1937 and 1946 sought to use their position to implement such items of the Gandhian programme as prohibition and the promotion of cottage industries. The ministries also became far more actively involved in the attempted resolution of industrial labour disputes than their bureaucratic predecessors.[59]

This expansion and reorientation of state responsibilities had enormous implications for the police. Alongside the existing burden of police work (which had already grown rapidly with the urbanisation of the 1930s and 1940s and with the development of industry and road transport), there were demanding new duties to perform. The task of enforcing prohibition, for example, fell to the police rather than revenue officials, and the policing of labour disputes created a heavy additional workload in the cities. The police were also required, at least in the conventions of nationalist rhetoric, to transform themselves from being the bully-boys of an autocratic Raj to the willing servants of a democratic nation state.

In practice, however, it is hard to see that any significant change in police methods and attitudes occurred after independence, though nationalist leaders like Nehru and Patel certainly claimed that it had, and cited the departure of European police chiefs as clear evidence for this.[60] Faced with a series of crises that threatened the unity and viability of the new nation-state under Congress direction – communal violence during and after Partition, communist insurrection in Telangana, unrest among industrial workers and peasants in many parts of the country – governments in New Delhi and the provinces shelved indefinitely any possibility of a radical overhaul of the police organisation they had inherited from the British. As the Indian Prime Minister, Jawaharlal Nehru, observed in November 1947, 'First things must come first and the first thing is the security and stability of India.'[61] While hastening the departure of its European personnel, Congress ministers took over the colonial police organisation (and its colonial mentality) largely intact, promoting to vacant senior posts Indian officers habituated to colonial policing roles and attitudes. The greatest value of the police to the new regime – as to its predecessor – was as an agency of coercion and intelligence, while the expansion of police responsibilities that followed from the wartime and post-war elaboration of state power tended to increase opportunities for police corruption and to perpetuate, even intensify, public antipathy towards the police.

Notes

1 R. J. Moore, 'The transfer of power: an historiographical survey', *South Asia*, 9 (1986), pp. 83–95.
2 For example, A. Gupta, *The Police in British India, 1861–1947* (New Delhi, 1979); P. Griffiths, *To Guard My People: the history of the Indian Police* (London, 1971).
3 M. Wynne (ed.), *On Honourable Terms: the memoirs of some Indian police officers, 1915–1948* (London, 1985), p. 60. Compare the abundance of sources available for the Indian Civil Service: D. Potter, *India's Political Administrators, 1919–1983* (Oxford, 1986), pp. 253–62.
4 E. Cox, *Police and Crime in India* (London, 1910), p. 7.
5 J. C. Curry, *The Indian Police* (London, 1932), p. 43.
6 Cox, *Police and Crime*, p. 22; cf. Griffiths, *To Guard My People*, p. 2.
7 For an assessment see D. Arnold, *Police Power and Colonial Rule: Madras, 1859–1947* (Delhi, 1986).
8 N. K. Bose, *Studies in Gandhism* (2nd edition, Calcutta, 1947), p. 68.
9 B. N. Mullik, *Nehru on Police* (Dehra Dun, 1970), pp. 31, 33.
10 D. Arnold, *The Congress in Tamilnad: nationalist politics in South India, 1919–1937* (London, 1977), chapter 4.
11 E.g., Cox, *Police and Crime*, especially chapter 2, 'The appalling state of the country at the commencement of British rule' and chapter 4, 'What passed for law and procedure under native government'.
12 Deputation of the Indian Police Association to the Secretary of State for India, 8 October 1931, India Office Records, London [IOR], L/S&G/7/455; Arnold, *Police Power*, pp. 70–8.
13 Indian Statutory Commission, *Report, II: Recommendations* (Calcutta, 1930), pp. 288–90; *Report of the Commission on the Superior Civil Services in India, 1924* (Simla, 1924).
14 Indian Statutory Commission, *Volume IX: Memorandum Submitted by the Government of the United Provinces* (London, 1930), pp. 120–6; *Volume X: Memorandum Submitted by the Government of the Punjab* (London, 1930), pp. 202–6; *Volume XII: Memorandum Submitted by the Government of Bihar and Orissa* (London, 1930), pp. 166–9. Cf. Wynne, *Honourable Terms*, p. 111.
15 Indian Statutory Commission, *Volume XV: Extracts from Official Evidence* (Calcutta, 1930), p. 244.
16 Indian Statutory Commission, *Report, II*, pp. 22, 48.
17 J. Darwin, 'Imperialism in decline? Tendencies in British imperial policy between the wars', *Historical Journal*, 23 (1980), pp. 673–7.
18 Haig to Viceroy (Lord Linlithgow), 24 December 1937, IOR, L/P&J/5/264; H. G. Hallett, 'The position of the police under the new constitution', 3 March 1933, IOR, L/P&J/7/1071.
19 Confidential report on conference of senior police officers, Simla, 23–6 May 1932, Tamil Nadu Archives, Madras, Under-Secretary's Secret File, 802, 16 December 1932, IOR, L/S&G/7/840.
20 Report on 1934 police conference, Tamil Nadu Archives, Government Order 1566, Home, 29 July 1936.
21 Gandhi in *Harijan*, 13 August 1938 and 28 November 1938, cited in D. G. Tendulkar, *Mahatma: life of Mohandas Karamchand Gandhi*, IV (New Delhi, revised edition, 1961), pp. 270–1, 309.
22 Undated office note, Lord Erskine, Madras, to Linlithgow, 5 August 1937, IOR, L/P&J/5/197; Haig to Linlithgow, 8 November 1937, IOR, L/P&J/5/264.
23 J. B. Irwin to Secretary, Governor-General, 16 May 1938, IOR, L/P&J/7/1071; Haig, 'Appreciation of existing position', 19 December 1938, IOR, L/P&J/5/266.
24 Intelligence Bureau report, 3 August 1939, and minute paper, 1529/39, IOR, L/P&J/7/1071.
25 Wynne, *Honourable Terms*, pp. 111–12; Arnold, *Police Power*, pp. 219–20.

26 Arnold, *Police Power*, pp. 94–5, 219; L. Brennan, 'The illusion of security: the background to Muslim separatism in the United Provinces', *Modern Asian Studies (MAS)*, 18 (1984), pp. 243, 263–4.

27 N. Mansergh (ed.), *The Transfer of Power, 1942–7*, II (London, 1971), pp. 451–513.

28 Linlithgow to L. S. Amery, Secretary of State for India, 24 August 1942, in Mansergh, *Transfer of Power*, II, p. 795.

29 Dow to Lord Wavell, Viceroy, 20 December 1946 and 11 January 1947, IOR, L/P&J/5/181.

30 P. Moon (ed.), *Wavell: the Viceroy's journal* (London, 1973), p. 366.

31 Colebrook to his mother, 9 April 1947, Colebrook Papers, IOR, MSS Eur. D. 789.

32 D. Arnold, 'The Congress and the police', in M. Shepperdson and C. Simmons (eds.), *The Indian National Congress and the Political Economy of India, 1885–1985* (Aldershot, 1988), pp. 214–15.

33 F. G. Hutchins, *India's Revolution: Gandhi and the Quit India movement* (Cambridge, Massachusetts, 1973), pp. 230–1. For further discussion of the police and the Quit India movement, see G. Pandey (ed.), *The Indian Nation in 1942* (Calcutta, 1988).

34 A. C. Bhuyan, *The Quit India Movement: the Second World War and Indian nationalism* (New Delhi, 1975), pp. 73, 108.

35 N. Mansergh (ed.), *The Transfer of Power*, VIII (London, 1979), pp. 38–44, 64, 147–8.

36 Gandhi, 'My idea of a police force', *Harijan*, 1 September 1940, *The Collected Works of Mahatma Gandhi*, LXXII (Delhi, 1978), pp. 402–4.

37 See Vallabhbhai Patel's 'serious objection' to a pictorial display of Quit India police 'atrocities' at Benares in January 1947: Patel to Pant, 31 January 1947, D. Das (ed.), *Sardar Patel's Correspondence, 1945–50*, V (Ahmedabad, 1973), p. 325. For the character and dilemmas of the Congress during this period, see C. Markovits, *Indian Business and Nationalist Politics, 1931–1939: the indigenous capitalist class and the rise of the Congress Party* (Cambridge, 1985); R. D. Shankardass, *The First Congress Raj: provincial autonomy in Bombay* (Delhi, 1982); Arnold, *Police Power*, pp. 213–29.

38 Moon, *Wavell*, p. 183.

39 Wylie to Wavell, 7 August 1946, Mansergh, *Transfer of Power*, VIII, p. 201; Colebrook to his mother, 23 October 1946, IOR. Colebrook Papers, Mss Eur. D. 789.

40 'Manpower shortage and the end of colonialism: the case of the Indian Civil Service', *MAS*, 7 (1973), pp. 47–73; cf. Potter, *India's Political Administrators*, chapters 3–4.

41 Gupta, *Police in British India*, pp. 470, 500, 551, 561.

42 V. Sahay, Home, Government of India, to R. E. Field, India Office, London, 19 August 1942, and G. C. M. Lewis, Minute, 10 July 1946, IOR, L/S&G/7/317; Secretary of State's memorandum on ICS and IP recruitment, 25 July 1946, Mansergh, *Transfer of Power*, VIII, p. 119.

43 A. K. Sinha, 'The police as I have known it', *The Indian Police Journal: Centenary Issue, 1861–1961*, p. 230; Wynne, *Honourable Terms*, p. 3; Arnold, *Police Power*, pp. 87–90, 97.

44 S. Sarkar, *Modern India, 1885–1947* (Delhi, 1983), pp. 418–25.

45 *The History of the Madras Police, 1859–1959* (Madras, 1959), pp. 429–30.

46 Bihar Fortnightly Report, first half September 1942, IOR, L/P&J/5/177; Bhuyan, *Quit India*, pp. 70, 187–8.

47 Bihar Fortnightly Report, first half October 1945, IOR, L/P&J/5/180.

48 Mansergh, *Transfer of Power*, VIII, p. 43.

49 Bihar Fortnightly Report, second half May 1947, IOR, L/P&J/5/182; Pyarelal, *Mahatma Gandhi*, volume 1, book 2 (Ahmedabad, 1965), pp. 312–14. The strike affected Bengal's police, too: Inspector-General, Bengal, to Director, Intelligence Bureau, 28 April 1947, in Das (ed.), *Patel's Correspondence*, V, p. 72. This and other reports also testify to growing communal divisions within the police in several provinces.

50 D. Arnold, 'The armed police and colonial rule in South India, 1914–1947', *MAS*, 11 (1977), pp. 101–25.

51 Quit India had, for example, brought home to the British the impracticality of relying upon major landholders (like the Maharaja of Darbhanga in Bihar) for effective support against the Congress: T. A. Stewart, Governor, Bihar, to Linlithgow, 12 October 1942,

IOR, L/P&J/5/177. Cf. Potter, *India's Political Administrators*, pp. 37, 42–3, for the former importance in policing terms of India's landed elites.

52 Gupta, *Police in British India*, pp. 469, 509, 547.

53 Stewart to Linlithgow, 25 August and 12 October 1942, IOR, L/P&J/5/177.

54 T. G. Rutherford, Governor, Bihar to Wavell, 11/12 November 1945, IOR, L/P&J/5/180.

55 Wavell to Cabinet, 5 November 1945, Moon, *Wavell*, p. 181; Wavell to Lord Pethick-Lawrence, Secretary of State for India, 12 July 1946, Mansergh, *Transfer of Power*, VIII, pp. 46–7.

56 Arnold, *Police Power*.

57 H. Knight, *Food Administration in India, 1939–47* (Stanford, 1954); B. R. Tomlinson, *The Political Economy of the Raj, 1914–1947: the economics of decolonization in India* (London, 1979).

58 Wavell to Winston Churchill, 24 October 1944, Moon, *Wavell*, p. 97; Tomlinson, *Political Economy*, pp. 162–3; Markovits, *Indian Business*, chapters 5–6.

59 Shankardass, *Congress Raj*, chapters 6–8.

60 Nehru in a curiously convoluted statement told police probationers at Mount Abu in October 1958 that with independence: 'There was no break as such but there was an enormous break all the same under the surface of things which seemed to be the same ... The whole relationship of the police with the public changed, even though people might not have realized it.' Mullik, *Nehru on Police*, p. 21.

61 Cited in Potter, *India's Political Administrators*, p. 125.

CHAPTER FOUR

Communal conflict and insurrection in Palestine, 1936–48

Charles Smith

On 18 February 1947, the British foreign secretary, Ernest Bevin, told the House of Commons that the British government was handing the responsibility of finding a solution to the problem of Palestine to the United Nations. 'We shall explain,' he said, 'that the Mandate has proved to be unworkable in practice, and that the obligations undertaken to the two communities in Palestine have shown to be irreconcilable.'[1] Bevin's announcement was the first public admission by a British statesman that the British government had failed in its aim of accommodating rival Arab and Jewish claims to Palestine, and, ultimately, of producing Arab and Jewish acquiesence to British rule of Palestine.

Bevin's exasperation was caused by the state of almost continual unrest in Palestine. The last twelve years of the mandate had been dominated by communal strife. In 1936 a general strike of the Arab population developed into a full-scale revolt, which took the British authorities three years to suppress completely. The end of Arab rebellion was immediately followed by rumours of Jewish unrest, and as the Second World War drew to a close, a Zionist revolt began, culminating in the withdrawal of Britain from Palestine in 1948, and the proclamation of the state of Israel.

Clearly, there was little consensus for British rule in the Holy Land. Yet, as was the case in Britain and throughout the empire, the principle that guided internal security policy was the idea that policing should be based on the consent of the population. Under the impact of revolution, this principle became more and more difficult to uphold. This was reflected in the Palestine police force, which, during this period, underwent dramatic changes in its role and composition, becoming increasingly militarised and reliant on British, rather than local personnel.

The early history of policing in Palestine

The development of the police force, however startling, did not represent a complete break with the past. From the very beginning of the Mandate, policing in Palestine was an uneasy compromise between the wish to govern with the consent of the population, and the need to rule by force. In July 1920 the British military administration in Palestine, which had ruled the country since its conquest from the Turks in 1917, gave way to a mixed British and Palestinian government, led by a British High Commissioner. A rudimentary police force was established, staffed mainly by Palestinians, and led by a small number of British officers recruited from the army. In March 1921 a Palestinian *gendarmerie* was added in order to reduce the expense of maintaining a large garrison in the country. As was the case with the police force and the government, most of the lower ranks were Palestinian, while the senior positions were filled by British officers. However, these arrangements soon proved unsuccessful. Less than two months later, in May 1921, Arab anger at increasing Jewish immigration led to the outbreak of serious anti-Jewish violence, which left forty-seven Jews and forty-eight Arabs dead. The disturbances gave police headquarters an early indication of how little they could rely on their Palestinian officers to police their own communities. Under the strain, the discipline of the force broke down, with Arab constables openly joining in the rioting and looting.

In March 1922, the British government therefore decided to raise a British *gendarmerie* of just over 700 officers and men, whose sole duty would be to provide support for the authorities in the event of further unrest. The existence of both a British and a Palestinian *gendarmerie*, plus the small garrison, meant that there were now three semi-military forces in Palestine. All three were therefore placed under the control of the new military commander in Palestine, Major-General Sir Hugh Tudor, the former chief of police during the civil war in Ireland, who arrived in Palestine in June 1922. He wished to staff the British *gendarmerie* with men he knew and trusted, so approximately three-quarters of the British *gendarmerie* were recruited from the disbanded Royal Irish Constabulary (RIC), and their auxiliary division, the notorious 'Black and Tans'. The roles of military and police commander were not separated until 1924, by which time the ethos, traditions and outlook of the police force in Palestine had been firmly established.[2]

During the next few years the country entered a relatively long period of peace, which enabled the authorities to attempt to create the basis of a regular, civil police force. In April 1926, the Palestine police force was formally established, divided into two separate sections, Part of the Palestinian *gendarmerie* was absorbed into a Palestinian section,

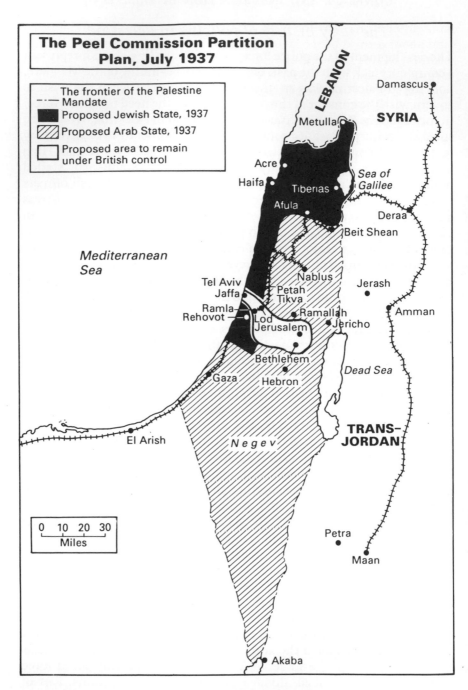

Palestine and the Peel Commission Partition Plan, July 1937

containing both Arabs and Jews. The British *gendarmerie* was abolished, and about a third of its members were drafted into a separate British section. Even so, their duties, training and disposition was still that of a riot squad, and they were little involved in regular police work, which was left almost entirely in the hands of Palestinians, supervised by British superior officers.[3]

In 1929, a dispute over access to the western wall in Jerusalem led to serious rioting breaking out again, which resulted in the deaths of 133 Jews and 116 Arabs, with hundreds more wounded. Once more Arab policemen either stood aside, or actively joined in, and until reinforcing troops arrived the unrest had to be contained by a handful of British policemen. When order had been restored, the British government appointed a commission, led by Sir Walter Shaw, to investigate the cause of the riots. Shaw devoted part of his report to the police force. He was extremely critical of the force, in particular the quality and quantity of intelligence gathered by the Criminal Investigation Department (CID). In fact, police intelligence was so bad that for twenty-seven of thirty-three days in September and October, the police had no information at all to publish in their daily situation reports. In the light of Shaw's remarks, the Colonial Office appointed Sir Herbert Dowbiggin, Inspector General of Police in Ceylon, to examine the performance of the force. Dowbiggin made major recommendations: an increase in the British section from its current establishment of 170, to 650, plus forty-six officers and inspectors, and a reorganisation and an improvement in the methods of the CID. He recommended a former colleague from Ceylon, Roy Spicer, to carry out the reforms, replacing the present commander, Arthur Mavrogordato.[4]

Shaw and Dowbiggin identified the central problem of policing in Palestine. Without good intelligence, the possibility of establishing an efficient civil police force, working with and for the local population, was minimal. But such intelligence could only be obtained with the co-operation of the population, something that was unlikely to happen unless the British government changed its policies in Palestine. In the absence of persuasion, the authorities had to rely increasingly on brute force to maintain British rule, upheld by the retention of a reliable British section.

When the dust had settled, Palestine again enjoyed a long and relatively uninterrupted period of peace. Spicer took the opportunity to emphasise the ordinary, civil aspects of police work. British policemen were sent to police stations throughout the country where they were expected to spend their time on criminal detection, rather than the square-bashing, physical jerks, and shooting practice that had previously occupied them.[5] By the beginning of 1936, Spicer's reforms seemed to have redefined the direction of the force. It now numbered 2,606 men, of whom 1,748 were Palestinian other ranks. Although the British section, with 709 other ranks, was still very large in comparison with most imperial police forces, it was better trained, and taking a larger part in ordinary police work. Spicer was even optimistic enough to suggest to the Colonial Office that they use the reformed British section as a source of senior officers for every police force throughout the empire.[6] Even so, the police force remained an uneasy coalition of police force and riot squad; the British section was still expected to provide emergency back-up to the civil authorities in the event of serious unrest. The problems confronting the force had not been resolved, but merely swept under the carpet. When communal rioting broke out in Jaffa in April 1936, this quickly became all too clear.

Policing in the Arab Revolt

Unlike previous outbreaks of trouble which had usually been confined to the main towns, unrest rapidly engulfed large areas of northern Palestine where most of the population was concentrated. Within a day or so of the beginning of the violence, an almost total strike of the Arab population began in support of nationalist demands for a representative government, an end to the sale of land to Jews, and a ban on further Jewish immigration into Palestine. When the strike failed to prompt any immediate concessions from the Palestine government, Arab militants formed small guerrilla units in the hills of northern Palestine and started to attack road traffic and police outposts. This was by far the most serious threat to British rule yet; by the beginning of June the High Commissioner, Sir Arthur Wauchope, told the Colonial Office that Palestine was already in a state of 'incipient revolution'.[7]

The police were not equipped, trained or prepared to meet a challenge of this magnitude. Their main tactic was the searching of Arab villages, usually protected by troops, where most of the gangs seemed to originate and draw support, weapons and supplies. However, co-operation from the villagers was minimal, so that the police had little idea who they were looking for or where arms might be concealed. Spicer and Richard Pierse, air officer commanding in Palestine who was also commander of the small British garrison, concluded that the villagers were being intimidated by the guerrillas into supporting their cause. Spicer and Pierse decided that they had to reply in kind. 'When one party used terror,' argued Spicer, 'the other party had to retaliate with the same methods.'[8] Taking care to conceal their intentions from Wauchope, who wished to end the unrest by negotiation, Spicer and Pierse ordered the police and troops to use 'Turkish methods' during search operations.[9]

Unfortunately for them, their plan back-fired. When he found out what had been happening, an enraged Wauchope ordered them to moderate the searches. Without good information, and unable to force the villagers to co-operate, search operations became a dismal failure and were abandoned altogether in July 1936.[10] Even worse, the tactics of Spicer and Pierse caused such resentment within the Palestinian section of the force that a few days after Wauchope's intervention, Spicer told Pierse that 'serious incidents' had occurred in police barracks in Jerusalem and Nablus, and that he could no longer rely on the loyalty of the Palestinian section.[11]

Even worse, many Arab policemen were actively helping the rebels. Confidential information on the security forces flowed freely to the guerrillas, to such an extent that both the army and the air force decided to keep the police in the dark about their future actions.[12] Rural posts, usually manned by Arab policemen, were now abandoned to the rebels, often without a fight.[13] To make good the deficit, the Colonial Office granted permission for the enlistment of 600 reservists, mainly from the Scots Guards, along with just over 3,000 Jewish auxiliary policemen who usually acted as drivers. There was also a small increase in the number of the British other ranks, so that it now totalled 915 men.[14] Thus the pattern was established; the absence of support by the population for the aims of the government resulted in a lack of assistance to the police from the population and a refusal of indigenous officers to obey orders. Control could only be maintained by the imposition of an alien body of men, most of whom had no police experience, and a greater willingness to use force.

Lacking in manpower and intelligence, short of transport and equipment, mistrusted by their colleagues in the army and air force, the police were increasingly left behind in the towns while the guerrillas were engaged by aircraft and troops. At the beginning of May, Pierse asked for reinforcements to be sent from Egypt and Iraq. Between then and October 1936, when the unrest ended, the garrison was reinforced twelve-fold.[15] Peace was restored by the despatch to Palestine of the first division of the army, with a subsequent threat to use the troops to impose martial law. The police had become largely irrelevant to the counter-insurgency effort.

Once the disturbances had been quelled, the British government sent a Royal Commission to Palestine, headed by Lord Peel, to seek a political solution to the problems of the country. In July 1937 the Commission reported, its main recommendation being the division of Palestine into separate Arab and Jewish states.[16] The Peel report also had a decisive influence on policing in Palestine. Peel scathingly dismissed the conciliatory approach of Wauchope, under whose regime the 'elementary duty' of maintaining law and order had not been discharged. If the population would not co-operate with the authorities by providing information, argued Peel, then there was little alternative but to use force. If trouble should reappear, martial law should be introduced under full military control. 'We are under no illusions as to what this means,' continued Peel. 'Innocent people may be sacrificed whilst the guilty escape.' Peel recommended the provision of barrack accommodation for every Palestinian police officer, to isolate him from nationalist influences, and the formation of a large mobile unit to be created by an increase in the number of mounted British police, or by the revival of the British *gendarmerie*.[17]

The first casualty of the Peel report was Spicer, who was removed from Palestine on the spurious grounds of fears for his health and safety. He was followed shortly afterwards by Wauchope, giving a similar excuse.[18] However, there was little time to digest Peel's recommendations before violence broke out again. The proposal to partition Palestine had outraged the Arab community. In September 1937 Lewis Andrews, the District Commissioner for Galilee, was murdered in Nazareth, an incident that marked the beginning of the 'second stage' of the Arab Revolt.

The report of the Peel Commission, which had been accepted by the Cabinet, now provided the framework for the British response to the revival of rebellion. Hundreds of suspects were interned without trial; the main nationalist body, the Arab Higher Committee, was declared illegal; and those of its leaders that could be found were arrested and deported. Even so, the murderers of Andrews escaped detection. This brought matters to a head between the police and the Palestine government, who shared Peel's concern with the quality of intelligence gathered by the CID.[19] The Colonial Office therefore asked Sir Charles Tegart, formerly of the Indian police force, a man who had gained considerable experience of guerrilla warfare in Bengal, to go to Palestine and examine the police force.

Tegart's report, presented in January 1938, covered familiar ground. Like Dowbiggin, it epitomised the dilemma between policing by consent and policing by force. On the one hand, it recommended the reorganisation and strengthening of the CID, with the achievement of greater efficiency by expert training, control and direction, and the development of closer relations between the government and the governed, particularly by regular visits to Arab villages. Tegart underlined the importance of involving Arabs in the force, as only they would be in a position to supply the authorities with reliable intelligence. On the other hand, Tegart supported Peel's proposal for the erection of barracks to house the entire Palestinian section of the police force; security could only be guaranteed at the price of isolating the Arab officers from their community. But

Tegart's most striking recommendation was for the creation of rural mounted units who would perform a similar function to the now defunct British section of the *gendarmerie* (although it would be a mixed British–Palestinian force). The sort of recruit required, wrote Tegart, was 'the tough type of man, not necessarily literate, who knows as much of the game as the other side'. These men should have military experience.[20]

In many ways Tegart's report was contradictory and confused. While it condemned the British section of the police force as 'neither policemen nor soldiers', his proposal for the creation of paramilitary rural mounted units was, in his own words, nothing less than a proposal to increase the 'buff' at the expense of the 'blue'.[21] Despite the muddle, Tegart's report echoed the sentiments of Peel; if Palestinians would not agree to being governed by the British, then imperial rule could only be maintained by using the big stick. In this sense the Tegart report was significant; it was another milestone along the road to the militarisation of the force and its alienation from the population it was supposed to serve.

Despite Tegart's report, the Arab rebellion continued to gain ground throughout 1938. By the autumn, the 'great retreat' of the British administration had begun as the rebels steadily gained control of more and more of the countryside. Yet again the Arab police proved unreliable and they had to be disarmed and moved to other duties, although a proposal to sack them was rejected by the new Inspector General, Alan Saunders, who feared that this would only drive them 'lock, stock and barrel' into the hands of the guerrillas.[22] Tegart's proposed rural mounted force had to be abandoned, as the mutual animosity engendered by the revolt destroyed any prospect of British and Arab policemen working together in the same units.[23] Thus, at the period of greatest danger for the British, the removal of Arab police from active duties meant that the strength of the security forces had been reduced by nearly 2,000 men – a situation made even more precarious by the possibility of war in Europe, which meant that there were no extra troops that could be spared for Palestine.[24]

Such a situation had two far-reaching consequences for the police. During the summer they had been steadily recruiting extra men for the British section, most of whom were army reservists.[25] By October the situation had deteriorated to the extent that the new High Commissioner, Sir Harold MacMichael, made a dramatic appeal to London for the immediate recruitment of another 1,250 men, all of whom should be ex-servicemen.[26] The Palestine authorities were now hanging on for dear life; the ability to fire a gun accurately was now much more important than any police experience. These new recruits had to be thrown straight into action, often with as little as ten days' training. During 1938, over 1,800 ex-servicemen swelled the ranks of the British section. It now contained 3,092 officers and men, the majority of whom had little or no police experience, outnumbering the 2,416 officers in the Palestinian section. There was also a huge increase in the number of Jewish auxiliaries, which now totalled nearly 12,000 men.[27]

Shortly before MacMichael's appeal, the necessity of co-ordinating the counter-insurgency effort had led the Palestine government to agree to placing the British section of the police under military control. The police were now organised into five companies concentrated at the main towns in Palestine, with the object of providing a fighting force to participate in military operations.[28] Once the Munich crisis was over, thousands more soldiers arrived in Palestine. The Palestine government moved aside, and the whole country was given over to virtual military control.

Despite being placed under the operational control of the army, the presence in Palestine of two complete divisions made it inevitable that the police played a secondary role in the counter-insurgency effort. Any likelihood of the police playing a more prominent role was firmly ruled out by army command. In practice they had little time for the British policemen, variously describing them as incompetent or unable to keep secrets, and even accusing them of cowardice.[29] Lieutenant-General Robert Haining, the commanding officer in Palestine, thought the police were so inefficient that he was even reluctant to agree to any increase in their numbers.[30] Both Haining and Bernard Montgomery, who was then a divisional commander in Palestine, were highly contemptuous of Saunders and campaigned openly in Whitehall for his removal.[31]

As had been the case in 1936, the force was again confined mainly to the towns where the police concentrated largely upon riot control, guard duties and patrolling, while the majority of operations against the guerrillas were carried out by the army and the Royal Air Force. But even in the towns the paucity of reliable police officers meant that control sometimes slipped from the police. In October 1938, for example, the Arab quarter of the old city of Jerusalem fell into guerrilla hands. Under military control, 'no-go' areas were not tolerated. Five days later, two units of troops, allegedly using Arabs as shields to protect their entry, successfully recaptured it and returned it to the safe-keeping of the police.[32] The police did not return to the countryside in any numbers until the end of the revolt in 1939, and the erection of a number of police forts, recommended by Tegart, had been completed.[33]

Whatever the truth behind the allegation that Arabs were used as human shields by the troops that reoccupied Jerusalem, this was only one of a vast number of accusations of brutality that accompanied the assumption of near-military control in Palestine. This inevitably affected the police force too. Under the military aegis, any constraining influences on those police officers who felt restricted by the conventions of normal police behaviour were quickly removed. As early as September 1938 MacMichael had noted the 'occasional emergence of black and tan tendencies' amongst the British section.[34] Suspects arrested for interrogation and held in police stations were now tortured as a matter of course; bastinado, suspending suspects upside down and urinating in their nostrils, extracting fingernails and pumping water into a suspect before stamping on him, became commonplace.[35] If the police or the army believed a road might be mined, local men were rounded up and forced to act as 'minesweepers' by sitting in vehicles that would be forced to drive along in front of police or military convoys.[36] The most notorious incident involving the police force came at the end of October 1938, when four British policemen shot, in cold blood, a prisoner they were supposed to be escorting between two police stations. Presumably, the policemen were so confident that their actions would receive official sanction that they murdered the victim in broad daylight, on open land, in full view of several European inhabitants. Their confidence was not misplaced; although they were all arrested, they were charged with manslaughter and only received derisory sentences which were all reduced on appeal. They were also allowed to resign from the force rather than be dismissed. It should also be noted that these were not young, poorly trained recruits; between them they had well over ten years, experience in the force.[37] In spite of the occasional unease of the Colonial Office, the Palestine government was generally prepared to condone the means of its police force (and of the troops) if the ends justified them.[38]

Policing during the Jewish Revolt

By the beginning of 1939 the draconian measures taken by the military had crushed the Arab Revolt. However, there was little time for the police to draw breath and regroup. Within a few months they faced a new crisis. In September war broke out in Europe. The army made it clear that they now wished to divest themselves of responsibility for internal security in Palestine; the police would now have to stand on their own two feet. Although the British section of the police force had been expanded, they would be unlikely to fill the manpower gap. Most of them had only joined on temporary two-year contracts, and MacMichael warned the Colonial Office that when their contracts expired almost all of them would wish to leave the police and rejoin the army.[39] The position was made even more threatening by warnings from numerous sources predicting that the end of the Arab Revolt would soon be followed by the beginning of a Jewish Revolt.

The Palestine authorities were thus faced with a shortage of men at the worst possible moment. MacMichael responded by taking emergency powers to extend the contracts of the temporary recruits, even against their will. When a number of policemen defied these orders they were arrested and sentenced to prison. Not surprisingly, this caused considerable resentment in the ranks. Meanwhile, in the summer of 1942 the military situation in the Middle East had seriously deteriorated as the Germans pushed deeper into Egypt. In June 1942 MacMichael acted. Although the police had been under the operational control of the army, they were still regarded as a separate body. MacMichael now placed the force under the Army Act. From then to the end of the war, the police were regarded as being a component of the armed forces, and were liable for military duties.[40]

Paradoxically, most of the recruits of 1938 that MacMichael had been forced to retain had proved to be almost entirely unfit for police work. One official admitted that, had it not been for the war, only 400 of the original 1,250 recruits would have had their contracts renewed.[41] Such problems were not confined to the ranks. Many of the leading officers had risen through the ranks after arriving in Palestine from Ireland when the British *gendarmerie* had been created in 1922. Saunders reported that over half his superior officers were so limited in their abilities that they could not be promoted, while seven of them were so incompetent that he asked for them to be transferred away from Palestine altogether. However, the manpower shortage was so serious that not only were most of these officers retained in Palestine, but MacMichael was even forced to recommend one of them, Raymond Cafferata, for promotion to the rank of superintendent.[42]

The police, therefore, were in a sorry state as a new revolt loomed. Morale was at an all-time low. The authorities responded with the usual remedy: yet another reorganisation of the force. In May 1943 Mac-Michael put forward a proposal for the reintroduction of a *gendarmerie* in Palestine. It would number 2,000 men and work alongside the existing British section of the police force, acting as a temporary body 'holding the fort' until the war had ended. Once again, recruits would be found by persuading the armed services to release men.[43] In November 1943 MacMichael's proposals were accepted by the War Cabinet, with the proviso that the Palestine government find a substitute for the word *gendarmerie* lest the public be in any doubt that the new force was an integral part of the civilian police force.[44] The details were left to the new Inspector General, Captain John Rymer-Jones (who had replaced Saunders in August 1943) and his deputy, Michael McConnell, to sketch out. The final appearance of the Police Mobile Force (PMF), as it was to be called, owed a considerable amount to the background and former experience of these two officers. Rymer-Jones had served with the army in Ireland in 1920, and McConnell, a former RIC man, had been a company commander with the original British *gendarmerie*. The PMF was to be organised, said Rymer-Jones, 'much like an armoured division...equipped with armoured cars, bren guns, mortars, and sten guns, et cetera'.[45]

The PMF, therefore, was more akin to an army unit than a police force. They were even clad in khaki battle dress and remained so long after the war had ended.[46] If it had remained a temporary body, as Mac-Michael and the Colonial Office envisaged, or a protective screen behind which the police force would carry out their normal duties, as the army wished, then the influence of the PFM on the police force might have been insignificant.[47] But Rymer-Jones had other ideas. He saw the PMF as the crack unit of the police force, leading the fight against terrorism.[48] In this way the paramilitary PMF came to be both a permanent fixture of the police force and its dominant influence.

The integration of the police force with the armed services, and the creation of the PMF, ensured that the military influence on the force was pervasive. Increasingly the police were seeing the problems of insurgency through military eyes. Nowhere is this more clear than in the training programmes in which the force now took part. In 1944, for example, the police and the armed services in Palestine took part in two joint exercises in which they confronted an imaginery Zionist movement determined to seize power. In exercise 'Cyrus', the participants were asked to imagine a situation in which the Jews were refusing to surrender their arms and were not prepared to co-operate with the authorities on such matters as transport and the distribution of food. Meanwhile the unrest was causing the Arabs to become restive, and they were attacking Jewish settlements and civilians. The problem set for the participants in the exercise was to organise mobile columns from units under their command, and to keep communications open.[49] The Arabs had been defeated in a military campaign; *ergo*, any Zionist revolt could be tackled in a similar manner. However, none of the skills developed on such courses were to have much relevance during the Zionist revolt.

Not everyone agreed with the direction the force was taking. At first the establishment of the PMF was greeted with little enthusiasm by many career police officers, who resented the continuing imposition of soldiers on the existing police structure, and who were jealous of the greater prestige attached to the new body by police headquarters.[50] This was part of a growing unease on the part of many officers prompted by the very rapid increase of the force in 1938, and the subservience of the police force to the army.[51] Many policemen complained that while they were expected to behave as soldiers, they were also denied any of the perks of army life, such as duty-free cigarettes and beer.[52]

In terms of their day-to-day duties, the PMF were mainly engaged in patrolling, escort, and cordon-and-search operations. They might have been an ideal unit for the maintenance of law and order if, as had been the case during the Arab rebellion, the enemy had been organised in armed guerrilla gangs and had worn semi-military uniforms. But Zionist insurgents were not so easily recognisable. They usually operated in small units, planting bombs and carrying out assassinations before melting back into the cities. The key to successful police operations was good intelligence which might enable the police to identify and locate the insurgents, and provide evidence to convict them. But the sort of operations carried out by the PMF were not capable of generating such information.

At first this did not seem to be too important, as the CID were receiving considerable information on the activities of the two militant Zionist organisations, the *Irgun zvai leumi*, and *Lehi*, which was eponymously known to the British as the Stern gang after its late leader, Abraham Stern. In November 1944, Lord Moyne, the British Minister-President in the Middle East, was assassinated by two members of *Lehi*. Fearing that such actions would damage the prospects for a favourable political solution in Palestine, Moyne's murder prompted the main Zionist body in Palestine, the Jewish Agency, and its military wing, the *Haganah*, to begin a short-lived period of co-operation with the authorities against the *Irgun* and *Lehi*. For a few months information flowed relatively freely, and the police were able to make a number of arrests.[53] However, by the summer of 1945 the political situation had changed when the new Labour government, contrary to all its previous promises, refused to establish a Jewish state in Palestine. Co-operation with the British authorities was withdrawn, and information began to dry up. Without the assistance of the Jewish Agency, the Criminal Investigation Department (CID) could make few inroads into the Zionist underground. In fact, quite the opposite was the case. The mass enlistment of the Jewish auxiliary policemen during the Arab Revolt had opened the door to Zionist infiltrators. By 1946 there were 650 Jews in the regular police force, most of whom were also members of the *Haganah*, drastically compromising operational secrecy.[54] Even worse, early that year the deteriorating security situation led to the withdrawal of British policemen from Tel Aviv, leaving control in the hands of Jewish officers. As the army pointed out, this meant that Tel Aviv had been handed over to the *Haganah*.[55]

Throughout 1946 the situation worsened. Thousands of would-be immigrants, arriving in pitiful, unseaworthy boats, continued to be turned away from Palestine, complicating relations with Washington and embarrassing the government in the eyes of the world. In July, the secretariat of the Palestine government, housed in the King David Hotel in Jerusalem, was blown up by the *Irgun*, killing over ninety people.

[74]

Meanwhile, the security forces were being constantly shot at, blown up or vilified by the Zionist organisations. In the absence of good intelligence, the police and the army had little to hit back with except large-scale cordon-and-search operations mounted in the hope, rather than the expectation, of arresting anyone. These tactics never succeeded in finding more than a handful of *Irgun* or *Lehi* members, and had little effect on their activities.[56] By August 1946 the Palestine government had lost patience. Sir Alan Cunningham, the High Commissioner, told the Colonial Office that the police needed 'some new ideas', and requested that they send to Palestine Sir Charles Wickham, a former Inspector General with the Royal Ulster Constabulary, who had recently served with the British forces during the civil war in Greece.[57]

Wickham found the force under tremendous strain. They were over-worked, lacking in experience, and operating without overall political guidance. Despite the creation of the PMF, an aggressive recruitment campaign on the part of the colonial authorities had failed to fill the vacancies in the force. In 1946 the police were functioning at barely half strength; even the PMF had only 733 officers and men, instead of the 2,000 envisaged when it had been established.[58] The lack of suitable volunteers for the force had led to a lowering of the age requirement; Wickham found that over 75 per cent of the recruits during 1946 were between 18 and 19 years of age.[59]

Wickham's report severely criticised the influence of the PMF on the force, and he recommended that it be immediately abolished. Patrol by armoured car was virtually the only tactic the police now employed. Such methods, he argued, isolated the police from the public they were supposed to serve and made the collection of information very difficult. He recognised that the creation of the PMF had led to a militarisation of the force with a subsequent loss of traditional police skills; during the previous twelve months, he wrote, new recruits to the force had received no training in police methods.[60] The army agreed with Wickham's assessment. 'It is no exaggeration to say that the police force in Palestine is quite ineffective', wrote Montgomery, now Chief of the Imperial General Staff: 'I think the reason is the force is wrongly organised. Part of it is trained to act as soldiers and [they] will never be any better than third-class soldiers.'[61]

The lack of training finally told in November 1946, when the strain of continual harassment suffered by the young and frightened police officers led to a collapse in the discipline of the force. On the night of 18 November, a police vehicle was blown up by terrorists, causing the death of four of its occupants. As a result a number of policemen went on the rampage in Tel Aviv. Jewish cars were stolen, several people were assaulted, a number of buildings were damaged, while a street was allegedly cleared by policemen firing their guns along it. A Jewish police patrol was also fired upon.[62] An even more serious incident occurred the following summer, after the hanging of two army intelligence officers by the *Irgun*. Four Jews were killed and fifteen injured when a grenade was tossed into a café in Tel Aviv from a police armoured car. Earlier that evening the armoured car had fired on a crowded Jewish bus and on a Jewish taxi. A massive cover-up by policemen from the depot where the armoured car was based ensured that no criminal charges were ever laid against those suspected of involvement.[63]

Despite the concern that many policemen shared with Wickham about the militarisation of the force, the report was received with hostility by most policemen, who resented the implication that they were too cowardly to be out on the streets mixing with the population. Being well armed and protected, they pointed out, was the only way to survive in Palestine.[64] Either way, although the PMF was dissolved, Wickham's report was overtaken by events. In January 1947 Cunningham attacked both the police and the military for their inability to protect the lives of British civilian officials in Palestine, and reorganised the government and administration of Palestine into easily defendable, protected areas.[65] By the end of February 1947 all British women and children had been evacuated from Palestine, while their men stayed behind. The men were confined in 'Bevingrads' where they lived lonely and miserable lives, protected by barbed wire and armed guards, forbidden to move outside except with an escort.[66] The same month came Bevin's announcement that Britain was handing the problem of Palestine to the United Nations, and from then until the end of the Mandate, police operations were largely confined to protecting the British withdrawal. The Colonial Office acknowledged that there was now no possibility of the police force carrying out their duties in the manner envisaged by Wickham.[67]

Yet in the few months that remained of British rule in Palestine, there was the curious case of the Farran affair, an event that in many ways summed up the process of the previous twelve years. At the beginning of 1947, the abduction and flogging of four soldiers by the *Irgun*, and the kidnapping of two British officials, one of whom was a high-ranking judge, left the Cabinet feeling angry and humiliated at this block to British prestige. This led them finally to accede to Montgomery's long-standing demands to lift the restrictions that controlled the level of force used in security operations.[68]

This was the context within which Nicol Gray, who had replaced Rymer-Jones as Inspector General in March 1946, evolved the idea of special police undercover units, to operate against the Zionist underground. Influenced by the wartime success of such organisations as the Special Air Service (SAS) and the Special Operations Executive, Gray, an ex-Royal Marine, appointed Brigadier Bernard Fergusson, who had served under Wingate in Burma, to form the units. Those policemen who heard of the proposals were horrified. Even Rymer-Jones, now back in England with the Metropolitan Police, was alarmed, and warned Fergusson that such tactics would end in disaster.[69] Fergusson ignored him and appointed two squads of ten men each, mainly recruited from the now disbanded SAS, one led by Alistair McGregor, an ex-soldier who had been in MI6, and the other by Roy Farran who had fought behind enemy lines in France.[70]

Rymer-Jones's worries were confirmed almost immediately. Fergusson's original proposals were unclear on the role of the squads: were they to infiltrate and gather intelligence, or were they to seek and destroy?[71] Both Gray and the Palestine government warned that the squads must stay within the bounds of the law.[72] If so, these orders did not communicate themselves to Farran. 'It was to all intents and purposes a *carte blanche* and the original conception of our part filled me with excitement,' he recalled. 'A free hand for us against terror when all the others were so closely hobbled!'[73]

The chain of command for the squads was also confused. Fergusson had stated that they would be answerable to the local superintendent of police.[74] Farran, meanwhile, felt that their secrecy would be compromised if they had to work with the CID.[75] Furthermore, the police force was still under the operational control of the army, and Fergusson admitted to Rymer-Jones that as commander of the squads, he would be mainly responsible to army command in Palestine and not to the Inspector General.[76] Neither had the squads any recognisable political objective. Their formation came at exactly the same time as the Cabinet had signalled their intention to withdraw from Palestine. Montgomery's pressure had merely succeeded in establishing units that had no logical or sensible role to play.

The squads started operating in April 1947, but before their performance could be properly judged a scandal blew up. In May, Alexander Rubowitz, a young member of *Lehi*, was abducted and never seen again. The squads were implicated, and the Palestine government decided to arrest Farran and try him for murder. Farran, however, was tipped off and fled to Syria, where he was granted political asylum. He was tracked down by Fergusson and two officers from his regiment, who persuaded him to return to Palestine to sort things out. However, Farran, despite Fergusson's promises to the contrary, was arrested as soon as he arrived back in the country. So two days later he escaped again, this time to Saudi Arabia. He subsequently returned to stand trial when word reached him that the Jewish underground were planning reprisals against other British officers.[77] Fergusson, meanwhile, had hesitated for five days after the flight of Farran before telling Gray what had happened. Gray then sat on the information for several days before finally confiding in Arthur Giles, the Deputy Inspector General and head of the CID. Giles immediately brought it to the notice of Cunningham. No report was made to London for nearly three weeks, to the fury of Arthur Creech-Jones, the Colonial Secretary.[78] When he was finally brought to trial, Farran was acquitted, Fergusson declining to give evidence on the grounds that he might incriminate himself. Once the trial had finished, Fergusson was ordered to resign and be out of the country within thirty-six hours.[79]

Conclusion

The Farran affair was a fitting conclusion to the history of British policing in Palestine. The Arab Revolt, followed shortly afterwards by the Jewish Revolt, had shown that there was little consent for British rule in Palestine. 'Our general security in Palestine,' recalled Oliver Lyttleton, Minister-Resident in the Middle East in 1941, 'rested more upon military strength than upon any consent of the inhabitants to the existing regime.'[80]

Nevertheless, from the very earliest days of the Mandate, policing by consent remained the ideal, the yardstick against which the success or otherwise of policing was measured. When Palestine was at peace, emphasis lay on the promotion and development of police skills such as criminal prevention and detection, usually augmented by attempts to wean the British section away from riot control, in the hope that it would become fully involved with regular police work. But when Palestine was disturbed, the authorities usually had to fall back on the coercive abilities of the British section, particularly as their Arab colleagues had shown on several occasions that they could not be relied upon. The Palestine police force, like most police forces, was an amalgam of coercion and persuasion; which aspect had the upper hand depended upon the stability of the internal security situation.

The state of almost permanent revolt that engulfed Palestine from 1936 was responsible for ensuring that the coercive side to policing predominated. This was accentuated in 1938 by military control of the force, and the mass recruitment of hundreds of army reservists, which decisively tipped the balance towards a militarisation. Under the impact of war, the police moved even further in this direction. Policing problems were then seen in almost military terms, evidence of which was the formation of the Police Mobile Force which, under the prompting of Rymer-Jones and McConnell, had such a decisive influence on the force.

The Arab and Jewish revolts merely illustrated that, all along, the velvet glove concealed an iron fist. Almost all of the very first recruits were enrolled because of their experience in fighting guerrilla warfare in Ireland. Many of these men stayed with the force to the very end, by which time they were in positions of responsibility, influencing its outlook and shaping its ethos. In a sense, the career of Raymond Cafferata symbolised the Palestine police force. A former 'Black and Tan', he arrived in Palestine when the British section of the *gendarmerie* had been formed in 1922. By 1939 he had risen near to the top of the force, despite the fact that his own commanding officer had described his police knowledge as poor and had recommended him for transfer away from Palestine. Both Rymer-Jones and McConnell, two of the most influential of all Palestine policemen, learnt their trade in Ireland. By 1943, ex-'Black and Tan' men held five of the eight positions of district commander in the force.[81] Seen in this light, the Farran case was only a logical extension of what had been created in the earliest days of the Mandate.

Notes

1 House of Commons Debates, Vol. 433, Cols. 985–94, 18 February 1947.
2 For a history of early policing operations in Palestine see 'Palestine and Trans-Jordan 1921–1936', Public Record Office, Kew [PRO] AIR 19/9; Memorandum by the Colonial Secretary, November 1921, PRO CAB 24/131; Middle East Department, 'Note on the Palestine Police Force', December 1946, PRO CO 537/2269; Palestine Police Force Annual Administrative Reports, 1931 to 1935, PRO CO 814/5–10; The Palin Report, PRO FO 371/23229; Harry Luke and Edward Keith-Roach, *The Handbook of Palestine* (London, 1922), pp. 202–3; Cd. 1540, October 1921, appendix 'A'; Cd. 3530, March 1930, pp. 12–14, 145–8; Brigadier Angus McNeil, 'Notes on the British gendarmerie', 3 January 1923, Middle East Centre, St Antony's College, Oxford [McNeil papers]; Edward Horne, *A Job Well Done: a history of the Palestine Police Force 1920–1948* (Leigh-on-Sea, 1982), chapters 1 to 7; Douglas V. Duff, *Bailing With a Teaspoon* (London, 1953); James Lunt, *Imperial Sunset: frontier policing in the twentieth century* (London, 1981), pp. 51–3; A. J. Kingsley-Heath, 'The Palestine Police Force under the Mandate', *Police Journal*, 1 (1928), pp. 78–88.
3 Geoffrey J. Morton, *Just the Job* (London, 1957), pp. 19–20.
4 Cd. 3530, March 1930, pp. 147–8; Committee of Imperial Defence, 20 December 1929, PRO CAB 5/7/339; High Commissioner to Shuckburgh, 22 March 1930, PRO CO 733/180/1; High Commissioner to Colonial Secretary, 17 November 1930, PRO CO 733/180/2; High Commissioner to Shuckburgh, 22 March 1930, PRO CO 733/176/5; Middle East Department, 'Note on the Palestine Police Force', December 1946, PRO CO 537/2269; Horne, *A Job Well Done*, pp. 159–62, 467–8; Cd. 5479, pp. 194–5.
5 Morton, *Just The Job*, pp. 19–20, 27–8.
6 Palestine Police Force Annual Administrative Report, 1935, PRO CO 814/10; Horne, *A Job Well Done*, pp. 169–70.
7 High Commissioner to Colonial Secretary, 2 June 1936, PRO CO 733/297/2.
8 Quoted in Tom Bowden, *The Breakdown of Public Security: the case of Ireland 1916–1921 and Palestine 1936–1939* (London, 1977), pp. 230–1.
9 Air Vice Marshal Richard Pierse, 'Abridged despatch on the disturbances in Palestine, 19 April – 14 September 1936', PRO AIR 5/1244, p. 25.
10 'Abridged despatch', pp. 46–7, PRO AIR 5/1244; and Palestine Police Force Annual Administrative Report, 1936, PRO CO 814/11.
11 General Staff, HQ, the British Forces, Palestine and Trans-Jordan, February 1938, 'Report on the military lessons of the Arab rebellion in Palestine 1936', pp. 12–13, PRO WO 282/6; 'Abridged despatch', PRO AIR 5/1244, p. 31.

12 Sir Henry Brooke-Popham to Ellington, 20 July 1936 [Brooke-Popham papers], Liddell Hart Centre for Military Archives, King's College, London, 11 June 1941; 'Report on the military lessons of the Arab rebellion in Palestine', PRO WO 282/6, pp. 51–2.
13 'Report on the military lessons of the Arab rebellion in Palestine', pp. 116–18.
14 Simpson to Furse, 7 February 1941, PRO CO 733/417/75015/46; Palestine Police Force Annual Administrative Report 1936, PRO CO 814/11.
15 'Report on the military lessons of the Arab rebellion in Palestine', pp. 116–18; 'Palestine disturbances 1936: report of the General Officer Commanding British forces in Palestine and Trans-Jordan', 30 October 1936, PRO WO 32/9401, p. 6.
16 Cd. 5479, pp. 380–96.
17 Cd. 5479, pp. 195–202.
18 Colonial Secretary to Battershill, 21 October 1937, PRO CO 733/332/10; Battershill to Colonial Secretary, 2 October 1937, PRO CO 733/332/11; Memorandum by the Colonial Secretary, 8 October 1937, PRO CAB 24/271/232; 13 October 1937, PRO CAB 23/89/37(37); Edward Keith-Roach, 'Pasha of Jerusalem', pp. 432–3 [Keith Roach papers], Middle East Centre, St Antony's College, Oxford; Sir Arthur Wauchope to Malcolm MacDonald, 2 November 1937 [MacDonald papers], Department of Palaeography, University of Durham, 9/9/13; Morton, *Just The Job*, pp. 58–9.
19 See High Commissioner to Colonial Secretary, 27 March 1937, PRO CO 733/333/2; Battershill to Shuckburgh, 12 October 1937, PRO CO 733/356/1; High Commissioner to Parkinson, 20 May 1937, PRO CO 733/332/11.
20 Tegart Report, PRO CO 733/383/75742.
21 Meeting with High Commissioner, General Officer Commanding, and Inspector General of Police, 7 January 1938 [Tegart papers], Middle East Centre, St Antony's College, Oxford, box 2, file 3.
22 Major Alan Saunders to Sir Charles Tegart, 20 October 1938, Tegart papers, box 3, file 4; 'Narrative despatches from the High Commissioner to the Secretary of State for the Colonies, reporting on the situation in Palestine, vol. 1', no. 10, 24 October 1938, PRO CO 935/21.
23 Battershill to Colonial Secretary, 9 October 1938, PRO CO 733/383/75742/1.
24 Note of a conference at the Colonial Office, 7 September 1938, PRO PREM 1/352.
25 High Commissioner to Colonial Secretary, 9 August 1938; draft letter by the Colonial Secretary to Mr Brusier, 18 August 1938; War Office to Crown Agents, 30 – July 1938; High Commissioner to Colonial Secretary, 14 September 1938, PRO CO 733/358/75015/1.
26 High Commissioner to Colonial Secretary, 20 October 1938, PRO CO 733/358/75015/1; Simpson to Furse, 7 February 1941, PRO CO 733/417/75015/46.
27 Palestine Police Force Annual Administrative Report, 1938, PRO CO 814/13.
28 High Commissioner to Colonial Secretary, 12 September 1938, PRO CO 733/358/75015/1; Battershill to Colonial Secretary, 9 October 1938, PRO CO 733/383/75742/1.
29 Sir Charles Tegart, diaries, Vol. 1, entry for 10 January 1938, Tegart papers; Tegart report, chapter 22, PRO CO 733/383/75742; Harris to Pierse, 5 September 1938, PRO AIR 23/765; 24 August 1938, PRO CAB 24/193/278, p. 24.
30 General Sir Richard O'Connor to Mrs O'Connor (no date), O'Connor papers, Liddell Hart Centre for Military Archives, King's College, London, 5/1.
31 Meeting between Haining, MacDonald and Luke, 20 August 1939, PRO CO 733/415/75982; Haining to Tegart, 6 July 1939, Tegart papers, box 4, file 4; Nigel Hamilton, *Monty: the marking of a general 1887–1942* (London, 1981), pp. 300–2.
32 H. W. Faure, 'Operations in the old city of Jerusalem, October 1938', *Guards Magazine* (Autumn 1979), pp. 99–103; Yehoshua Porath, *The Palestinian Arab National Movement: from riots to rebellion, Vol. 2, 1929–1939* (London, 1977), p. 240; Horne, *A Job Well Done*, pp. 237–8; General Sir Richard O'Connor to Mrs O'Connor, 18 October and 22 October 1938, O'Connor papers, 5/1; Keith-Roach, 'Pasha of Jerusalem', pp. 445–6, Keith-Roach papers, Middle East Centre, St Antony's College, Oxford.
33 Tegart report, chapter 3, PRO CO 733/383/75742; HQ, British Forces in Palestine and Trans-Jordan, 'Despatch on the operations carried out by British forces in Palestine and Trans-Jordan', 3 August – 31 December 1939', 16 February 1940, PRO WO 201/169;

Note of a meeting between General Ironside and the Colonial Secretary, 27 February 1940, PRO CO 733/417/75015/43.

34 High Commissioner to Colonial Secretary, 5 September 1938, PRO CO 733/358/75015/1.

35 Roger Courtney, *Palestine Policeman: an account of eighteen dramatic months in the Palestine Police Force during the great Jew–Arab troubles* (London, 1939), p. 214; General Sir Richard O'Connor to Mrs O'Connor, 3 November 1938, O'Connor papers, 5/1; Ogden to Baggally, 8 September 1938, PRO FO 371/21881; Internal note by Parkinson, 20 May 1939, PRO CO 733/413/75900/3; Memorandum by Lees (no date), PRO CO 733/75156/71/B.

36 General Sir Neil Ritchie, 'Palestine retrospective', 25 August 1939, Ritchie papers, King's Own Royal Regiment Museum, Lancaster; Charles Groves, *History of the Royal Ulster Rifles, Vol. 3* (Belfast, 1950), p. 29; Hugh Foot, *A Start in Freedom* (London, 1964), pp. 52–3; 'Narrative despatches from the High Commissioner to the Secretary of State for the Colonies reporting on the situation in Palestine, Vol. 1', No. 10, p. 24, October 1938, PRO CO 935/21.

37 See PRO CO 733/75156/71/B.

38 See, for example, High Commissioner to Shuckburgh, 20 October 1938, PRO FO 371/21865; High Commissioner to Colonial Secretary, 29 August 1942, PRO CO 733/434/75015/54.

39 High Commissioner to Downie, 19 April 1940, PRO CO 733/416/75015.

40 Hutchinson to War Office, 19 December 1940, PRO CO 733/416/75015; High Commissioner to Colonial Secretary, 26 October 1940, Simpson to Furse, 7 February 1941 and note by Bennett, 24 February 1941, PRO CO 733/417/75015/46; Draft telegram (by Colonial Secretary?), 27 November 1942, PRO CO 733/434/75015/50; Horne, *A Job Well Done*, pp. 243–50.

41 Simpson to Furse, 7 February 1941, PRO CO 733/417/75015/46; Meeting between Simpson, Gater and Battershill, 28 July 1942, PRO CO 733/433/75015/3.

42 Saunders to Tegart, 23 February 1939, Tegart papers, box 3, file 4; High Commissioner to Colonial Secretary, 17 October 1940, PRO CO 733/416/75015/A.

43 High Commissioner to Colonial Secretary, 24 May 1943; Note for the Colonial Secretary before his meeting with the High Commissioner, September 1943; Note of a meeting between Colonial, Foreign and War Office officials, 10 December 1943 and Commander-in-Chief, Middle East, to War Office, 20 December 1943, PRO CO 733/434/75015/55; Memorandum by the Colonial Secretary, 16 November 1943, PRO CAB 66/43/WP (43)510.

44 19 November 1943, PRO CAB 65/36/158(43).

45 Horne, *A Job Well Done*, pp. 85, 515; interview with Brigadier John Rymer-Jones, 19 August 1986.

46 Horne, *A Job Well Done*, p. 264.

47 General Staff, Force HQ, Jerusalem, 'Memorandum regarding a gendarmerie or a semi-military force for Palestine', January 1939, PRO WO 106/5720; High Commissioner to Colonial Secretary, 24 May 1943, PRO CO 733/434/75015/55.

48 Interview with Rymer-Jones, 19 August 1986.

49 'Exercise Cyrus', 2 and 3 February 1944, and 'Exercise Scylla', 25 July 1944, PRO WO 169/15849.

50 Horne, *A Job Well Done*, pp. 519–20; Bernard Fergusson, *The Trumpet in the Hall* (London, 1970), p. 202.

51 Fergusson, *The Trumpet in the Hall*, pp. 34–5; Memorandum by A. J. Kingsley-Heath, 7 March 1939, and Memorandum by Saunders (no date), both in Tegart papers, box 2, file 1.

52 Simpson to Furse, 7 February 1941, PRO CO 733/75015/46.

53 Fo co-operation between the British authorities in Palestine and the Jewish Agency after the murder of Lord Moyne see Security summary, Middle East, no. 210, 29 November 1944, PRO FO 371/40128; Memorandum by the Colonial Secretary, 23 November 1944, PRO CAB 66/58/WP(44)678; Weizmann to Churchill, 18 December 1944, PRO CAB 66/59/WP(44)746; 24 November 1944, PRO CAB 65/48/155(44)1;

High Commissioner to Colonial Secretary, 20 September 1946, PRO FO 371/52559. For an account of the attitude of the Jewish Agency and the *Haganah* towards the *Irgun* and *Lehi* see J. Bowyer Bell, *Terror out of Zion* (Dublin, 1979), pp. 125–35.

54 Middle East Department, 'Note on the Palestine Police Force', December 1946, PRO CO 537/2269; Efraim Dekel, *Shai: the exploits of a Haganah intelligence* (New York and London, 1959), p. 15; Yehuda Bauer, *From Diplomacy to Resistance: a history of Jewish Palestine 1939–1945* (New York, 1973), pp. 11–13; Yehuda Bauer, 'From co-operation to resistance: the haganah 1938–1946', *Middle Eastern Studies* (1966), pp. 182–210; Morton, *Just the Job*, p. 119.

55 General Sir Hugh Stockwell, note on the British presence in Tel Aviv, 15 August 1946, Stockwell papers, Liddell Hart Centre for Military Archives, King's College, London, 6/2; David Clark, 'The colonial police and anti-terrorism: Bengal 1930–1936, Palestine 1937–1947, and Cyprus 1955–1959' (D.Phil. thesis, Oxford, 1978), p. 207.

56 See, for example, High Commissioner, 9 January 1947, and 'Summary of recent searches in Palestine' (no date or author), PRO CO 733/477/3.

57 High Commissioner to Colonial Secretary, 1 August 1946, PRO CO 537/3847. Army Command in Palestine remarked that intelligence on the *Irgun* and *Lehi* was 'insufficient [to] permit of any preconceived plan for their extermination'. Memorandum by Lieutenant-General Barker, 'Military actions to be taken to enforce law and order in Palestine', 22 June 1946, PRO WO 261/568.

58 The establishment of the British section of the force was now 5,453, but actual strength was only 2,993. See Middle East Department, 'Note on the Palestine Police Force', December 1946, PRO CO 537/2269; Minute by Clark, 4 November 1946, PRO CO 537/1696.

59 'Palestine Police: Report by Sir Charles Wickham', PRO CO 537/2269. For a discussion of the recruitment problems of the force, see Clark, 'The colonial police and anti-terrorism', pp. 242–51.

60 'Palestine Police: Report by Sir Charles Wickham'.

61 Montgomery to Simpson, 2 December 1946, Montgomery papers, Imperial War Museum, BLM 177/9.

62 Clippings from the *Daily Mail* and the *News Chronicle*, both 19 November 1946, and High Commissioner to Colonial Secretary, same date, PRO CO 733/456/8/2.

63 High Commissioner to Colonial Secretary, 15 November 1947, and police report, 8 September 1947, PRO CO 733/477/4.

64 Letter to the author from Edward Horne, 29 March 1986.

65 High Commissioner to Colonial Secretary, 29 January 1947, PRO CO 537/3870.

66 Richard Graves, *Experiment in Anarchy* (London, 1949), pp. 56–7; Rex Keating to Cyril Connor, 23 April 1947, Keating papers, Imperial War Museum, 86/16/1.

67 Internal note (anonymous), 26 June 1947, PRO CO 537/2269.

68 For the controversy over the 'new directive' to the High Commissioner and the security forces in Palestine see Memorandum by the Colonial Secretary, 7 January 1947, PRO CAB 129/16/CP(47)3; 15 January 1947, PRO CAB 128/9/6(47)2; Meeting of the Chiefs of Staff, 20 November 1946, PRO CAB 79/53/169; Colonial Secretary to the High Commissioner, 29 January 1947, PRO CO 537/2298; Colonial Secretary to the High Commissioner, 20 January 1947, PRO FO 371/61762; the whole of file PRO CO 537/1731; Montgomery, diary, part IV, chapter 26, and part V, chapter 33, Montgomery papers, BLM 177/1 and BLM 178/1; and Field-Marshall the Viscount Montgomery of Alamein, *Memoirs* (London, 1958), pp. 466–70.

69 Brigadier John Rymer-Jones, unpublished autobiography, p. 151, Rymer-Jones papers, Imperial War Museum (uncatalogued), and interview with Rymer-Jones, 19 August 1986.

70 Nicholas Bethell, *The Palestine Triangle: the struggle between the British, the Jews, and the Arabs 1935–48* (London, 1979), p. 302.

71 Memorandum by Fergusson, 12 February 1947, PRO CO 537/2270; Fergusson, *The Trumpet in the Hall*, p. 210.

72 Interview with Gray (August 1977) in Clark, 'The colonial police and terrorism', p. 235; Sir Henry Gurney to Colonial Secretary, 26 June 1947, Cunningham papers, Middle East Centre, St Antony's College, Oxford, box 2, file 1.

73 Roy Farran, *Winged Dagger* (London, 1948), p. 348.
74 Memorandum by Fergusson, 12 February 1947, PRO CO 537/2270.
75 Farran, *Winged Dagger*, pp. 348–9.
76 Rymer-Jones, unpublished autobiography, p. 151, Rymer-Jones papers, Imperial War Museum.
77 Fergusson, *The Trumpet in the Hall*, pp. 228–39, and Farran, *Winged Dagger*, pp. 352–68.
78 See the telegrams between the High Commissioner and the Colonial Secretary, 17 to 20 June 1947, Cunningham papers, box 2, file 1; Bruce Hoffman, 'Jewish terrorist activities and the British government in Palestine, 1939–1947' (D.Phil. thesis, Oxford, 1985), pp. 126–7.
79 Fergusson, *The Trumpet in the Hall*, pp. 238–9. For a discussion of the Farran affair see David Charters, 'Special operations in counter-insurgency: the Farran case, Palestine 1947', *Journal of the Royal United Services Institute*, 124 (1979), pp. 56–61.
80 Oliver Lyttleton, Lord Chandos, *The Memoirs of Lord Chandos* (London, 1962), p. 222.
81 Rymer-Jones, unpublished autobiography, p. 116, Rymer-Jones papers, writes that four of the six district commanders were ex-'Black and Tan' men. If the head of the transport section, and a police officer who was seconded to the Arab Legion are added to the figure, then the total is five out of eight. These five were Raymond Cafferata, James Munro, James Kyles, Eric James and Alfred Barker. Horne to author, 6 April 1989.

CHAPTER FIVE

Political intelligence and policing in Ghana in the late 1940s and 1950s

Richard Rathbone

Until the riots of 28 February 1948 occurred, the Gold Coast's police force had played a relatively slight role in the country's politics. From their inception they had, it is true, attempted to contain local 'disturbances', but the acquisition of political intelligence, a role usually associated with a specialist unit, the Special Branch, had not been part of their general duties. In every respect the February riots were a major disaster for the police. The Commissioner had, after all, personally sanctioned the ex-servicemen's demonstration and march which had eventually led to the tragic shooting at the Christiansborg crossroads, and he had done so because he 'was satisfied that untoward incidents arising from this large assembly of men were improbable'.[1] His satisfaction was not shared by the officer commanding the Accra contingent of the Royal West African Frontier Force who had, on his own initiative, put his troops on standby at dawn on 28 February. The army's reading of the entrails proved to be a better assessment of the ways that things might work out. In the event an ill-equipped, under-manned and very frightened police detachment eventually fired upon the crowd; the rest is history.[2]

Amongst other things, the riots showed, as Sir Reginald Saloway, a Deputy Governor under Sir Charles Arden-Clarke, was later to write, that 'the forces of law and order were utterly inadequate'.[3] The police were obviously required, under the pressure of the new circumstances, to reform and to reform fast. Some reforms predated the riots. For example, a Police Mobile Force had been set up in 1947 and was to be used no fewer than 200 times between December 1947 and September 1951.[4] But amongst the changes directly influenced by the crisis was the drafting in of a large number – twenty-one – of police officers from Palestine and three others from British Guiana, Mauritius and Uganda;[5] a new police wireless network was in operation by March 1949 and the Special Branch was beefed up as part of a general expansion of the police force which saw it double in size between the end of 1947 and 1952.

On 27 February 1950 the Secretary of State wrote a report on 'Recent Developments in Colonial Police Forces'. This was based on a report completed by a Colonial Police Adviser appointed on 1 November 1948, a mission triggered by the shock of the February riots. In 1950 the Secretary of State wrote: 'The attention of Colonial Governments was drawn in 1948 to the need for establishing or strengthening intelligence services and special branches'.[6] While that Report repeated the comments of the Adviser that such functions were still far from satisfactory, it is clear that not the least significant aspect of the February riots was a rapid change in the Colonial Office's attitude towards intelligence gathering.

In the Gold Coast itself the relationship between the crisis of 1948 and the changing nature of intelligence gathering is made clearer in a long typescript letter from the Colonial Secretary, Scott, to the Chief Commissioner, Ashanti, Butler on 13 April 1948. Marked 'Top Secret', it reads:

> We now find ourselves having to deal locally with political movements operating not only across internal administrative boundaries but in some cases also across colonial and international boundaries. In these circumstances it is essential that we should have a continuous supply of political information carefully collected from every part of the Gold Coast ... We must in future be better prepared, so far as political and security intelligence is concerned, then [sic] we have been in recent months. Some steps in this direction have already been taken. These include the immediate reinforcement of the C.I.D. and the Special Branch ... and the setting up of an 'Intelligence Co-ordination Committee' which now meets each week at Police H.Q. ... It is proposed that the Special Branch ... should collect all security intelligence (i.e. about any groups or individuals taking part in subversive activities ...) and any political intelligence that comes its way.

The letter is an interesting piece of evidence. Seeking as it was to improve intelligence gathering and to create a structure in which that could happen with the support of Butler, it heaps lavish but, one suspects, slightly hypocritical praise on the relevant skills of political officers serving under Butler. It, however, presents us with a definitional problem which I have yet to resolve. In stressing the tasks allocated to the Special Branch, Scott went on to remind Butler that 'the political administration should collect only political intelligence unless asked to help the Special Branch in collecting security intelligence about specific matters'.[7] This interesting letter raises more questions than it answers. While it is clear that Political Officers continued, as before, to collect the bulk of the administration's political information, how was the distinction between 'security' and 'political' intelligence drawn? As some of the later evidence in this chapter implies, there is much to suggest that they did

[85]

D

significantly overlap. Special Branch was surely collecting 'political' as well as 'security' intelligence? While I have not encountered the kinds of demarcation disputes which enliven the pages of the Le Carré *oeuvre*, the distinction, or rather its lack of definition, must have created an atmosphere ripe for squabbling and localised chaos.

The argument that 1948 marked a serious change in approach is further reinforced by a secret minute written on 14 July 1948 which reads: 'Following the Gold Coast disturbances the head of MI5 Overseas department recently paid a visit to three of the four West African territories; as a result of his tour a Security Liaison Officer has been appointed with H.Q. in Accra to co-ordinate security intelligence for the region.'[8] That this attachment to the West African Council was 'a representative of MI5', probably a Colonel Stephens, is confirmed in a Top Secret paper entitled 'Progress for Defence Planning'.[9] More shadowy is an MI5 man called Kellar who was sent out to assess the intelligence situation on 18 March 1948, and seems to have been responsible for the posting of Stephens to the West African Council.[10] Attempts to further identify him have as yet failed. His name appears several times in a security context which identify him as belonging to MI5 (see PRO CO 537/3558 and PRO CO 537/2760).

Lastly, to clinch the novelty of this increase in intelligence activity, a secret letter from the Governor Sir Gerald Creasy to the Colonial Office in May 1948 contains important information on the new, post-riots structure of intelligence gathering in the Gold Coast, and refers to the fact that: 'To improve the collection of security intelligence we have already reinforced the special branch of the CID.'[11]

By the end of 1948 the Special Branch was, therefore, one of the agencies collating and selectively distributing summaries of its intelligence information. These secret summaries provided an extremely important element in the clutch of working papers used by the weekly meetings of a newly-constituted Intelligence Co-ordination Committee (later to be streamlined and renamed the Central Security Committee or CenSec) which was concerned with political intelligence. Its members were the Governor, the Colonial Secretary, the Officer Commanding the Gold Coast Regiment, a Security Liaison Officer and the Commissioner of Police. As far as can be discerned, its other working papers included the reports of Local Intelligence Committees, chaired by the provincial Chief Commissioners, which produced reports based very largely upon more detailed reports or 'SitReps' from District Commissioners and local police officers. Sadly for the historian, most of these potentially rich primary sources were destined for destruction. Only on rare occasions can one compare the 'raw material' with the Chief Commissioners' digests and analyses. Frustratingly, I have seen only *some* of these which were classified in the Chief Commissioner, Ashanti's files as the S0060 and S0070 series. These, the 'Local Intelligence Committee Reports' for Ashanti, survived in incomplete form and did so entirely by happy accident.

Each report was required to be destroyed in the first week of each quarter. A counterfoil was appended to each of the sixteen numbered, cyclostyled copies and this was supposed to be returned to the Central Security Committee in Accra after each batch was burnt. Those I was able to consult still proudly bore their counterfoils, a powerful warning about the vulnerability of apparently 'fail-safe' precautions. The Central Security Committee's own productions, the 'Political Intelligence Summaries', again marked 'Secret' should, for obvious reasons, have largely disappeared in Ghana. Some but not all of their contents can, however, be consulted at the Public Record Office in the CO 537 series, where edited versions are variously called 'Political Intelligence Summaries', 'Reports' or 'Notes'.[12]

Those files I was able to consult in Ghana boasted no class numbers but all had the following post-script: 'It was laid down that copies of the Summary should be destroyed six months after publication. All holders should now destroy copies of Issue Numbers ... by fire and complete and return the certificate below.'[13] The certificates on those 'Summaries' I saw were, disconcertingly, no longer on the Summaries. It seems likely that the certificates were indeed duly returned to Accra (although I found no trace of them in the Ghana National Archives in Accra) but, through oversight perhaps, the 'Summaries' were not destroyed. The completeness of the limited amount of material used in this chapter must, accordingly, be extremely doubtful. Additionally it is frequently impossible to be sure of the authorship of the documents, for the signatories seem to have delighted in illegibility. These cabbalistic squiggles could unfortunately represent the names of any of the possible authors. Additionally, despite strenuous efforts, it proves impossible to discover which of the senior police officers were seconded for Special Branch work. There is no more confidence possible about the provenance of the information presented and its authenticity. But some inferences may and will be drawn.

I have chosen to look at some aspects of intelligence-gathering and dissemination and, especially, the role of Special Branch in the run-up to, and the immediate aftermath of, the Gold Coast's first general election in 1951. The political history of this period of Ghanaian history is sufficiently well known to make a lengthy prologue redundant. The brief and essential facts are these: having initially rejected the constitution devised by the all-African Coussey Committee as 'bogus and fraudulent', the energetic Convention Peoples' Party (CPP) of Kwame Nkrumah eventually committed itself, after an abortive attempt at a national strike better known as 'Positive Action', to contesting those elections. As I have tried to show elsewhere, this was in many ways a welcome decision for the senior British political authorities as it betokened a shift away from the threatening atmosphere of confrontation which had haunted the Gold Coast from February 1948.[14]

What emerges from the rather attenuated police records of the period is, not least, the absence of any agreed 'colonial' view of the significance of these processes. Elements within the colonial administrative structure – the Governor, the Secretariat, individual Regional Commissioners and, of course, the police – had sharply differing opinions about what was happening and what would happen. Each attempted in various ways to convince the others, and the Colonial Office, of the validity of their own analysis. The police, it seems, remained profoundly uneasy about the CPP at the very time that some, but assuredly not all, field administrators and other members of the Political Service were learning to live with it. By the end of 1950, when the co-operation of the CPP branch officials was being greeted by some if not most administrators with relief if not actual pleasure, the police remained convinced that the CPP was not quite the reformed, constitutional political party it sought to present itself as. As late as 30 November 1950, only weeks away from the general election, a Special Branch summary talks of the CPP as continuing to have as 'one of its most cherished beliefs ... that by divers forms of agitation and coercion, self-rule can be wrested from the British Government ... at no distant date'.[15]

Their perceptions had, however, moved a slight distance from an earlier set of fears, informed not least by the more general apprehensions of the 1940s, that the CPP was both utterly insurrectionary and communist. The slightly more relaxed tone seems, and only seems, to have emerged from confidences the Special Branch seems to have enjoyed from a 'deep throat' on the CPP's Executive Committee. The same 'Summary', for example, reported a recent closed Executive meeting (for which there is, so far as I know, no public record, but which oral information confirms) in which Kojo Botsio succeeded in convincing his Party colleagues:

a) that every effort should be made to avoid imputations of Communist sympathy or connection.
b) that it must strive to prove, through the elections, that the Party represented the bulk of the electorate.
c) that the Party must so conduct itself prior to and during the elections that charges of intimidation and mal-practice (sic) could not be laid at its door.[16]

[88]

Within the reportage of the Special Branch for this period, and indeed throughout at least some of the terminal colonial period, it seems pretty certain that at least one member of that Party Executive was sharing confidential material with the Special Branch either consciously or unwittingly. Whatever the provenance of their information, some of the fears of the Special Branch by the end of 1950 revolved around a concern that the CPP leadership was not entirely in control of its membership – a fear shared by some of that party's Executive. Throughout October 1950 for example, several significant members of the CPP made speeches of an undoubtedly inflammatory nature which were described by the Special Branch as 'deviationism', a concept (and an idiom) they surely must have picked up from the deliberations of the CPP Executive itself. In the run-up to the election, the Special Branch appeared consistently worried that 'Party discipline has deteriorated since Positive Action'.[17]

It is, however, extremely easy to be misled by the slightly more positive tone of such reportage. There is a persistent note of sometimes whimsical and often unpleasant sarcasm in the Special Branch's treatment of the Party, and African politics and politicians in general. Examples abound, but perhaps the following give some of the flavour of this. The Special Branch spent a good deal of time working up dossiers on political activists and, by the end of 1950, candidates for the General Election.[18] Commenting on one such candidate, who because he is still alive I shall identify no more closely, their report states: 'On the soap-box is a loquacious and scurrilous orator. At party jamborees is occasionally found dressed in a sort of pyjamas of CPP colours.'; and further: 'Intellectually is about average "Standard VII" but gives the impression of mental instability and may well be psychopathic.' Other commentary on individuals in this series includes the delicious Buchanish description: 'one of the three most dangerous men in Bekwai'! But more seriously, the general tenor suggests the creation of files of a potentially damaging nature for these aspirant Assemblymen. Previous convictions were cited, as were educational and career backgrounds. Character assessments based upon crude psychological stereotypes accompanied the more obviously objective data. Politicians are variously described as:

> Vain and given to ill-controlled outbursts of frenzied enthusiasm. Suffers to some extent from an inferiority complex and often lacking in courtesy in consequence ...

> Where personal relationships are concerned at least one officer, to use his own words, would 'prefer a barge pole'.

> ... his public spirit quotient is nil.

[89]

Part initial *try to accelerate* *note - try and black politicians ridiculeous*

But for his undoubted hold over the 'rough boys' he would be an amusing, if rather tiresome nonenity. Of small stature, he has no personal presence or dignity.

Five months in Colonial Lunatic Asylum in Accra in 1928 on certificate of Dr. 'A'. He is self-styled at various times 'The Great Lion of Judah' and other remarkable titles ... The fact that 'X' is the son of a fetish priest and has supernatural powers may influence some of the voters. He does, however, seem fairly normal at the moment, though his letters written in the past lead one to doubt his mental stability.

With Europeans he is polite but reserved, arousing some irritation with his exaggerated 'Oxford accent' and other mannerisms.

There is a great deal more in the same vein; much of it is equally footling and much of it similarly offensive.[19]

Now it is obviously the duty of Special Branch officers to keep *au fait* with the political situation in which they operate. Much of the data they generate is certainly ephemeral or of little interest and importance. The authors of this material took themselves seriously, more seriously perhaps than their opposite numbers in Botswana in the 1950s. The late Michael Crowder, who consulted this sort of material in the Maseru Archives, told me that it was classified there, delightfully, as 'TerGos' or Territorial Gossip!

With dossiers of the sort I have been quoting from, much hangs on who reads them and of course what those readers do with the information they contain. From the circulation list of a series of 'Personality notes' drawn up by the Special Branch on thirty-seven of the thirty-eight members elected (as opposed to nominated) to the new Assembly, we can discern the limited scope of this readership. Only twenty copies in all were prepared. Ten of these were for internal police distribution and included a file and a spare copy. Outside the immediate ranks of the Gold Coast police the other ten copies went to the Chief Secretary, the Chief Commissioners of the Colony, Ashanti and the Northern Territories, the Commissioners of Police in Gambia, Nigeria and Sierra Leone, Sir Percy Sillitoe, the Colonial Office (via MI5) and the local Security Liaison Officer (the convenor of the local Central Security Committee).[20] It is clear from the known history of the period that the Governor and successive Chief Secretaries chose to follow their political noses and certainly had the statesmanship to ignore the more obviously absurd and partisan material.

But their approach was schizophrenic. On the one hand CenSec demanded of the country's District Commissioners that they 'report any evidence they have discovered of the infiltration of communist propaganda into their districts and on any local reactions'.[21] On the other, they reported to Whitehall that 'it is appreciated that Communist influence touches this country very little as yet, but there may be attempts to increase it in future'. The same document sets out the guidelines given to senior colonial officers when dealing with the visiting press. They must insist that 'there is no direct evidence of organised Communism in the Gold Coast though it is obvious that some of its methods have been adopted and its jargon of anti-imperialism and anti-colonisation [sic] is being used'.[22] I would account for this manifest ambiguity in the following way: Arden-Clarke and those close to him remained unconvinced by the particularity of the 'red menace' accusations throughout the terminal colonial period. The evidence shows clearly that they attracted a great deal of repeated criticism in Westminster and hence in Whitehall for their scepticism about what was clearly a hallowed belief in London. Much of the attention Gold Coast officials devoted to the issue of communism was at the behest of London and was, I believe, a tight-lipped performance designed to satisfy their masters and to disarm their critics.[23]

Nonetheless, the circulation list certainly suggests where some of the more dissentient voices in the Gold Coast, most notably that of the Chief Commissioner, Ashanti, found some support and some outlet for their unease with either the entirety or the details of the policy of rapid decolonisation. Such reports, like all such documents, were of course not value-free accounts of 'the facts' but were nuanced by and charged with political intent. The uses to which the rather wider and distant readership put these data can only be guessed at. Circulation lists for the large variety of political intelligence documents appear to have altered over time. The material in them did not always satisfy all arms of government. On 19 April 1950 Brigadier C. R. Price of the Ministry of Defence, for example, complained to the Colonial Office that '... what we feel we also need ... are any situation telegrams from the various colonies where the "cold war" is in progress indicating that trouble may be about to break out. In one or two cases fairly recently the first we have heard, in this office, of trouble for example in West Africa, is from an announcement on the BBC news or in the Press.'[24] *do rci office in Bril don really seem to know what was going on*

There is much that is striking about these reports. The Gold Coast electorate had, by the time this series of documents were in circulation, just elected a new government. Both the Assembly and the Executive Council were by then dominated by African members, and the administration was headed by an African Leader of Government Business, Kwame Nkrumah, who was by coincidence freed from prison on the date-line of the document referred to above. There is no evidence that I know of that suggests that any African government minister in the 1951–4 administration ever saw, in its entirety, the material produced by the Special Branch in that period; and because of its tone it seems

[91]

virtually certain that the Leader of Government Business never saw the reports on himself which, *inter alia*, indict him for his 'lack of moral courage' and his 'mediocre intellect'. Although I have, over the years, spoken to a number of the African veterans of that CPP dyarchic administration, none has expressed anything other than surprise at the existence of such material. I am equally persuaded that Nkrumah, both as Leader of Government Business and later as Prime Minister, was later, but only later, selectively seized of those aspects of Special Branch's work which enabled him to lean so heavily upon the activists within the Western Province branch of the CPP and upon the Ghana Trades Union Congress.[25] Not the least significant element of that aspect of the CPP's 'centralisation' was the persistent indictment of and legislation against such activists' allegedly close relationships with agencies, institutions and individuals in the Eastern Bloc. Interestingly, this 'crackdown' on the left in 1953–4 was strongly urged by the Colonial Office on both Nkrumah and Arden-Clarke, both of whom were for local political reasons only too happy to oblige. However it seems highly unlikely that the country's Prime Minister was ever privy to the *entire* scope of Special Branch's work throughout the terminal colonial period, not least because he remained under its surveillance even as Leader of Government Business.[26]

It is a crucial aspect of Ghana's particular history of decolonisation that, in its most essential visible and less visible forms, law and order remained under British control until March 1957 although the police force and its Special Branch was being rapidly Africanised. This was once again far from accidental. In his memorandum to Cabinet on 18 February 1954, Lyttleton reported with satisfaction that 'the Governor's reserve powers are now fully safeguarded and Defence (including the police) ... are firmly in his hands'.[27] There was of course nothing new about this policy. As early as January 1950 the problem had been addressed, and a letter from Gorsuch in the Colonial Office to J. Wheeler at the Ministry of Defence makes this clear. Gorsuch was attempting to ease Ministry of Defence worries about constitutional changes in the pipeline and he quoted Arden-Clarke's earlier comment that 'defence cannot be divorced from internal security and one of the principal instruments in the maintenance of internal security is the Police. There will be some opposition locally to the police being under an ex-officio member and not an elected minister but I regard it as essential that at this stage defence, internal security and police should remain in the Chief Secretary's portfolio'.[28] On the same day Gorsuch wrote again to Wheeler, this time secretly pointing out that he had no need for concern. 'You will see that so far as matters of defence and internal security are concerned, there is in effect a double safeguard; the portfolio is to be allocated to an official ...

and the Governor retains … his reserve power … together with his power of veto over legislation.'[29] Lyttleton had already made it clear that this was not a negotiable position. Reporting to the Cabinet on 4 September 1953, he wrote: 'As I told my colleagues, I shall not agree to any arrangements that does not [sic] reserve to the Governor overriding control of the police.'[30]

Nor was such a triumph unique to Ghana. Lyttleton, this time writing in the midst of the negotiations for Nigeria's new constitution, wrote in manuscript to Churchill ('My Dear Winston' and 'Yours ever, Oliver') from Government House in Lagos that 'the fact that the Police, the Judiciary and the Civil Service are all effectively safeguarded mean [sic] that we retain all the control over all the subjects that matter to us'.[31] As the Minister of State reminded the House of Commons on 28 April 1954, whilst the new constitution allowed the Gold Coast's Cabinet responsibility for internal self-government, this was 'subject to the continuing reserved powers of the Governor and his responsibilities for external affairs, Togoland, defence and *in certain matters concerning the police*' [my emphasis]. This at the very least should condition the historian's rather sloppy use of the concept of 'internal self-government' which Ghana enjoyed between 1954 and 1957. More particularly, this particular separation of significant state powers created considerable problems for the Prime Minister when he sought, from the end of 1954, to control the extra-parliamentary campaigns of the National Liberation Movement.[32]

But this is not the only point of interest. The intelligence function of the Gold Coast police not only persisted throughout the period of dyarchy and internal self-government, it also provoked a sense of apartness from the polity amongst the Special Branch officers themselves. In its twenty-seventh monthly 'Summary', the Branch reflected on what it saw as its dilemma in a fashion which seems to suggest the perceived problems of serving two masters:

> although there is a long term possibility that the CPP edifice may crumble and fall, the current trend is towards some form of totalitarianism or, more precisely, mob rule. If the Police Force retains its impartiality and individuality no doubt it can withstand the worst potentialities of such a development, but if, on the other hand, there is excessive interference by the Executive as to whether members of the CPP shall or shall not be prosecuted for criminal offences (of which there has been some indication recently) then the Force is well on the way to becoming the cat's paw of a dictatorship. No doubt the new Constitution has got to be made to work – 'regardless' one might almost say – but if the Police Force is to become a pawn in the game, it would be a bold man who would predict the consequences in the Force itself and in the country at large.[33]

This set of apprehensions remained firmly on the front burner. In April 1951 a conference of colonial Police Commissioners was held at the Police College at Ryton-on-Dunsmore. It was addressed by the Secretary of State who said amongst other things:

> the waging of the 'cold war' has inevitably increased the importance and responsibilities of Police Forces ... they must now shoulder most of the burden for extirpating or at least of keeping under supervision and control the internal canker of communist inspired subversion and treachery ... when a colony reaches the more advanced phases of development towards self-government, an acute clash of loyalties may arise ...[34]

There is, of course, a strong suggestion of posturing as well as analytic confusion here. All sorts of signals, including coded messages about mundane matters like pay and conditions, lie buried in such self-presentation as the thin blue line of democracy. But Special Branch were only one element of a much wider colonial establishment whose political attitudes ranged from an enthusiastic and excited welcome for radical change, to a more conservative, anti-nationalist and pro-chiefly set of views held by those who were ultimately only too happy to see the emergence of the conservative ethnicity of the National Liberation Movement in 1954 as firm evidence of 'I told you so'. At the same time this sense of being somehow above the political arena and beyond the reach of all but those parts of the government which Special Branch judged to be trustworthy, namely some of the residual British colonial elements, persisted until independence and seems not to have been unique to them. It provides us with yet another useful gloss on the real nature of the 'Westminster Model' in the terminal colonial period which manifestly differed considerably from anything that would have been recognised by Walter Bagehot or Erskine May.

There was a great deal that was concealed from African ministers in the terminal colonial period. Sadly some of material which would help us to understand the volume and nature of what was kept back remains 'retained by the department' and thus not open to consultation. Hints, however, do emerge with some frequency. Although dating from after the period under consideration, an intriguing outgoing telegram from the Colonial Office to the Secretariat in Accra, for example, talks of 'our surprise that your latest telegram ... was no. 65 in the Secret and Personal Series. We had regarded this series as one which should in no circumstances be disclosed to the [Gold Coast] Cabinet'.[35] The advent of Africans into the Executive Council and Ministries in large numbers appears to have altered the style of communication in security matters. E. Hanrott wrote secretly to G. E. Sinclair of the Gold Coast's Ministry of Defence and External Affairs in July 1951 that 'for obvious reasons your Political Intelligence Notes are more reticent than they used to be and ... there is a greater risk than formerly of our diverging from a true appreciation of the local facts'.[36] Clearly one of the implications of fairly rapid constitutional change was that the more open information flows were more guarded than they had previously been. Throughout the period up to March 1957, however, Special Branch and other forms of police intelligence betray this same *disengagée* sense of being outside and somehow above the control of the elected government in their secret documentation.

The distance felt by the Special Branch from elected members is most apparent in the extraordinary documentation they provided the readership referred to above about the members of the 1951–4 Legislative Assembly. Although few of us will have seen how the domestic Special Branch treats British Members of Parliament, it is difficult to believe that they are quite so partisan and clumsily vituperative as the fifty-seven-page document the Gold Coast's Special Branch drew up after the first general election.[37] All the material that I have seen shows, unsurprisingly, a devoted presentation of the 'criminal antecedents', the 'form' of the new MLAs. No single offence against the Illiterates' Protection Ordinance or against the laws on obstruction, irrespective of their anti-quity or slightness, eluded their careful research. Similarly there is strong internal evidence which suggests the transmission of personal data from the United Kingdom to the Gold Coast as the material on those activists who had worked and studied there is rich. This in turn tells us something about the British security interest in bodies like the West African Students' Union, the West African National Secretariat and other inter-nationalist 'student organisations'. Special Branch were, understandably given the tenor of the times, especially interested in those with apparent links with the British Communist Party, the World Federation of Demo-cratic Youth and other 'alarming' groups. Special Branch in the Gold Coast certainly intercepted mail, especially mail from Eastern Europe. In one 'Summary' they refer to a 'flood of Communist literature into the country' and were holding, they reported, 8,000 'copies of various Communist publications'.[38]

The career records of each Member of the Legislative Assembly emerge in great detail from the pages of this Special Branch dossier and I am persuaded that a significant amount of this material was accurate if highly selective. At the same time it is perfectly obvious that some of this material cannot be described as accurate. What is more noteworthy in these appraisals is the clearly partisan nature of personal comment and the apparent commitment to amassing material that could perhaps prove 'useful' in times to come. While it cannot be proved that this was the intention, it is hard to read such files without such a suspicion

[95]

emerging. In their analyses of new Assemblymen, the Special Branch showed no preference for particular members or particular parties. With only very limited exceptions, the tone is hostile and the dossiers cluttered at times with hearsay evidence of misdemeanours and past irregularities. The qualification must be a limited one. Special Branch found little or nothing to complain of only in the cases of Kwesi Plange (Member for Cape Coast), Emmanuel Dadson (Tarkwa), J. E. Hagan (Cape Coast rural), W. E. Arthur (Saltpond), E. K. Bensah (Agona), R. A. Ampadu (Kwahu), I. D. Osabutey-Aguedze (Ga-Adangme), J. K. A. Quashie (Anlo) and A. B. Boakye (Amansie). That is to say that the Special Branch had negative files, sometimes, as we shall see extremely negative files, on no fewer than twenty-eight of the thirty-seven Members of the Legislative Assembly examined, and it is clear from the summary information that some of that source material was indeed copious.

Although the personal remarks are perhaps the most arresting, the Special Branch's preoccupation with communist connections was both predictable and obvious. Nkrumah, they concluded was fundamentally:

> a Communist but having realised that the broader aspects of Communism have little appeal in this Colony, he has revised his programme to suit the present situation and has given a nationalist flavour to what are basically Communist ideologies and techniques ... Like Botsio, Nkrumah has received much literature from the WFDY and the IUS and before his imprisonment was in touch with a number of racial agitators in the United Kingdom and America ... his recent sojourn in prison appears to have led him to believe that ... Communist technique will not benefit himself or his Party ... he wishes to disentangle himself, outwardly and temporarily at any rate from Communist trappings.

It is important to remember that Special Branch were not writing about some obscure colonial agitator but, rather, about the Leader of Government Business of the Gold Coast, a title amended in 1952 to that of Prime Minister to more appropriately fit the role.

Other figures were similarly tainted by contact with pernicious creeds. J. K. Lamptey (Sekondi-Takoradi) had embraced 'the ideologies of such organisations as the African League, the Pan-African Federation and the European and Colonial Oppressed Peoples Association (later the Congress of Peoples against Imperialism) ... He has maintained contact with a number of his United Kingdom associates, notably Fenner Brockway'. Anthony Woode (member for Sefwi and a committed left-winger later to be expelled from the Party) had 'made several wild speeches seeming to show absorption of Communist propaganda. Known to be receiving communist literature'. J. E. Erzuah (Ankobra) was of concern because he had been Vice-President of the Nzima Youth Association 'which applied for affiliation to and was accepted unconditionally into the membership of the communist dominated International Union of Students at their 5th Council meeting in Prague in August, 1950'.

In this respect it is rather surprising to find the most damning allegations made against Kojo Botsio who hardly emerges as a firebrand in the analysis of most academic writers. Botsio had attracted police attention when, after getting his Diploma of Education from Oxford, he had become Warden of the West African Students' Union in London. Special Branch alleged that he has used this position to 'spread Communist doctrine amongst African Students in the United Kingdom'. Botsio certainly got to know Nkrumah and other African exile politicians whilst the former acted as the Treasurer of the West African National Secretariar (the files on which still remain endorsed 'retained by Department' in the PRO). What is more interesting is the internal evidence from Botsio's dossier that the British Special Branch intercepted WANS mail as they cite, *inter alia*, correspondence between WANS and Botsio after he had left the United Kingdom but intercepted at the 'London end'.

Botsio returned to the Gold Coast to take up the post of Vice-Principal of Akim Abuakwa State College in Kibi whose Principal from 1947 was W. E. Ofori-Atta, one of the United Gold Coast Convention 'Big Six' and, after 1951, UGCC member for one of the two Akim seats, the other being held by Ofori-Atta's uncle, J. B. Danquah. Botsio was thus a prominent client of the Akyem royal family and J. B. Danquah in particular – hardly a connection much enthused by Marxism-Leninism. Nonetheless Special Branch reported Botsio's classes in civics at the State College as opportunities at which he 'imbued his students with Communist ideas and idealogy [sic]'. Botsio's role as the CPP's first General Secretary was built on his organisational techniques which Special Branch believed were based on 'the basic training in Communism he received in the United Kingdom and the text book on which he mainly relied was Stalin's 'On Organisation' – particularly the section of it dealing with the establishment and maintenance of cadres'.

Botsio's private life proved unexceptional but his personal modesty was, they claimed, 'apt to obscure from the casual observer a somewhat vindictive character prone to unscrupulous intrigue'. Although one is tempted to recognise in such remarks evidence of some real expertise in unscrupulous intrigue, comment of more interest in terms of Special Branch's *modus operandi* emerges in a later section on what they called, rather coyly, 'Outside Influences'. Botsio, we learn, had been in touch

with many Communist and left-wing organisations in the UK and in Europe. He was instrumental in affiliating the CYO [the Committee on Youth Organisations, the proto-CPP] to the WFDY [the World Federation of Democratic Youth] and has for some years been regularly receiving literature from the IUS and the WFDY. Since his release from prison [in connection with his involvement in Positive Action], however, he appears to have been looking mainly to George PADMORE [caps, in the original] Fenner BROCKWAY [again in caps, in the original] and the Congress of Peoples against Imperialism for guidance as to the manner in which the CPP should approach the new Legislative Assembly.[39]

That the Special Branch felt apprehensive about communism is hardly surprising. The preoccupations of security forces and politicians in much of the western world had been shaped in the aftermath of the European war and by the emergence of the Soviet Union as the controller of such huge tracts of Europe. Security priorities emerged in the conspiratorial atmosphere of rubble-strewn cities like Vienna and Berlin and the fears were underlined by the blockade of Berlin, the illegal transmission of nuclear data and the outbreak of war in Korea in June 1950. Only months earlier, Senator Joseph McCarthy had commenced his bitter campaign to expose 'fellow-travellers' in the State Department; in February 1950 Klaus Fuchs was found guilty of passing secrets to the Soviet Union, and in February of the same year Bruno Pontecorvo had slipped into Eastern Europe. Soviet imperialism was not perceived as anything so slight as a slogan. It was within such panicked security services that colonial policemen received their training. Ideas were given flesh by service in 'hot spots', and it is interesting to note that a significant proportion of the Gold Coast's European police officers had seen service in the pre-war Caribbean and Palestine, and were to proceed, after the Gold Coast, to places like Kenya, Aden and Cyprus. So far as West Africa was concerned it is clear, with hindsight, that the 'red menace' had little substance. At the time it seemed real enough to some; some CPP activists undeniably addressed one another as 'Comrade', and some but not many had nibbled at the edges of Marxism-Leninism. Although there is real evidence to suggest that the Governor never took such Special Branch evidence of communism very seriously, there were those who did, not least the Labour Secretary of State for the Colonies, his Minister of State and the Parliamentary Under-Secretaries of State. Anti-communism is a factor of immense significance in late colonial history and sadly an almost totally ignored one.

While there is nothing to link the strong opinions of the Special Branch with a vigorous press campaign in Britain over this period, there are at least some resonances. Just before the Gold Coast elections, two British Conservative Members of Parliament visited the Gold Coast with a member of the Conservative Central Office Research Department. They, as befits a fact-finding visit, found some facts. But they also later paraded some myths which they had also collected. These, rather than the facts, found a public forum in the form of a luridly entitled article in the London *Daily Telegraph*. Entitled: 'Red shadow over the Gold

Coast', their article discerned in the CPP 'the latest technique of the *Politbureau* allying itself with the *Ju Ju* of darkest Africa'.[40] Even more closely mirroring the Special Branch 'line' was an article in the *Financial Times* on 7 March 1951 written to cover the Gold Coast election results. The anonymous editorial stated that 'Its [the CPP's] organisation and inspiration, far beyond local ability, is remarkable. Where does it come from? ... It is both directly and indirectly inspired by the Communists. Directly by Moscow, indirectly and far more dangerously by some Communists in London'.[41]

Whether such ideas were simply the common currency of those most hostile to or most threatened by political change in the Gold Coast and Africa more generally, or whether there was some tactical 'leaking' by those with access to the more detailed material with which this piece is concerned, must remain a matter of speculation. But in a general fashion it is important to recognise that in the antagonistic politics which characterised the British colonial administration's extremely divided positions on Gold Coast politics after February 1948, all sides, both doves and hawks and flocks of more indeterminate birds, used their contacts in the press, business and parliamentary worlds to carry on their local battles. It is hard to believe that the police, or at least all of those in receipt of police intelligence or a sight of it, were so principled as to be above such manoeuvring.

The police were concerned with communism. But they also had not much more affection for their colonial neighbours. The Gold Coast, hemmed in on three sides by French administration, might and perhaps should have felt the comfort of being bordered by allies. This was not so. The French connection created unease when it emerged and there is little evidence of a close relationship, at least in the late 1940s and early 1950s, between the French and British security services. Cross-border travel by Gold Coast politicians was viewed with great suspicion, but the lack of hard evidence about what they did once in Francophone West Africa suggests both a lack of liaison and an unease with the machinations of a friendly power. Nkrumah, whose father was from the Ivory Coast and whose birthplace is a short distance from that border, visited Abidjan in September 1948, but the Special Branch could only conclude that his was 'an abortive attempt to secure support for his projected West African National Congress'.[42] J. K. Lamptey also 'recently visited the Ivory Coast and met leaders of the RDA', but the rest is silence. Much more alarmingly, it seems, G. O. Awuma (Member for Akpini-Asogli), a former member of the Togobund, and more recently a leading figure in the Togo Union, had travelled in 1948 in Europe. Rather ambiguously, the Branch claimed that 'at the time there was good reason to believe that his expenses were being paid by the French'. By January 1950, Awuma was on his travels again, this time to Paris. He had sought, the Special Branch alleged, to 'arrange accommodation in that city through Fenner Brockway ... It was alleged that one of Awuma's objectives would be to contact d'Arboussier of the RDA on behalf of the African League and to inform him that the League 'meant business' ... In April 1950 he visited Lomé where he was introduced to and entertained by French Government officials and shown over various government buildings.' Awuma took photographs of these buildings, they alleged, and promised he would show them to the people in British Mandated Togoland 'so that the latter might realise how far ahead of the British were the French in matters of colonial development and administration'. Special Branch believed that Awuma had 'in the past been in the pay of authorities in French Togoland and in view of his recent election to the Legislative Assembly, the French may well consider him to be a person worth cultivating'.[43] While there may have been truth in this allegation, we are left with the unanswered question of who the Special Branch was using in French Mandated Togo!

In conclusion it must be readily admitted that there remain serious problems about how such material can be integrated into the more general and perhaps better known facts about this period of Ghana's recent history. Irrespective of our feelings about the outrageous quality of some of the Special Branch's reportage, the very fact that political intelligence-gathering had acquired such a momentum after February 1948 indicates that at least the nature of the colonial state had been radically changed. It was no longer the rather weak apparatus that had proved so incapable of predicting, let alone resisting, the considerable pressures it was subjected to in the last months of 1947 and the first of 1948. Part of that weakness was an over-reliance by the Secretariat and the Governor on the political awareness of Provincial Commissioners.[44] They, as events in 1948 showed, were single-mindedly satisfied with the political appraisals of those paramount chiefs in whom they placed trust. Before 1948, the Secretariat, and certainly after the end of Alan Burns' governorship, the Governor, had very limited alternative sources of information. The greater use of the Special Branch and the creation of CenSec were, not least, intended to fill this yawning gap. The emergence of this alternative pole of information-gathering undoubtedly sapped the once virtually untouchable power of Chief Commissioners, the 'barons' of the pre-1948 Gold Coast. Given that the entire structure of local government was to be utterly changed between 1950 and 1957, this was a shift of some considerable significance. It also adds a further element to Richard Crook's elegant and persuasive argument that Indirect Rule institutions in the Gold Coast were already regarded as wretchedly inefficient and increasingly anachronistic.[45]

Secondly, the nature of this material suggests that the interpretation of 'dyarchy' which characterised the governance of the Gold Coast up to independence must be tempered with a more open realisation of the maintenance of some elements of total and unalloyed British control. To some extent historians have looked at this with a rather naive belief that much of that continuing presence was to a large extent formal and a 'natural' bedfellow for a government that was not fully independent before March 1957. It is said, for example, that it was only natural that such a state should continue to have its external relations handled by the colonial power. But the continued British hold over internal security and over an army which remained mainly officered by British personnel and subjected to a high degree of control from London does not quite succumb to this logic. It seems quite clear that the CPP's ability to continue holding on to office owed not quite everything to the ballot box. While it might appear over-dramatic, the CPP also remained in office because it met with qualified colonial approval. As events in British Guiana in 1953 were to show, constitutions could be withdrawn and popularly-elected politicians and parties could be removed.[46] The independence of the Special Branch in the Gold Coast must, I think, be seen partly in the light of the possibility of radical policy changes.

Thirdly, data of this kind contributes to the destruction of any persistent, simple mythology of monolithic colonial attitudes and establishments. Special Branch were, not least, playing institutional politics within a profoundly divided service. The colonial establishment in the Gold Coast after the Second World War was consistently a house divided. The internal battles were bitter and the weapons deployed were sometimes subtle, sometimes crude, but nearly always outside the compass of 'British fair play'. A number of files in the PRO contain 'private letters' from aggrieved members of the Gold Coast political service with claims and proofs that their seniors had got things dangerously wrong – a most irregular activity. Special Branch were almost certainly not alone in their campaigns or their opinions. Such internal warfare remains a neglected theme in the growing canon of studies of 'decolonisation'.

Lastly, the kinds of material used in this chapter suggest, perhaps, the power of the police in post-independence states. In Ghana, as can be seen, the Commissioner had access to thick files on political luminaries and doubtless on many others within the state. That kind of data is a powerful political resource and allows those with the keys to the filing cabinets to twist arms, to cajole, to blackmail and to influence decisions. The rise of John Harlley during and after Ghana's first coup in 1966 is, perhaps, partially explained by his own personal, J. Edgar Hoover-ish control of just this resource. Again this remains a seriously under-investigated area in modern African studies, but perhaps there are good reasons for that.

Notes

My thinking about many of the issues raised in this chapter benefited greatly from the comments of my friends and colleagues at the SOAS African History Research seminar, the Cambridge University African Studies Centre Seminar and the Walter Rodney Seminar at Boston University who were subjected to an earlier version of this. Most of all I appreciate the comments of the late Professor Michael Crowder whose friendship I was privileged to enjoy. I am no less indebted to the long, perceptive and generous written comments of Professors John Dunn, Anthony Low and Donal Cruise O'Brien, and Drs David Anderson and David Killingray. Any merit the piece might have should be credited to their insights but the faults belong exclusively to the author.

1 *Report of the Commission of Enquiry into disturbances in the Gold Coast*, Chairman A. Watson, Public Record Office, Kew [PRO], Col. No. 231, para. 37, p. 11. Poor Commissioner Ballantine's career in the Gold Coast did not survive this misjudgement and he was replaced by M. K. N. Collens who had previously been Commissioner of the Nigerian Force. This constituted a strange lateral move in terms of seniority and suggests the perceived seriousness of the Gold Coast's security situation.

2 For more detail on these events see Watson Commission Report and Richard Rathbone, 'The government of the Gold Coast after World War II', *African Affairs*, 67 (1968), pp. 209–20, and Richard Rathbone, 'The transfer of power in Ghana' (unpublished Ph.D. thesis, University of London, 1968), pp. 78–80, 83.

3 'Gold Coast into Ghana: some problems of transition', *International Affairs*, Vol. XXXIV (1958), pp. 49–56. Saloway, who acted as Officer Administering the Government in the absence of the Governor, was well qualified to make this judgement.

4 This calculation is based on the monthly 'Intelligence Summaries' to be found in the PRO CO 537 series.

5 This transfer of personnel is covered by a long sequence of telegrams to be found in PRO CO 537/4406.

6 This report covers developments up to December, 1949 and was circulated to all colonial governments. It is to be found in PRO CO 537/5439.

7 I copied this letter from an unclassified bundle of correspondence in the files of the Chief Commissioner of Ashanti in Kumasi, Ghana.

8 E. Hanrott to (indecipherable), 14 July 1948, PRO CO 537/3653.

9 This paper dates from 18 October 1948 and is signed by J. C. Morgan, in PRO CO 537/4108. Stephens is identified in a number of tangential comments in papers concerning relations between the West African Council and the British consulate in Dakar, to be found in PRO CO 537/3648.

10 Attempts to further identify him have so far failed. His name appears several times in unspecific and tangential terms in PRO CO 537/2760 and CO 3558.

11 Creasy to Cohen, 7 May 1948, PRO CO 537/3648.

12 The PRO may well contain far more detailed material but serious historians remain checked by the very high incidence of files being either retained or being subject to time limits in excess of the normal thirty years in the important CO 537 series as well as, more obviously, in the CO 1035 series which deals with intelligence, security and police matters.

13 For further details on this material see the relevant parts of the annotated bibliography in my PhD thesis, 'Transfer of power'. There were of course many different kinds of intelligence summary, for example the FO's INTEL series and the Secretary of State's TONIL series for colonial governors. As befits this rather undercover world, they had a depressing, for the historian that is, propensity to keep changing their names.

14 See Rathbone, 'Transfer of power', pp. 129–35 and 136–40.
15 'Special Branch Summary', no. 22, October 1950, but dated 30 November 1950, File SF 873, Vol. VII, copy no. 3. In the files of the Chief Commissioner, Ashanti.
16 *Ibid.*
17 *Ibid.*
18 This large dossier is called 'Pen-Portraits' and is classified as SB SCO 135, no date but almost certainly mid-January 1951. In the files of the Chief Commissioner, Ashanti.
19 From *ibid.*
20 Cover-sheet to 'Personality Notes – members of the Gold Coast Legislative Assembly', SF 873, Vol. VIII, 12 February 1951. Files of the Chief Commissioner, Ashanti. In view of some of the things said below about liaison or lack of liaison with the French, it is worth pointing out that a severely edited version of the monthly 'Intelligence Summaries' was sent to the French Colonial Office after June 1949. These, according to a list of what had to be edited out, excluded 'references to actions in the intelligence sphere by the West African police forces'. Secret dispatch from Gorsuch to West African Governors, 1 June 1949, PRO CO 537/4726.
21 'Special Branch Summary', No. 27, April 1951, SF 873. Vol. VIII. Files of the Chief Commissioner, Ashanti.
22 *Political Intelligence Report*, 5 February 1951. Secret. PRO CO 537/7233.
23 My evidence for this interpretation leans heavily on CO 537 series and the DO 35 series in the PRO, and especially DO 35/6178, although the latter mostly relates to the period *after* that with which I am concerned here. I remain reasonably certain of this conclusion.
24 C. R. Price to C. J. Barton, 19 April 1950, in PRO CO 537/5302.
25 See Rathbone, 'Transfer of power', pp. 150 and 183–5.
26 For example there is clear evidence that he was 'tailed' in the 'Colonial Political Intelligence Summary', no. 3, March 1951, p. 12, CO 537/6798.
27 Cabinet Memorandum, Secret. C(54)62, 18 February 1954. PRO PREM 11/1367.
28 Gorsuch to Wheeler, 10 January 1950. PRO CO 96/821/6, and DEFE 7/422.
29 Gorsuch to Wheeler, 10 January 1950, PRO CO 537/5814.
30 Cabinet Memorandum, Secret. C(53)244, 4 September 1953. PRO PREM 11/1367.
31 Undated (possibly 24 January), but clearly written during the completion of the 1954 constitutional negotiations in Lagos, PRO PREM 11/1367.
32 See Rathbone, 'Transfer of power', pp. 251–2.
33 SF 873, Vol. VII, 30 November 1950. Files of the Chief Commissioner, Ashanti.
34 For the report on that conference see PRO CO 537/6941. In September 1951 Colonel A. E. Young, the Commissioner of Police for the City of London, and Chief Superintendent F. J. Wilson of the Metropolitan force, were appointed to advise the government on the future organisation, training and methods of the Gold Coast Police Force – see PRO CO 537/6801. It is also clear that from about June 1952 a working party had been established in Accra to sort out the position of the police in the later stages of colonial constitutional development. See PRO CO 537/6960.
35 CO to Governor, Accra, Secret telegram dated 8 June 1953, PRO CO 554/684.
36 Hanrott to Sinclair, 17 July 1950, PRO CO 537/7181. A nice minute from W. Gorrell Barnes to Sir John Martin on 14 July 1953, PRO CO 936/192, adds another dimension to the issue of concealment. He argued that some parts of a dull paper on Anglo-French co-operation were 'quite unsuitable to be shown to African Ministers in West Africa. My reason for taking this view is not that the document reveals "secrets" but rather that the range of subjects ... and the wording ... give it something of an "imperialist" flavour which would be liable to create an unfortunate impression in the minds of African Ministers ... If any West African Governor subsequently asks for a document which he can show to West African Ministers ... then we shall presumably have to draft some document with a rather different flavour ... Alternatively we could suggest to them that ... nothing occurred to be worth reporting to West African Governments'. I quote this at length because it seems that the changing nature of communication between the Colonial Office and local Secretariats following radical constitutional change would be an interesting research topic.

37 'Personality Notes', SF 873, February 1951. Files of the Chief Commissioner, Ashanti.

38 SF 873, Vol. VII, 30 November 1950. Files of the Chief Commissioner, Ashanti.

39 All the quotations in the preceding paragraphs are taken from 'Personality Notes', SF 873, February 1951. Files of the Chief Commissioner, Ashanti.

40 *Daily Telegraph*, 17 November 1950. My suggestion of leaks, nods and winks is nicely supported by a challenge the Colonial Office made to an outrageous question asked by Lord Milverton in the House of Lords on 29 March 1950 which suggested that communists had infiltrated the British Council and the public service. Sir Thomas Lloyd demanded in an unusually cross personal letter to the retired Governor on 5 April that Milverton reveal his sources. On 14 June Milverton replied that 'I have information in writing from a responsible Nigerian Police Officer upon which the general statements made by me are made.' PRO CO 537/6553.

41 *Financial Times*, London, 7 March 1951.

42 Quotation from 'Personality Notes', SF 873.

43 *Ibid.*

44 See Rathbone, 'The government of the Gold Coast after World War II'.

45 Richard Crook, 'Decolonisation, the colonial state and chieftaincy in the Gold Coast', *African Affairs*, 85 (1986), pp. 75–106.

46 See T. J. Spinner, *The Political and Social History of Guyana 1945–1983* (Boulder and London, 1984).

CHAPTER SIX

Policing during the Malayan Emergency, 1948–60: communism, communalism and decolonisation

A. J. Stockwell

From a law-abiding dependency to insurrection: a failure of intelligence?

During the Malayan Emergency the police force was largely Malay while the police problem was fundamentally Chinese. This situation was the outcome of, firstly, the pre-war ideology and practice of colonial government, secondly, the plural society it administered, and thirdly, the cultural traditions and political attitudes of the overseas Chinese.

From their intervention in the Malay States in the late nineteenth century to their defeat by the Japanese in 1942, the British elaborated a doctrine of trusteeship and operated a dual administration on the principle that 'Malaya was a Malay country'. Malays, being 'sons of the soil', were absorbed within the Residential System as junior partners; all others, particularly the Chinese immigrants, were regarded as 'birds of passage' who, though vital to the development of 'modern Malaya', were not rooted in it. Swettenham was appreciative of the Chinese contribution to the Malayan economy, but he and his contemporaries dismissed any suggestion to treat them as a 'Malayan community'. While he accepted that Chinese 'energy and enterprise have made the Malay States what they are today', he insisted that it 'is almost hopeless to expect to make friends with a Chinaman, and it is, for a Government officer, an object that is not very desirable to attain' since those Chinese found in Malaya 'only realise two positions – the giving and the receiving of orders'. Taking pains to learn the language and to respect the religion and customs of the Malay was the duty of every British official seeking 'to understand the inner man', but dealing with the Chinese was 'a lesson more easy to learn'. He was also convinced that the Chinese 'are the easiest people to govern in the East for a man of determination, but they must know their master, as he must know them'.[1]

This ambivalent attitude to the Chinese in Malaya infused British

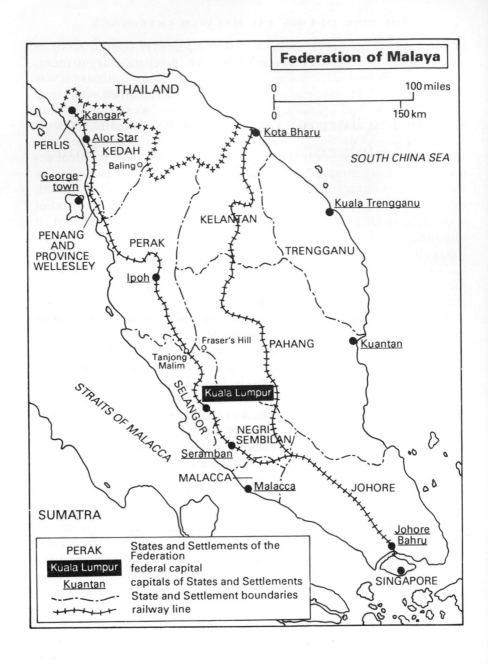

The Federation of Malaya

administration until 1942 and, despite the post-war commitment to multi-racialism, lingered until independence. A separate department, the Chinese Protectorate was set up to deal with Chinese affairs (it was replaced by the Chinese Secretariat in 1946), but it remained something of a specialism, and promotion to the higher reaches of the Malayan Civil Service tended to be via the 'Malay-language stream'.[2] During the 1920s and 1930s Swettenham's picture of stability and prosperity was clouded by depressed rubber and tin prices and the political activities of Kuomintang and communist agents amongst overseas Chinese. In addition census figures revealed both an absolute growth of the Chinese population in Malaya and an increasing proportion of second-generation Chinese residents. These developments served, if anything, to reinforce Britain's pro-Malay policy. Sir Cecil Clementi, ironically the one Governor/High Commissioner (1930–4) who knew China and Chinese, endeavoured to contain the Chinese 'menace' by elevating the status of the Sultans and involving Malay aristocrats more actively in routine administration.

Pre-war policing bore the hallmarks of wider colonial practice in Malaya. Firstly, there were some 250 British officers who learned Malay, were trained for Malayan conditions and made their careers in the Malayan Police Force. Secondly, for a population that rose from 3·3 millions in 1921 to about 5 millions twenty years later, the rank-and-file of the force numbered approximately 10,000 and consisted of Malays and Indians. The latter were Sikhs and Punjabis, not the Tamils who supplied the labour for plantations and public works. Thirdly, despite the fact that a significant proportion of Malayan crime emanated from the Triads, few Chinese (apart from some valuable detectives) joined the force and only a small minority of European police officers knew any of the Chinese dialects. In the inter-war period, however, 'turbulent Chinese' were easily controlled and, where necessary, removed through the operation of the Banishment Ordinance. Looking back from the stressful days of the 1950s, observers concluded that before the Second World War the peoples of Malaya had been essentially law-abiding.[3] Indeed, a pre-war handbook presented service in the Malayan Police as an attractive prospect for a European. The Force was 'in very good heart, keen on the work, very successful with it'. An officer could count on the loyal support of the men under his command, one half of whom were 'kindly and courteous' Malays while the other half were drawn from 'the military races of India ... steadfast, trustworthy men who respond with intelligence and with eagerness to proper treatment from the right sort of British officer'.[4]

Contrast that testimonial of 1929 with this *cri de coeur* from March 1946: 'now I dare not go out. You might ask why this is. I say, quite honestly, because there is violence in the land, because in the small towns and villages of Malaya, the gun and pistol rule.'[5] Why had Malaya moved from an apparently law-abiding state to a lawlessness that defied policing? The answer is to be found in the wartime dislocation of both Malayan society and the colonial system.

More than three-and-a-half years of war and Japanese occupation had wrought major changes throughout the peninsula: Chinese had fled the invaders to squat on jungle fringes; others had migrated to towns from disused mines and plantations; the infrastructure had all but collapsed, and so too had disease control, with malaria reaching almost epidemic proportions.[6] Malaya, which previously had imported food and textiles, now faced grave shortages of rice and cloth. These privations aggravated hitherto latent racial antagonisms. Moreover, British defeat and Japanese rule aroused political awareness. In the anarchic interregnum between the Japanese surrender on 15 August 1945 and the restoration of the British regime in September, and even during the subsequent seven months of over-rule by the British Military Administration (BMA), these tensions spilled over in rice riots, communal clashes and political protests. The Malayan Peoples Anti-Japanese Army (MPAJA), which was dominated by Chinese communists, meted out summary justice to collaborators and held sway in the country until the BMA managed to establish its nine regional commands. Then, in the first half of 1946 the hitherto quiescent Malay community mounted a mass non-cooperation campaign against novel British proposals to offer citizenship to Malaya's Chinese.

As they attempted to reimpose their authority and prepare the ground for the ambitious (but, as it turned out, short-lived) Malayan Union constitution, the British found that in virtually every field of colonial administration they lacked the resources and expertise to cope satisfactorily with problems which, at least in their extent and intensity, they had not encountered during the 1930s. As regards the police, the force as a whole was seriously under strength. The echelon of Europeans had been decimated by war or internment, and many officers who returned to Malaya were in poor shape and low spirits. Former prisoners of war distanced themselves from those who had had the good fortune to evade Japanese detention, while 'old Malayans' as a group distrusted newcomers from other dependencies. Moreover, the leadership wanted incisiveness and was ingrained with pre-war views and priorities.

Turning to the Asian members of the Force, the British discovered that the Malay constables, whom both British and Japanese had employed for rural policing, had had their confidence sapped by changes of regime and MPAJA reprisals. The reliability of Malaya's Indians was similarly suspect; many had suffered at the hands of the Japanese, others had been turned by the anti-British Indian National Army. Furthermore, as India moved rapidly to independence, the British bowed before Congress resistance to the deployment of Indian soldiers and policemen in South-East Asia, with the result that Indian membership of the Malayan Police Force declined dramatically. By late 1953, for example, Indians and Pakistanis accounted for only 5 per cent of the rank-and-file of Regular Police. Finally, the Force had a feeble grip on Chinese affairs; in 1946–8 it lacked both knowledge of, and hence power over, the potentially most troublesome community in Malaya.

Analyses of the origins of the Malayan Emergency have focused upon the extent to which the police appreciated the intentions of the Chinese-dominated Malayan Communist Party (MCP). Critics of the police have charged it (and more especially its intelligence branch, the Malayan Security Service [MSS]) with failure to foresee the insurrection which was launched in mid-1948. Others have argued that the fault lay, not in the provision of intelligence, but in the reluctance of High Commissioner Gent to act upon it.[7] Short has presented a third view: intelligence reports were numerous but too general to be a useful guide to action. By frequently crying wolf, the MSS itself contributed to the atmosphere of official complacency; by bombarding the High Commissioner with awful prognostications, it omitted to pinpoint communist objectives. Obsessed with the possibility of Indonesian subversion of the Malays, Colonel Dalley (Director of the MSS) tended to hedge his bets when required to pronounce on Chinese activities. The security service was almost entirely dependent upon the highly placed double-agent, Loi Tak, and neglected the cultivation of Chinese agents at grassroots level The upshot was that, when Loi Tak absconded in March 1947 and his place as Secretary-General of the MCP was taken by Chin Peng, the British were more or less bereft of a source of accurate information. Quite simply, the police were unable to penetrate the MCP at key moments between March 1947 and June 1948.[8]

We should, however, not fault the Malayan Police for failing to find what may not have existed in June 1948, namely a specific plan for an armed rising. Although Cold War warriors explained the insurrection in terms of a world-wide attack upon colonies which was inspired by Moscow (the so-called Zhdanov doctrine), regionally orchestrated through Calcutta (at conferences in February 1948) and nurtured (in the case of Malaya) by Peking, these assumptions have since been questioned, emphasis being placed upon the local circumstances within which the MCP operated, and note being taken of the Party's proclivity to react to, rather than to initiate, confrontation with the colonial administration. It has been suggested that the federal government itself contributed significantly to the timing and the shape of the outbreak. By declaring

a State of Emergency for the whole of Malaya on 18 June and by proscribing the Party on 23 July 1948, it actually endowed the MCP with
a much-needed *casus belli*, thereby completing the transformation of
lawlessness into insurrection.[9]

The British now expected trouble elsewhere in the empire. Perceiving
connections between the Malayan insurrection and the more or less
simultaneous uprisings in Burma, Indonesia and the Philippines, together
with the war in Indo-China, the Colonial Office instructed all governors
to improve their police forces, particularly the intelligence and special
branches.[10] When, for example, the governor of North Borneo proposed
to appoint 'an experienced Chinese police officer with training in Special
Branch work' on the grounds that with 'the increasing tempo of events
in the Far East it is imperative that all possible steps should be taken
to gain an insight into Chinese political activities and thought', the
Colonial Office could only concur, although it did wonder where a recruit
with such qualifications would be found.[11]

The police forces of Britain's South-East Asian territories were
desperately short of Chinese-speaking officers as well as Chinese constables, and the problems of gathering intelligence and of enlisting
Chinese assistance would continue to hamper police work in Malaya
long into the 1950s. The immediate effect of the Emergency, however,
was to thrust paramilitary tasks of counter-insurgency upon the already
hard-pressed Malayan Police.

Paramilitary operations: towards a police state?

A new era of Malayan policing opened with the appointment of Colonel
W. N. Gray as Commissioner of Police in August 1948. Gray came to
Malaya after a wearing stint in Palestine where he had run his force
on military lines.[12] In Malaya he insisted that terrorism was primarily
the responsibility of the police, not the military, and that policemen
should be taught to shoot. Under Gray the Malayan Police Force expanded enormously and quickly. The numbers of full-timers rose from
about 11,000 in 1947 to nearly 73,000 at their peak in 1952 of which
32,000 were Regulars and the remaining 41,000 were the (predominantly Malay) Special Constables. In support were part-time Auxiliaries
and Kampong Guards whose numbers grew from approximately 17,000
in 1948 to over a quarter of a million by 1952. It was a costly development and, after the prices boom of the Korean War subsided, the force
was cut back: in the last three years of British administration the combined size of the Regular Police and Special Constabulary hovered at
the 48,000 mark, while the number of part-timers dropped to less than
155,000.[13]

During 1948–52 the emphasis of policing shifted from 'normal' to 'paramilitary' duties. Throughout the Emergency the Malayan Police and its auxiliary forces provided the bulk of the manpower for internal security and bore the brunt of government casualties: three policemen died for every soldier killed by the insurgents. Their first priority was the protection of dollar-earning rubber and tin. In 1949 the police moved on to the offensive and took part in jungle sweeps. The task of guarding mines and estates was now mainly assigned to Special Constables. Later, notably after the start of the Briggs Plan in mid-1950, the police played the major role in resettling squatters and defending New Villages in order to deprive the communists of food and information. Both civil and military authorities recognised 1950 to be the critical year in the campaign, and by June 1951 High Commissioner Gurney (1948–51) and the Director of Operations (General Briggs) agreed that the turning-point had been reached. We now know that this was something of a false dawn, but even at the time it was clear that all was not well with the Malayan Police Force.

First of all, the morale of European officers was at a low ebb. 'Old Malayans' were bitter about what they saw as a seizure of the force by 'Palestinians', for, in addition to Gray, seven others had been appointed to senior positions. Gray's abrasiveness, his sometimes inappropriate Palestinian methods and his refusal to use armoured vehicles worsened the mood, as did deteriorating conditions of service at a time when the relatively few experienced officers were subjected to ever-increasing work-loads. Secondly, the efficiency of the force had been impaired by its rapid expansion. The time devoted to training (especially language instruction) had been reduced, with dire consequences for intelligence. Moreover, organisation had grown unwieldy; centralisation suffocated local initiatives while, at the top, there were disputes between Gray (who threatened to resign in October 1950)[14] and the Director of Intelligence, Sir William Jenkin (who did resign the following October). Thirdly, there was discord between the civil, police and military authorities, with Gray contesting the views of General Briggs on police organisation and those of both Briggs and Gurney as regards resettlement. Finally, because Gray insisted that 'all members of the Force had to be trained to fight' and refused to admit that there was a fundamental difference between 'operational' and 'purely police' duties,[15] concentration upon counter-insurgency had damaged police relations with the public.

It was because of dissatisfaction with and within the Force that the Police Mission to Malaya was appointed towards the end of 1949. Its three members had wide knowledge of policing but were strangers to Malaya: Sir Alexander Maxwell, the Mission's chairman, had recently retired after a decade as Permanent Under-Secretary at the Home Office

(1938–48); J. F. Ferguson was Chief Constable of Kent (1946–58); and R. L. Jackson, who had been Secretary of the Metropolitan Police Office since 1946, would later serve as Assistant Commissioner CID at New Scotland Yard (1953–63). John Gullick was seconded from the Malayan Civil Service to act as Secretary to the Mission. The three men visited Malaya between 27 November 1949 and 12 February 1950, and their published report was broadly supportive of Gray's achievements since August 1948. They did, however, draw attention to deficiencies in morale and conditions of service, in intelligence and CID, and were especially perturbed by developments which subordinated 'the claims of ordinary police work' to the 'more urgent claims' of counter-insurgency, thereby provoking public complaint that 'the Force is ceasing to be a Police Force and is becoming a paramilitary organisation'.[16]

Maxwell, Ferguson and Jackson presented the metropolitan view of policing. Those engaged in counter-insurgency deployed force to destroy the enemy, whereas, they argued, officers fulfilling normal police duties were obliged to preserve peace with minimum force and to win the trust and co-operation of the people.

> The policeman must be helpful to members of the public: he must develop the qualities of forebearance and restraint: he must be impartial and even-handed in his treatment of people of all types and positions. His whole bent must be towards preserving the framework of law and order within which civil life goes on. The contrast between that bent and the attitude of mind required for war-like objectives is such that *training for jungle operations can do little or nothing to develop the habits of thought and action required for ordinary police work* [my emphasis].[17]

To assist the return to 'normal policing', the Mission made specific recommendations concerning training programmes and the recruitment of Chinese. Observing that the 'lack of Chinese-speaking junior officers is a serious weakness in the Force at present', they stressed 'the importance of resuming the pre-war arrangements for enabling a proportion of European officers to acquire a knowledge of the Chinese language'. They also emphasised the 'responsibility resting on the Chinese in Malaya to take a larger share of the work of policing the country'. While acknowledging the valuable service rendered by Chinese in the Detective Branch, they regretted that their 'negligible' presence in the Uniform Branch (the Branch which was, after all, 'in daily touch with the public') imposed 'disadvantages both on the police and on Chinese members of the community'. Since the Uniform Branch had customarily been regarded by British and Malays alike as a Malay preserve, they were 'glad to learn that the principle has been accepted that Chinese should be eligible for the Uniform Branch' and also to discover 'a large measure of support for the policy' amongst both Malay and Chinese community leaders. What was now necessary was a 'determined effort ... to introduce a proper balance into the composition of the Police Force'[18] but, as we shall see, drives to recruit Chinese would have meagre results.

Good public relations through 'normal policing' were impeded by serious obstacles which, though identified by 1950, had yet to be removed. They included: an excessive emphasis upon the paramilitary role of the police, inadequate training and language expertise within the Force, Chinese mistrust of the authorities, and the arrangement which placed the police under the direct orders of government instead of fostering a sense of responsibility to the public. On this last point we should note that Emergency regulations gave the police extraordinary powers of search and arrest, control of the movement of persons and traffic, and the authority to impose curfews and collective punishments (as, for example, imposed by Templer on Tanjong Malim in March 1952). At the time of Lyttelton's tour of the Federation in late 1951 it was estimated that some 6,000 persons were being held in detention without trial.[19] R. Ramani, an Indian member of the Federal Legislative Council, protested against the 'new despotism of the executive and the newer despotism of the police',[20] and Tan Cheng Lock, another member of the Legislative Council as well as founder-president of the Malayan Chinese Association (MCA), regularly complained about the loss of civil liberties suffered by the majority of law-abiding Chinese.

Perhaps the most frequently cited critic of what he saw as 'the omnipresence of the police' during the regime of General Templer (High Commissioner 1952–4) was Victor Purcell. Sinophile and Chinese scholar, former Malayan Civil Servant turned Lecturer in Far Eastern History at Cambridge, Purcell became honorary adviser to the Malayan Chinese Association in November 1951. It was as adviser to the MCA that in August 1952 he departed for a tour of Malaya in the company of Francis Carnell, Oxford's expert on colonial constitutions. The Colonial Office, anxious that the 'safe' MCA should succeed in winning the allegiance of Malaya's Chinese without at the same time aggravating Malay fears, cautioned Purcell before he left England against over-exuberant advocacy of Chinese rights. Perhaps because he had received a false signal from MI5 that Purcell was coming out as 'a paid trouble-maker', Templer took an instant dislike to Purcell.[21] The feeling was reciprocated and each man embarked upon a personal vendetta.

In a series of articles and in the introduction to *Malaya: Communist or Free?*, Purcell declared that the 'police impregnated and coloured Malayan life as fluorescein will colour a stream', that there 'was no human activity from the cradle to the grave that the police did not superintend', and that the 'real rulers of Malaya were not General Templer or his troops, but the "Special Branch" of the Malayan police'.[22] For his part, Templer hounded 'that disgusting creature, Dr. Purcell' and Carnell of 'pernicious' views. When he accused Carnell of 'insinuating' subversion into Malayan students, the Colonial Office considered ways of banning them from courses in colonial administration at Oxford. It was for the Cambridge don, however, that Templer reserved most of his vitriol: 'It seems that Purcell, largely in order to vent his personal spite against me, may be infusing poison into successive batches of students from Malaya, and into any other students who come his way. This strikes me as fundamentally evil and I hope you will have the matter thoroughly investigated.' Templer added: 'What is the good of all the work we are trying to do if at the same time we nurse vipers at our bosom?'[23]

Both Purcell and Templer over-indulged in invective and each grossly exaggerated the damage that the other was doing to Malaya. For all his illiberal appearance, Templer was in fact committed to political advance and police reform. Moreover, his arrival in Malaya early in 1952 coincided with the replacement of Gray by Colonel Arthur Young. Indeed, in stressing Young's shock at finding 'what he called a "Police State"',[24] Purcell weakened his attack upon Templer, for Young was commenting upon the situation which the new High Commissioner, like the new Police Commissioner, had inherited, not created.

'Normal policing': towards a Malayan nation?

Arthur Young, Commissioner of Police in the City of London from 1950 to 1971, represented the metropolitan rather than the military tradition of British policing. Until he left Malaya in April 1953 he was engaged in the restoration of 'normal policing'. Although he did not always succeed in his overseas secondments, in Malaya 'Young's genius lay in presenting the image of the ideal London bobby; and in transforming that ideal into a Malayan reality.'[25] Discussion of the swing away from paramilitary policing must start, however, with the crisis that overtook Malayan government in October 1951.

The assassination of Sir Henry Gurney en route to Fraser's Hill on 6 October 1951 brought to a head Anglo-Malay exasperation with the Chinese community. Two days before his death Gurney, who in contrast to the racism he is reputed to have displayed towards the inhabitants of Palestine was deemed to have 'no anti-Chinese bias whatever',[26] raged against those Chinese who 'live comfortably and devote themselves wholly to making money ... but can spare nothing for the MCA anti-Communist efforts'. Chinese reluctance to co-operate with the police was glaring and stemmed, Gurney argued, not from government hostility towards them, but from their own selfishness:

the Government wished to recruit up to 10,000 Chinese for service in the Police. There was full prior consultation with leading Chinese, but as soon as the men were called up, the cry was all for exemptions, 6,000 decamped to Singapore and several other thousands to China ... Leading Chinese have contented themselves with living in luxury in Singapore etc. and criticising the Police and security forces for causing injustices. These injustices are deplorable but are the fault not of the Police but of those Chinese who know the truth and will not tell it.[27]

The problem of Chinese indifference to counter-insurgency and their unwillingness to enter the Police Force was discussed in late October 1951 at a series of top level meetings with, in turn, the Malay Rulers, chief ministers of the Malay states (*mentri mentri besar*), and with MCA and other Chinese leaders.[28] The mood of the Malays and some British officials was for sanctions (including the confiscation of property) against unco-operative Chinese. Chinese leaders, on the other hand, argued that Chinese co-operation should be won by government displays of trust, not extorted by punitive measures. While they admitted the urgent necessity to recruit more police from their community, they insisted that, since both the perpetrators and victims of insurgency were largely Chinese, 'this was essentially a Chinese problem' which would be solved only 'by placing confidence in the Chinese leaders by putting them in the position of influence, if not of power, and by supporting them and listening to their advice when it was offered'.[29] Such parading of communal claims, however, produced few constructive proposals for the enlistment of Chinese support for the policing of Malaya.

In December 1951 the new Conservative Secretary of State, Oliver Lyttelton, descended on Malaya. The result was a shake-up of personnel, an overhaul of administration (though not of long-term policy),[30] a revitalisation of counter-insurgency and a redirection of policing.[31] Templer combined the posts of High Commissioner and Director of Operations, and Young replaced Gray as Commissioner of Police. The priorities of the new regime were intelligence and police reform. Templer believed intelligence to be the key to victory and appointed a non-executive Director of Intelligence responsible for the co-ordination of all the civil and military agencies in Malaya and answerable solely to the High Commissioner. For the first time during the Emergency the various bodies engaged in counter-insurgency were provided with an intelligence *system*.[32]

Police reform proceeded on four fronts: (i) pay and conditions of service; (ii) organisation and training; (iii) provision of equipment, particularly armoured cars;[33] and (iv) the reinvigoration of 'normal policing'. Operation Service was mounted by Templer and Young to win public acceptance of the Malayan Police as a 'Service' rather than a

'Force'.[34] It was caught up in the campaign to win the 'hearts and minds' of the people. Recruitment of Chinese to the uniform branch of the regular Police Force, like concessions on federal citizenship or the promotion of multi-racial politics, was an aspect of 'nation-building'.

Morale soared, organisation improved and a training programme was announced in June 1952.[35] However, because counter-insurgency continued to interrupt 'normal policing', the Chinese responded sluggishly to exercises in public relations. The recruitment drive, launched by Templer over Radio Malaya after he had been in the country less than two months, was a case in point. At that time there were only 800 Chinese in the uniform branch of Regulars, and the High Commissioner hoped to draw in a further 2,000. In his broadcast he endeavoured to appeal to economic self-interest and Confucian loyalties:

> But I put it to you that unless we can together wipe out the Communist terrorists and free the people of this country from the threat of sudden death, extortion or mutilation, then your economic standards will cease to matter for you will be under the yoke of slavery; and your parents, wife and family will be no more than cherished memories. Family life finds no place in Communist doctrine. Children are taught to go against their parents.[36]

Eager to establish themselves in the eyes of both British officials and sceptical Malays as credible community leaders who were worthy of responsible positions, MCA members worked hard at recruitment but with disappointing results. For example, of the 300 or 400 recruits expected from Selangor, only thirty-six came forward.[37] In 1953 government retrenchment consequent upon the post-Korean collapse in commodity prices led to the application of the following formula to police recruitment: the number of Chinese enrolled each month should equal the number of Malays up to a maximum of eighty recruits from all races. At the end of the year the Federal Executive Council lowered the monthly ceiling to sixty but raised the Chinese share to two out of every three recruits. In order to steer Chinese towards the uniform branch, a limit of 550 was placed on the number of Chinese serving as plain-clothes policemen.[38] Nonetheless, at this rate it would take decades to right the lop-sidedness of the Force, as figures for the rank and file of Regulars on 1 November 1953 showed: – [39]

Malays	19,729 (including 358 plain clothes)
Chinese	1,824 (" 414 " ")
Indians & Pakistanis	1,162 (" 163 " ")
Others	219 (" 15 " ").

Some of the reasons for Chinese reluctance to join the Malayan Police have already been mentioned and it is now time to discuss them more fully. The first set of reasons embraced British attitudes and the practice of colonial rule. An essentially Malayophile administration had been customarily ignorant of Chinese languages, had concentrated on controlling rather than involving the Chinese community, and had regarded the Police Force as a British–Malay preserve. Heavy police casualties at the hands of mainly Chinese insurgents meant that officers found it 'hard to be courteous and forebearing' in their dealings with Malaya's Chinese.[40]

A second explanation is to be found in the communalism of Malaya's 'plural society': 'the rank and file of the Police Force is almost entirely composed of Malays who do not speak Chinese and who, generally speaking, are unsympathetic to Chinese.'[41] Though accepted in principle by all community leaders, the call for more Chinese policemen failed to excite popular enthusiasm. Malay were suspicious of any Chinese attempt to enter any field where they had hardly trod before, while Chinese were loth to become identified with an 'alien' Force. Moreover, although three-quarters of their community had been born in Malaya or Singapore, the Chinese were indifferent to the concept of service to the 'Malayan nation'. Indeed, by the time the first federal elections took place in July 1955, a startlingly small proportion of the Chinese community had bothered to become federal citizens and gain the vote: although 37 per cent of Malaya's population, the Chinese accounted for only 11·2 per cent of the electorate.[42]

The culture and experiences of the overseas Chinese provide a third reason for their unwillingness to join the Malayan Police. In the bleak aftermath of Gurney's assassination, the Acting High Commissioner noted a number of such factors lying behind 'the present non-cooperative attitude of the great bulk of the Chinese'.[43] One of these was the absence of a tradition of protective and uncorrupt policing in China where banditry was 'endemic'; another was the fear that open collaboration with the Federation government would sooner or later be reported back to Peking, leading to victimisation of relatives in China; a third was the recollection of Britain's surrender to Japan in 1942, coupled with uncertainty about her ability to defend Malaya in the 1950s. There were other considerations too, such as family commitments, economic self-interest, poor police pay (at one point it was suggested that the MCA might consider subsidising the families of recruits) and sheer dislike of the uniform worn by constables.

The Malayan Police Force was reviewed at intervals during the Emergency: by Gray shortly after his arrival in August 1948; by the Police Mission in 1949–50; and by Lyttelton, Templer and Young in 1951–2.

[117]

E

The last examination before the Federation moved into the final phase of decolonisation was carried out by Colonel Muller, the Inspector General of Colonial Police, who visited Malaya in February and March 1955, and reported to High Commissioner MacGillivray (1954–7) in July. Whereas Lyttelton had encountered an 'intolerable' situation in which 'the organisation of the police was in utter disorder', Muller expressed confidence in the force.[44] He was 'most impressed' by the specialist branches (including Special Branch), observed 'high morale' in every section and hesitated 'to suggest any radical changes in an organisation which is now working smoothly'.

Nevertheless, Muller did point to three major problems awaiting solution: the first was the racial imbalance and poor quality of the rank-and-file; the second lay in the field of criminal investigation; and the third was the continuing burden of work still borne by each Officer Commanding a Police District (OCPD). Here we might consider further Muller's views on the first two of these difficulties.

Muller noted that 'the average standard of the constable struck me as being very low'; for while he was 'extremely smart in drill', he was 'very backward as a policeman'. This defect was related, he argued, 'to the problem of bringing more Chinese of the right type into the force'. In spite of the 'very strenuous efforts' that had already been made, the few Chinese constables in the force were 'of very poor quality (mostly rubber tappers) and unsuitable, and I believe they have already proved to be unreliable'. Muller felt that the way forward lay in the creation of a special Urban or Town Police Force. This was a scheme which W. L. R. Carbonell had been working on since he succeeded Young as Commissioner of Police in 1953.[45] By demanding of its cadets a higher standard of education and in turn offering them better conditions of service, this Force was intended to attract more Chinese of 'the right type'. Since the scheme would risk discriminating against Malay police, 'who [would] still be the more suitable material for the rural areas', it would also be necessary 'to take positive action to build up the average quality of the Malay Police'.[46]

As regards criminal investigation, Muller proposed that 'the time [had] now come when a higher priority must be given to this branch of the work'. Accepting that '[i]nevitably everything [had] been subordinated to anti-terrorist operations', he nonetheless insisted that 'the top priority for the police [was] still "the fulfilling of their normal functions in the populated areas"', by which he meant that 'the police should aim at giving the same normal service as would be expected were there not terrorists'. Like others before him, he declared that effective criminal investigation 'would surely assist in "the fight to win the hearts and minds of the people"'.[47]

For all Muller's optimism about the health of the Malayan Police, officials in the Far Eastern Department of the Colonial Office interpreted his findings more gloomily. Excessive centralisation of management, a poor rate of crime detection and, most disturbingly, racial imbalance within the Regular Force still impeded community or 'normal' policing. J. S. Bennett commented: 'The impression which one gets from his report, of an over-militarised (or at any rate over-centralised) police force giving little attention to the main police job of dealing with crime, is not a reassuring one.'[48] In so far as his 'very limited knowledge' went, C. Y. Carstairs was 'inclined to agree' with this judgment: 'The pursuit of this Emergency has no doubt tended to the creation of a rather more military or "gendarmerie" force than is consistent with usual police ideas.'[49]

Decolonisation and the Malayanisation of the police

In July 1955, the month Muller submitted his report, the Alliance of Malay (UMNO), Chinese (MCA) and Indian (MIC) parties won fifty-one of the fifty-two elected seats in the first federal elections and Tunku Abdul Rahman became Malaya's first Chief Minister. By the time the Federation government had prepared its response to Muller, the independence conference was gathering in London (January–February 1956). The British authorities in Malaya shared Muller's anxiety about Chinese indifference to police work, the more so as it was 'a matter of political importance to the present elected Government'.[50] The Chinese role in Malayan policing was, however, fading as a perennial problem of colonial rule, and re-emerging as one of the long-term 'challenges of independence'.

In late 1955 an issue of greater moment than the optimum composition of the police force was the question of its effective control during the transition between 'self-government', which the Alliance claimed to have already achieved by their electoral landslide, and 'independence' which Malayan politicians now demanded by August 1957.

As early as April 1951 the Conference of Colonial Police Commissioners at the Police College, Ryton-on-Dunsmore, had considered the repercussions of constitutional advance upon colonial policing.[51] They foresaw two dangers: one was of the Police Force becoming merely the agent of the political party in power; the other was the possible clash between a policeman's duty to the Force and his allegiance to the political leaders of his people. The subsequent working party on the position of the police in the later stages of colonial constitutional development, which was chaired by Sir Charles Jeffries of the Colonial Office, concluded that no constitutional safeguard was proof against 'the establishment of a "police state" in which the Force is merely an instrument of the Government of the day and of a partisan policy'. The working party did recommend, however, the creation of Police Service Commissions in order to supply a measure of protection from political pressures.[52]

British concern with 'police impartiality', or rather with the insulation of the force from indigenous politicians, was first roused by events in the Gold Coast. Oliver Lyttelton was adamant that in West Africa there could be no concessions over the governor's reserve powers, British control of the police or African access to CID reports and intelligence, with the result that the 'internal self-government' achieved by the Gold Coast before 1957 did not include African control of police and internal security.[53]

During the hectic five months between the federal elections and the opening of the Lancaster House conference on constitutional advance in Malaya, British officials in London and Kuala Lumpur grappled with the question as to whether or not they should recommend the transfer to Malayan hands of internal security and police. These deliberations took place in the context of the improved security position in Malaya, the Alliance's commitment to independence by August 1957, Tunku Abdul Rahman's offer of amnesty to communist insurgents and his talks with MCP leader, Chin Peng.

Officials were faced with a choice between two courses of action. On the one hand they could follow the Gold Coast path and insist that the High Commissioner retained ultimate responsibility over the police. Alternatively, they could share the responsibility with Malayan politicians, transferring police administration while keeping operational control. In much the same way that concessions were granted to provincial India during the inter-war years, a proposal for 'dyarchy' in Malayan policing could be justified on the grounds that it would associate elected leaders more closely with the cause of public order and thus blunt their political radicalism.[54]

The British were anxious that the efficiency of internal security should not be impaired by clumsy management or political ineptitude. The major cause for alarm was Tunku Abdul Rahman's meeting with Chin Peng at Baling on 28–29 December 1955. At a time when the communists were in military disarray, the last thing the British wanted was a negotiated settlement by which the MCP slid into the political fold under cover of partnership with the Alliance. Indeed, Chin Peng subtly held out the prospect of peace 'as soon as the elected Government of the Federation obtains complete control of internal security and local armed forces'.[55]

By the turn of the year, MacGillivray (High Commissioner), Carbonell (Commissioner of Police), D.C. Watherston (Chief Secretary) and General Bourne (Director of Operations) were unanimous that the balance of advantage lay in transferring responsibility for the police to the Malayan Minister for Home Affairs by August 1956. Malayan prosperity and the absence of significant industrial unrest meant that local conditions were propitious. Moreover, since full internal self-government was definitely on the way, they believed that the sooner Alliance leaders got experience of policing the better it would be for the future security of the country. Furthermore, it was felt that elected ministers, rather than colonial officials, ought to bear the brunt of implementing measures of retrenchment that would include police redundancies.[56]

The clincher for ministers in London was the argument that projected a link between disappointing the Alliance and a serious deterioration in security. Should H.M.G. refuse to surrender responsibility for internal defence and police, then the Lancaster House conference might break up, and if this happened, Alliance leaders would 'not return to Malaya with the determination to rally the country in an all-out effort against Communist terrorism' but would be 'more likely to seek a settlement with the Communists on terms which might in the end constitute a new and greater threat to internal security'.[57] The Secretary of State accepted the High Commissioner's advice and informed his colleagues that, 'internal security will in any case be better safeguarded if controlled by co-operative local Ministers than if we retain nominal control in the face of constant opposition from Ministers and, as a result, probably also of growing unreliability among the great mass of the locally-recruited members of the internal security forces themselves'.[58] So it was that the means adopted by Lennox Boyd to safeguard British interests in Malaya differed from those previously taken by Lyttelton to secure the same objective in the Gold Coast.

The Cabinet approved this strategy.[59] Even so, the British moved faster than they had really intended; at Lancaster House they accepted August 1957 as the target-date for independence and agreed to the immediate transfer of internal defence and security to a Malayan Minister (the Tunku himself).[60] Ministerial power was, of course, far from absolute: a Police Service Commission was to be established, the High Commissioner continued to have full access to intelligence and Special Branch machinery, and Europeans still occupied senior positions in the Force. For the sake of future stability in the region, the British hoped there would not be a general exodus of expatriate officers, particularly from the Special Branch, and exempted the police from the Malayanisation schedule since there were 'not sufficient experienced Malayans in the Force at the moment to be able to take over all the senior posts within four years from now'.[61] For his part, Tunku Abdul Rahman succumbed neither to Chin Peng's blandishments nor to the

demands of his more radical supporters. He had stood his ground at the
Baling talks in December 1955 and he now resisted pressure for the
speedy Malayanisation of top jobs in the police. Three months before
independence day, he reassured Macmillan, 'you can trust us to deal
fittingly with the Communist terrorists in Malaya'.[62]

Many of the features, functions and failings of the colonial force have
been replicated since independence in the RMP (Royal Malaya/Malaysia
Police).[63] Like the colonial police, the RMP performs a paramilitary role,
is centrally organised and has extensive powers of arrest of persons and
seizure of property. It played a significant part in ensuring the survival of
the state through the last years of the Emergency (which ended officially
on 31 July 1960), during confrontation with Indonesia (1963–6) and in the
communal disturbances of May 1969. Like its predecessor, the RMP has
been accused of acting as the instrument of repressive government, in-
fringing civil liberties and neglecting 'normal policing'. Over the past
twenty years communalism has replaced communism as the major threat
to internal security, and the prime task of the RMP has become the
prevention or suppression of racial conflict. It has also periodically campaigned to project itself as a 'national institution' that is 'above race'.
The Force has ceased to be a Malay preserve and was generally considered
to have acted with greater professionalism and impartiality than the
military during the race riots of 1969.[64] It was, so the government has
explained, in order to avoid a repetition of 13 May 1969 that the police
detained 106 people under the Internal Security Act in October 1987.[65]

Notes

1 F. A. Swettenham: *Malay Sketches* (London, 1895), p. 1; *The Real Malay* (London, 1900),
pp. 38–9; *British Malaya* (London, ed. 1948), p. 232. Cf. Robert Heussler, *British Rule
in Malaya: the Malayan civil service and its predecessors, 1867–1941* (Westport, Conn.,
1981); Khasnor Johan, *The Emergence of the Modern Malay Administrative Elite*
(Singapore, 1984); Victor Purcell, *The Memoirs of a Malayan Official* (London, 1965);
Emily Sadka, *The Protected Malay States 1874–1895* (Kuala Lumpur, 1968); A. J.
Stockwell, 'The white man's burden and brown humanity: colonialism and ethnicity
in British Malaya', *Southeast Asian Journal of Social Science*, 10, i (1983), pp. 44–68.
2 Purcell, *Memoirs*, pp. 95–6.
3 Colonel W. A. Muller (Inspector General of Colonial Police), Report on inspection of
Federation of Malaya Police, 10 February – 19 March 1955, to Sir D. MacGillivray,
5 July 1955, Public Record Office [PRO] CO 1030/168.
4 C. W. Harrison (MCS retired), *Some Notes on the Government Services in British
Malaya* (London, The Malayan Information Agency, 1929), pp. 90–4; see also Sir Charles
Jeffries, *The Colonial Police* (London, 1952), pp. 78–9. For a history of policing in Malaya
before the Second World War see Patrick Morrah, 'The history of the Malayan Police',
Journal of the Malayan Branch of the Royal Asiatic Society, 36, ii (1963 [1968]),
pp. 5–172; see also J. M. Gullick, 'Syers and the Selangor Police 1875–1895', *Journal
of the Malayan Branch of the Royal Asiatic Society*, 51, ii (1978), pp. 1–57.

5 Letter in *The Sunday Times* (Kuala Lumpur), 3 March 1946, cited in Cheah Boon Kheng, *Red Star Over Malaya: resistance and social conflict during and after the Japanese occupation of Malaya, 1941–1946* (Singapore, ed. 1987), p. 170.

6 Brigadier H. C. Willan (Deputy Chief Civil Affairs Officer, Malaya), 'Report on the Military Government 12–30 September 1945', Arkib Negara Malaysia BMA/TS Com 58/9; *Malayan Union Annual Report*, 1946 and 1947; T. N. Harper, 'Custody and intercession: social welfare policy in post-war Malaya', unpublished paper presented to the Conference of the Association of South East Asian Studies in the UK (ASEASUK), Selwyn College, Cambridge, March 1988.

7 Malcolm MacDonald (Governor General, SE Asia, 1946–8) thought that Sir Edward Gent (Governor, Malayan Union 1946–8; High Commissioner, Federation of Malaya, 1948) had received adequate warning from the MSS, and was instrumental in getting Gent 'recalled for consultations' in late June 1948. Gent was killed when his plane crashed on the approach to London.

8 Anthony Short, *The Communist Insurrection in Malaya 1948–1960* (London, 1975), pp. 65–94. Short's book started out as an official history and he had full access to the confidential and secret papers of the Malayan Government in Kuala Lumpur. A recently released file at the PRO interestingly reveals that the controversial questions relating to the outbreak of insurrection which Short fully discusses were also aired, though superficially and inconclusively, in the Colonial Office's Far Eastern Department early in 1955; PRO CO 1030/16. Colonel Dalley's collection of MSS Political Intelligence Journals for 1946–8 have been deposited at Rhodes House Library, Oxford.

9 E.g. Ruth McVey, *The Calcutta Conference and the South-East Asian Uprisings* (Ithaca, 1958, mimeo); Short, *Communist Insurrection*; M. R. Stenson, *Repression and Revolt* (Papers in International Studies, SE Asian Series, No. 10, Ohio University, 1969, mimeo); Stenson: *Industrial Conflict in Malaya: prelude to the communist revolt of 1948* (London, 1970); *The 1948 Communist Revolt in Malaya: a note on historical sources and interpretation. With a reply by Gerald de Cruz* (Singapore, 1971); Richard Stubbs, *Hearts and Minds in Guerrilla Warfare: The Malayan Emergency, 1948–1960* (Singapore, 1989).

10 Creech Jones's secret despatch of 5 August 1948 to colonial governors is referred to in a North Borneo file for 1950 (PRO CO 537/6027). The despatch itself is probably at PRO CO 537/2768 for 1948 (file 14882) which is continued for 1949 by CO 537/4401 but both files have been 'retained', as has CO 537/2793 (14882/24 for 1948) on Malaya. Papers on organisation for research into political intelligence in the colonies at CO 537/2676 (14355/5 for 1948) have also been 'retained'.

11 Sir Ralph Hone to James Griffiths, secret, 3 July 1950, together with Colonial Office minutes, PRO CO 537/6027. Before his appointment as Governor, North Borneo (1949–54), Hone had been Secretary-General to the Governor General, SE Asia (1946–8) and MacDonald's Deputy Commissioner General, SE Asia (1948–9).

12 William Nicol Gray (1908–88) was a former officer in the Royal Marines and, after his time as Inspector General of the Palestine Police (1946–8), was designated Inspector General of the Gold Coast. Before taking up the West African post, however, he was invited to Malaya in an advisory capacity and, on the strength of his report on counter-terrorism, was asked to fill the vacancy left by H. B. Langworthy who had resigned as Commissioner of Police soon after the start of the Emergency. See Short, *Communist Insurrection*, pp. 120–1.

13 These figures, compiled from Annual Reports, are taken from Paul E. Stanborough, 'War by committee: counter-insurgency, the Malayan example, 1948–1957' (M.Litt. thesis, Oxford, 1987), Annex E, p. 217. Possibly because of a rapid turnover within the Force, police numbers vary from file to file and report to report; the figures here at least indicate the relative strength of the Malayan Police over the years and between its branches.

14 Gray to Chief Secretary, Federation of Malaya, top secret and personal, 21 October 1950, PRO CO 537/5973.

15 Note of a conference between senior officials (chaired by the Acting High Commissioner and attended *inter alia* by Malcolm MacDonald) and the Malay Chief Ministers, 26 October 1951, PRO CO 1022/148.

16 *Report of the Police Mission to Malaya, March 1950* (Kuala Lumpur, Government Press, 1950); a copy is at PRO CO 537/5417. I should like to acknowledge my debt to Mr John Gullick, secretary to the Mission, who has greatly enlarged my understanding of its deliberations.

17 *Report of the Police Mission to Malaya.*

18 *Report of the Police Mission to Malaya.* In 1949 the Police Adviser to the Colonial Office examined Singapore and (so it appears from the Singapore government's reaction to his report) made recommendations similar to those of the Police Mission to Malaya, notably that 'the original "militaristic" basis on which Colonial Forces have been built must give place to an organisation on purely civil lines so that the Police shall enjoy the confidence and good-will of the public'. As in Malaya, 'progress towards this most desirable end' had been impeded by the Japanese occupation and communal divisions. However, the Singapore government argued that the gulf between the overwhelmingly Chinese public (approximately 75 per cent of the island's population) and an 'alien' force (mainly composed of kampong Malays) justified retention of 'the tried military model' of policing. W. L. Blythe (OAG, Singapore) to Secretary of State, secret, 31 December 1951, PRO CO 968/278.

19 Oliver Lyttelton, *The Memoirs of Lord Chandos* (London, 1962), p. 372.

20 Short, *Communist Insurrection*, p. 159.

21 Purcell to J. J. Paskin, 23 June 1953, PRO CO 1022/85.

22 Victor Purcell, *Malaya: communist or free?* (London, 1954), p. 14. Copies of articles and letters to the press by Purcell and Carnell are in PRO CO 1022/85. See also Short, *Communist Insurrection*, pp. 379–87, and John Cloake, *Templer, tiger of Malaya* (London, 1985), pp. 307–9.

23 Templer to Lyttelton, secret, 23 October 1953, PRO CO 1022/85.

24 Purcell, *Communist or Free?*, p. 14.

25 Short, *Communist Insurrection*, p. 354. Colonel Arthur Young (1907–79; knighted 1965) was Commissioner, City of London Police, 1950–71; visited the Gold Coast to make recommendations on police reorganisation, 1951; served as Commissioner of Police in Malaya, 1952–3, and Kenya, 1954; and was seconded as Chief Constable, Royal Ulster Constabulary, 1969–70.

26 M. V. del Tufo comments on Gurney's 'political will' handed to Lyttelton during the latter's visit to Malaya in December 1951, PRO CO 1022/148. For Gurney's attitudes towards the peoples of Palestine see Charles Smith, chapter 4, above.

27 'A note in the handwriting of the late Sir Henry Gurney recently found amongst his private papers and known to have been written two days before his death' (copy), PRO CO 1022/148.

28 PRO CO 1022/148, cf. Short, *Communist Insurrection*, pp. 324–5.

29 Note of a meeting with Chinese leaders at King's House, 28 October 1951, PRO CO 1022/148.

30 See A. J. Stockwell, 'British imperial policy and decolonization in Malaya, 1942–52', *Journal of Imperial and Commonwealth History*, XII, 1 (1984), pp. 68–87, and 'Insurgency and decolonisation during the Malayan Emergency', *Journal of Commonwealth and Comparative Politics*, XXV, 1 (1987), pp. 73–81.

31 Lyttelton's Cabinet paper reporting his mission to Malaya has been 'retained' (ref. PRO CAB 129/48, C(51)59). He did, however, publish a lively, if somewhat inaccurate account of the visit in his *Memoirs of Lord Chandos*, pp. 361–83. The report of Hugh Fraser, his Parliamentary Private Secretary who accompanied him on the trip, is available. This mainly deals with nuts-and-bolts issues: as regards the police, Fraser noted the need to retrain Special Constables and the poor morale and efficiency of the Force (excepting some very good senior officers), PRO CO 1022/22.

32 Cloake, *Templer*, pp. 227–30.

33 Gray's resistance to the use of armoured vehicles, on the grounds that they inhibited the police from fighting back during an ambush, had been particularly controversial.

34 Cloake, *Templer*, p. 233.

35 PRO CO 1022/168.

36 Text of Templer's message to the Malayan Chinese broadcast on Radio Malaya, 31 March 1952, PRO CO 1022/149.
37 *Ibid.*, extract from Monthly Review of Chinese Affairs, August 1952.
38 PRO CO 1022/169.
39 *Ibid.*
40 Commissioner Gray as reported in note of conference with Chief Ministers of the Malay States, 26 October 1951, PRO CO 1022/148.
41 Extract from secret savingram from the Federation of Malaya to the Secretary of State, 30 October 1951, *ibid.*
42 S. Sothi Rachagan, 'The apportionment of seats in the House of Representatives', in Zakaria Haji Ahmad (ed.), *Government and Politics of Malaysia* (Singapore, 1987), p. 63. By the elections of 1959 the Chinese share of the electorate had increased to 34·5 per cent through the operation of the citizenship provisions of the independence constitution.
43 Extract from secret savingram from the Federation to the Secretary of State, 30 October 1951, PRO CO 1022/148.
44 Lyttelton, *Memoirs of Lord Chandos*, p. 372; Muller, Report, PRO CO 1030/168. Walter Muller (1898–1970) was in the Ceylon Police Service, 1920–38; Commissioner of Police, Trinidad, 1938–48, and Tanganyika, 1948–51; Inspector General of Colonial Police, 1951–7, and a member of the Kenya Police Commission, 1953.
45 William Carbonell (b. 1912) was about twentieth on the seniority list of the Malayan Police Force when Arthur Young picked him out as his successor (Cloake, *Templer*, p. 232). Carbonell served as Commissioner from April 1953 until his retirement in 1958, the year following Malayan independence.
46 Muller, Report, PRO CO 1030/168.
47 *Ibid.*
48 Bennett to Carstairs, 21 July 1955, *ibid.*
49 Minute by Carstairs, 22 July 1955, *ibid.*
50 Acting High Commissioner to the Secretary of State, confidential, 16 January 1956, *ibid.*
51 PRO CO 968/283 and /284.
52 'Report of the working party on the position of the police in the later stages of colonial constitutional development', confidential, 22 April 1953, PRO CO 968/284.
53 For an early statement of Lyttelton's 'sticking points' and 'the bare essentials' which 'cannot on any account be conceded' see his minute of February 1953, PRO CO 554/254, printed in A. N. Porter and A. J. Stockwell, *British Imperial Policy and Decolonization, 1938–64, volume 2, 1951–64* (London, 1989), p. 198. See also Richard Rathbone, chapter 5 above.
54 Direct reference was made to Gold Coast arrangements, see minute by M. L. Cahill, 23 December 1955, PRO CO 1030/75, and 'Conference on constitutional advance in the Federation of Malaya. Memorandum by the Secretary of State for the Colonies', January 1956, PRO CAB 134/1202, reprinted in Porter and Stockwell, *British Imperial Policy, volume 2*, p. 408. The Indian experience does not appear to have been explicitly cited in this instance, but for the parallels compare David Arnold, 'Police power and the demise of British rule in India, 1930–1947', chapter 3 above.
55 Transcript record of the final session of talks at Baling, 29 December 1955, PRO CO 1030/29. I am also grateful to Anthony Short for his unpublished paper, 'Bullets to ballots? The Malayan peace negotiations, 1955' (June 1988).
56 MacGillivray to A. M. MacKintosh, secret, 28 December 1955, PRO CO 1030/73.
57 MacGillivray to J. M. Martin, secret telegram, 9 January 1956, *ibid.*
58 'Conference on constitutional advance', PRO CAB 134/1202.
59 Lennox-Boyd's paper, 'Constitutional advance in Malaya', was drafted in the Far Eastern Department (PRO CO 1030/70), approved by the Colonial Policy Committee on 12 January (PRO CAB 134/1202, CA(56) 2nd meeting) and went before full Cabinet on 17 January 1956. The final version which was presented to Cabinet has been withheld (it should be at PRO CAB 129/79, CP(56)12) but the Cabinet conclusions are open at PRO CAB 128/30 pt. II, CM 4(56)3. See also H. O. Hooper to Prime Minister, 11 January 1956, PRO CAB 21/2883.

60 Cmd. 9714, *Report by the Federation of Malaya Constitutional Conference held in London in January and February, 1956*, Parliamentary Papers (1956–7) XIII, p. 893. Cf. Harry Miller, *Prince and Premier* (London, 1959), pp. 197–9.
61 David Watherston to J. B. Johnston, confidential, 1 June 1956, PRO CO 1030/230. Cf. minute by A. M. MacDonald (Colonial Office), 10 March 1956, *ibid.*
62 Tunku Abdul Rahman (in Madrid) to H. Macmillan, 28 May 1957, thanking him for lunch at 10 Downing Street on 23 May, PRO PREM 11/1929.
63 See Zakaria Haji Ahmad, 'The police and political development in Malaysia', in Ahmad (ed.), *Government and Politics*, pp. 111–27.
64 'Underscoring their determination to be firm but fair, the police with its newfound popularity among Chinese was placed in control of Chinese neighborhoods, while the army was concentrated in Malay areas.' Karl von Vorys, *Democracy Without Consensus: communalism and political stability in Malaysia* (Princeton, 1975), p. 348. At note 10 on the same page von Vorys also claims: 'The police was an integrated body. On May 13th only 39% of the entire force and 214 out of 723 Assistant Superintendents of police were Malay.' Contrast this with Zakaria Haji Ahmad's more recent assessment ('Police and political development', p. 120) that the Force is 'overwhelmingly Malay in the rank-and-file, but more ethnically mixed in the officer corps'.
65 For a report on the Malaysian Government's White Paper, *Towards Preserving National Security*, which gave the official explanation for the arrests and was presented to parliament on 23 March 1988, see *Far Eastern Economic Review*, 7 April 1988, pp. 36–7.

CHAPTER SEVEN

Crime, politics and the police in colonial Kenya, 1939 – 63

David Throup

The politics of African nationalism in Kenya is a topic that has not lacked for scholarly attention. Alongside the many contemporary, or near contemporary studies, of the Mau Mau rebellion and the political process of the transfer of powers which followed its suppression, a spate of recent literature has excavated new sources, re-examined old arguments and presented new interpretations of the causes and consequences of the events of the 1940s and 1950s.[1] Historians still remain as far from a consensus on their understanding of Mau Mau as ever, yet it is apparent that attention is now focused upon broader questions of civil order during the 1950s rather than the more specific politics of nationalism: we have become more interested in the manner in which the colonial state in Kenya was able to continue to function through the Emergency, and the extent to which Africans supported or opposed notions of civil order and the rule of law in this period.[2] Taking up these questions, this chapter is concerned with the role of the colonial police in the post-war period, from the beginnings of the political disturbances that heralded the Mau Mau movement in the late 1940s, through the Emergency itself, to the political settlement that led to Kenya's independence in 1963.

The approach will be essentially chronological, starting with a review of the expansion and reform of the Kenya Police up to 1951. In the midst of a programme of modernisation after 1945, and with their responsibilities being ever widened as the colonial state sought to impose its authority in new areas and in new ways, the Kenya Police found themselves confronted firstly by a dramatic increase in urban crime and then by the rapid escalation of political difficulties; the growing militancy of African trade unions and also the activities of newly-formed political parties drew the police into arenas where they lacked experience and training. With only a weak hold on many rural areas, and compelled to leave parts of urban Nairobi unpoliced, the Kenya Police made a hesitant transition from criminal investigation to effective political policing.

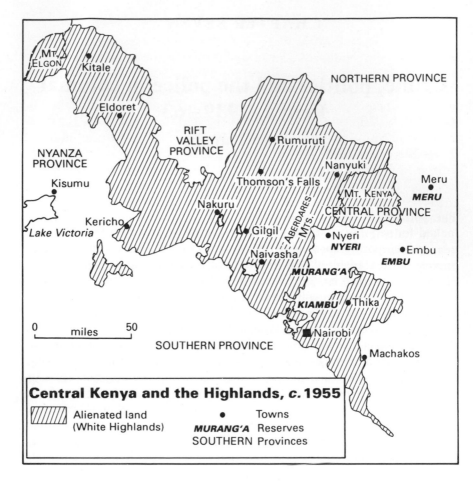

Central Kenya and the Highlands, *c.* 1955

The Emergency altered the priorities of the colonial state, and as the second section moves on to discuss, this had a profound effect upon the police. Special Branch were crucial in the policing of Mau Mau, and the experience of police intelligence-gathering in one particular area, Embu, will be analysed in detail. The final section examines the role of the Kenya Police in the transfer of powers between 1959 and 1963, and considers the extent to which policing policy became embroiled in the politics of the last days of colonial rule.

From criminal investigation to political policing

During the Second World War the Kenya Police were presented with two major new challenges. The first of these was the expansion of police jurisdiction into the African Reserves of the Colony, areas that until 1943 had been under the sole authority of the district administration and their ill-equipped and poorly trained Tribal Police. As an experiment, the force was firstly introduced into the African Reserves of Kiambu, Nandi and Narok towards the end of 1943, and in 1944 to Kericho and Kisii. It was not until 1949 that new police stations were established in the Mukogodo, Elgeyo, Teita, and Maasai areas or that the police operated in all parts of the populous Abaluhya Reserve. Even then large areas of the Coastal and Rift Valley Provinces remained without police detachments.[3]

The halting and partial nature of this expansion reflected the complex organisational changes required for such a significant extension of policing authority. One of the most important elements of this was the increasing number of Africans recruited and promoted to positions of command: by 1949 there were 58 African non-gazetted officers and 496 African sergeants (compared to 59 in 1938). African rank-and-file similarly expanded from 1,821 members to 4,212, making a total African enlistment of 4,766 by 1949. The ethnic composition of the force, however, changed little with this expansion. Indeed, the pattern of pre-war recruitment continued to be visible in the predominance of Kamba recruits making up nearly one-quarter of the establishment and numbering 1,144 junior officers, sergeants and constables. Luo (607), Kipsigis (436) and Nandi (329) provided the next largest numbers of recruits. By contrast, Kikuyu, with only 112 members, still formed less than 2·5 per cent of the police force in 1949.[4]

Along with expansion in numbers came new structures of command and dispersement. A new provincial police organisation, introduced in 1942, was designed to improve supervision of the expanding force with a Superintendent in command of each province. More junior Assistant Superintendents were in charge in each district. The introduction of provincial commands was intended to improve liaison with Provincial Commissioners and facilitated closer co-operation between police units in different districts. In practice the Kenya Police were not always welcomed by the political branch of the colonial administration, many of whose officers valued their 'intimate' local knowledge of the populations with whom they worked. The police may have aspired to a similar intimacy, but they could rarely achieve it. The introduction of the Kenya Police into the Reserves excited considerable resentment, particularly in Central Province. In Machakos, Kitui and Nyanza, where it might have been expected that Kamba and Luo constables would be posted to their home districts, more than half the detachments came from other ethnic groups. As a result, the rural population saw the force as an alien unit and placed even less confidence in it than they had in the Tribal Police which, although widely viewed as lackies of the administration and the chiefs, comprised local men who had to live in the community. The problem was particularly acute in Kiambu, Murang'a and Nyeri – the three Kikuyu Reserves – where the sophisticated local population resented the intrusion of illiterate Kamba, Luo and Kalenjin constables.[5]

If the Kenya Police initially found difficulty in adapting to their increased responsibilities in the countryside, they were equally uncomfortable in the towns during the 1940s. Here, in the shape of a rapidly rising rate of urban crime, lay the second major challenge confronting the Kenya Police. Urban crime escalated dramatically during the war and this, combined with a fall in the rate of convictions for housebreaking and burglary, caused great alarm in Nairobi. The city's 'crime scare' provoked several debates in the Legislative Council and demands for resolute action. European spokesmen suggested that there was 'a growing class of habitual criminals' in the larger towns. Certainly, the number of incidents reported nearly trebled to 11,220 between 1938 and 1945, while the overall conviction rate fell by half. These widely reported figures did much to fuel European perceptions of a rising 'crime wave', despite the expansion of the police force over the 1940s.[6] Of course, Kenya was not the first territory to find that an expanding police force tends to reveal more crime; yet the social and economic transformations promoted by the demands of the war, especially in Nairobi, did contribute to a real increase in crime. Offences against property in Nairobi increased from 1,201 in 1940 to 4,993 by 1949, and in the White Highlands from 3,017 to 7,274, while offences against the person trebled in Nairobi and doubled in Mombasa and the settled areas over the same period. Burglaries and property thefts were concentrated in the colony's two major towns – Nairobi and Mombasa – which reported more than half the total number of crimes. These two cities offered the highest wages to workers, but also contained high numbers of unemployed: during the 1940s Nairobi's population grew by 17 per cent per annum, more than doubling between 1940 and 1947. By contrast, the provision of municipal housing remained virtually static, while rent costs spiralled upwards. Over the 1940s the extent of Nairobi's social problems was transformed dramatically and this made a very direct impact upon policing.[7]

Despite the emphasis given in public debate to serious crime and the emergence of organised criminal gangs, it was the prosecution of minor offenders against local ordinances in the urban areas and European Settled Areas that dominated police time: 29,362 convictions, for example, were secured in 1944, and 28,729 the following year. These local ordinances restricted Africans from remaining in urban areas for more than seventy-two hours without a permit; forbade the purchase and consumption of hard liquors; deported 'vagrants' back to their home districts; required African share-croppers (or squatters) on European farms to work 270 days per year and regulated their cultivation rights and the number of livestock that they could keep; and many other things besides.[8] While European residents worried about the threat of burglary, they saw the mass of Nairobi's Africans, many apparently unemployed and illegally resident in the city, as the source of crime and as evidence of a growing 'disorder'. Thus, over the 1940s the police became ever deeply enmeshed in enforcing the most unpopular decisions of settler local government authorities, both throughout the White Highlands and in Nairobi, devised to regulate the activities of Africans. Poorer Africans, especially Kikuyu, who flocked to the burgeoning shanty-towns around the capital as they were dispossessed by European and African commercial farmers, were common offenders against local ordinances. With so many Nairobi Africans barely surviving on irregular forms of casual employment, or earning their living as illegal brewers, unlicensed hawkers, prostitutes or petty criminals, the police were identified by the European community as the agency responsible for 'cleaning up' the city; in contrast, the African residents of Nairobi more commonly viewed the police as agents of colonial oppression. When the Municipal Council, supported by European residents, introduced increasingly stringent regulations controlling African access to Nairobi in the immediate post-war years, relations between the police and Africans deteriorated even further The Vagrancy (Amendment) Bill of May 1949 empowered the police to repatriate anyone who had failed to secure permanent employment after three months' residence in Nairobi, and the Voluntarily Unemployed Persons (Provision of Employment) Ordinance, which was approved in January 1950, enabled the police to arrest and deport to the Reserves anyone suspected of being unemployed or a vagrant.[9]

Legislation was intended to empower the police, but the extent to which they were able to 'order' the daily life of Nairobi in the 1940s was severely circumscribed. In order to control the capital more effectively, the city's police structure was reformed in September 1947. Until then, the municipal area had been an extra-provincial enclave, separate from the neighbouring parts of southern Kiambu and western Machakos, which were densely populated rural areas from where many people went to work in Nairobi or supplied food and charcoal to the city's residents. Faced by the growth of crime, a new Nairobi Police District was created, incorporating the neighbouring parts of Kiambu, Machakos, Thika and Maasailand, improving police co-ordination against criminal gangs which it was believed operated from outside the municipal border.[10] But only with this reorganisation was the first police station built in Nairobi's African locations, when the new station at Shauri Moyo was placed under the control of one of the new African Inspectors, James Juma. Juma and his force of five constables could do little to combat crime in the area or, indeed, to hinder the activities of Kikuyu gangs which controlled prostitution, organised protection rackets and intimidated the location's non-Kikuyu residents. African Nairobi, especially in the hours of darkness, was generally abandoned by the police, who devoted their energies to protecting the European residential areas and the central business district, only a few blocks from River Road, which marked the border between European and African areas. In the context of mass unemployment and widespread poverty, crime was an understandable response on the part of many desperate members of the African community. Many small entrepreneurs, attempting to avoid municipal regulations or licence fees, were viewed as criminals. Respectable members of the African community in Nairobi complained about police harassment over labour passes and residence permits. Many such 'respectable' African citizens sympathised with the dispossessed vagrants who were attempting to find accommodation and jobs.[11]

The problems of urban Nairobi during the 1940s were recognised as a matter for serious concern by the colonial government, but the police were more willing than the administration to admit that African criminality stemmed from economic grievances. Reviewing the rising crime rate of Nairobi in his Annual Report for 1951, Commissioner of Police O'Rorke warned that:

> The cost of essentials has increased greatly throughout the year; it is doubtful whether wages have kept pace with this increase. The drift of Africans from their reserves to towns increases from year to year in far greater numbers than employment offers; parental and tribal control deteriorates yearly, and virtually does not exist outside native areas, and honesty and industry are all too soon pushed overboard by the temptations and expenses of town life. These are the factors which send urban crime soaring.[12]

The Colony's progress, argued O'Rorke, brought 'greater opportunities, incentive and means for the commission of crime'. Cheap transport facilities had extended criminals' opportunities. More and more of them were educated and had worked in the urban business sector, while the low level of African wages, even among skilled workers, and the contrast with the Europeans' high post-war standard of living, encouraged crime. Part of the problem lay in the fact that Nairobi's industrial area had by 1950 expanded beyond the borders of the municipality and the operational zone under the control of the capital's police. Warehouses, factories and shops offered more lucrative and easier targets than private homes, and were in locations that were rarely patrolled.[13] By 1950 Nairobi recorded about 40 per cent of Kenya's crime, although it had only 5 per cent of the population. The per capita incidence of crimes was even higher in Mombasa, where there were 53 crimes per 1,000 people in 1952. Even making allowance for the criminal propensity of large urban areas, the police command considered that the capital produced 'fully twice as much crime as it should'. 'There can be no doubt,' O'Rorke observed,

> ... that the proximity of the Kikuyu Reserves to the City is the cause of far too much crime – and crime of a serious nature ... Overcrowding on the land, and considerable unemployment in a City where incentives and opportunity to crime are far too great, all combine to make the Nairobi area – so far as crime is concerned – a festering sore which grows no better.[14]

O'Rorke was concerned that budgetary restraints had prevented more rapid modernisation and delayed essential reforms, yet even he acknowledged that 'improved policing alone will not provide the final solution to a crime problem, which so largely stems from economic circumstances, dissatisfaction, ignorance and idleness'. Although he identified the economic roots of much of Nairobi's crime, the Police Commissioner, like the administration and City Council, underestimated the depth of Kikuyu grievances.[15]

Throughout the 1940s the expansion of police responsibilities and the efforts of the police to contain a rising rate of urban crime were hampered by problems of recruitment. It was difficult to attract suitable recruits for ordinary police work, especially in Nairobi. And when good recruits were secured, it was difficult to keep them: salaries were low, the cost of living (especially for those in Nairobi) was high, housing was poor, there was widespread public distrust and suspicion of the police, and good job opportunities for former policemen as nightwatchmen, bank messengers or drivers combined to generate a high turnover of manpower in the force. Recruitment of educated African school-leavers was an especially difficult area. Although 1,158 new recruits joined the force in 1949, receiving training at the newly-opened police college in Nyeri, their general calibre was failing to keep pace with the increasing sophistication of the more developed African areas. Of the new constables, 54 per cent were literate in Swahili, but only 7 per cent could speak English. The force had historically drawn most of its recruits from the less developed parts of the country, and most of its Kamba, Kipsigis and Nandi recruits were illiterate, while those who could read and write tended to come from the Luo, Abaluhya and Kikuyu areas.[16] Educated young Africans, like Asians, were reluctant to start at the bottom and to undergo the same basic training as less sophisticated recruits. Those who did join did not want to remain patrolling the beat, but preferred to become charge officers or clerks. Many European officers, moreover, suspected the loyalty of educated Africans, who were less deferential and more politically aware. Such attitudes were prominent in the force: the 1949 Police Annual Report defended the status quo, pointing out that 'the worth of the illiterate policeman should not be under-estimated as it is within this element that there is found the greater reliability and manliness and sense of responsibility and discipline'.[17]

Police training did not emphasise intellectual ability. For the first three months all recruits received intensive drill and physical training. Only then did they begin to receive lectures on first aid and police duties. Later in their careers, more experienced constables might receive specialised training in wireless telegraphy and car driving, or instruction as sergeants or African Assistant Inspectors. Even the most experienced African officers with the rank of Senior Inspector, however, received only three-quarters of the salary of European Assistant Inspectors, unable to speak any of the vernacular languages. African salaries ranged from £100 for Assistant Inspectors to a maximum of £330 for Senior Inspectors with a minimum of five years' experience, whereas European Assistant Inspectors started at a minimum of £400, rising to £840. African police salaries compared unfavourably with those of Nairobi clerks. Yet, despite these inequalities, the number of African Inspectors grew from only six in 1940 to 65 by 1946, and to 115 three years later, although most of these were promoted from within the force and the proportion of English-literate recruits remained low. Very few had passed the Secondary School Certificate. From December 1950, the least well qualified recruits received a two months' pre-training course during which they learnt rudimentary Swahili and elementary school subjects. The number of educated recruits was so small that a few experienced, but barely literate, senior Sergeants with many years' experience had to be promoted to the Inspectorate 'to stiffen the rank with men of proved personality and power of command'.[18]

The shortcomings of the Kenya Police were vividly exposed in the report compiled early in 1950 by W. C. Johnson, the Inspector General of Colonial Police. For a population of approximately 5·3 million, Kenya had 5,935 police, 1,214 of whom were permanently stationed at Headquarters or serving as a special Railways and Harbours' detachment, while another 1,138 men were deployed in the Northern Frontier area in a paramilitary role. Johnson noted with dismay that this left only 3,583 police for the remaining territory, including Nairobi and Mombasa.[19] He was equally critical of the fact that virtually no administrative assistance was given to Officers-in-Charge of Provinces, so that 90 per cent of their time was absorbed by routine administration with the result that they were out of touch with the executive work of their subordinates.[20]

Inspector General Johnson also thought that Kenya had too many European Inspectors, many of whom were undertaking duties which were appropriate for sergeants and corporals. By contrast, more Asian officers were urgently required. Literacy, he believed, should not be the main criterion for selecting African NCOs, nor even for African Inspectors. Johnson, too, put less emphasis upon intellectual calibre: there was 'a definite field in the more remote police posts, for the type of practical man who, although not educationally qualified, is respected by the rank and file as a leader with a fund of local knowledge and native ability'. But he also argued that the training system needed to be reformed: 'The basic syllabus,' he reported, 'is not designed on a modern conception of policing a colonial territory. The emphasis is heavily weighted upon the para-military subjects of drill, musketry, etc.' He found it particularly strange that 'the non-literate receives only a fourth of the instruction given in practical police work that is given to the literate'. Training for the European Inspectorate, amounting to only thirteen weeks, was also viewed as deficient. Johnson recommended they should receive a course on basic police duties before leaving Britain and be seconded to selected British Forces for five months before departing for Kenya.[21]

The most significant of Johnson's recommendations concerned the formation and training of a Criminal Investigation Department (CID). Until 1950 crime work was undertaken by investigation teams at station and divisional levels, which required a disproportionate number of officers, many of whom had no special training for the task. As a beginning, Johnson suggested that a competent Headquarter's officer should supervise the CID and develop an experienced group to deal with such crimes in Nairobi. Five or six men should be sent on detective training courses at Hendon, run by the Metropolitan Police. Another important specialist unit, Special Branch, was praised for the work it achieved despite the handicap of no proper provincial network for intelligence-gathering.[22]

Johnson's report heralded a period of reform for the Kenya Police, directed with enthusiasm by Police Commissioner O'Rorke. Between 1950 and 1952 O'Rorke devoted particular attention to improving the quality of the CID and other technical departments. During 1951, five conferences of senior provincial officers and other independent units, such as the CID and Criminal Records Office, were held. Recruitment of Asian officers was increased, and more Africans were promoted to higher rank. Attempts were made to improve the education of African recruits. English classes were introduced at the larger police stations, a force text book was devised by staff at Nyeri, and fifty NCOs and constables were trained at the Jeanes School in Kabete to act as instructors. As part of his reforms, O'Rorke modelled the Nyeri training centre's curriculum upon methods used in Britain. Recruits were subjected to a regimen of discussion groups, debates, brief talks, staged demonstrations and film shows, were taken to inspect the scenes of crimes, given 'practicals' on how to cope in major incidents, and taken on visits and briefly attached to District forces.[23]

European officers also felt the burden of new standards. Senior officers were dispatched to attend courses at the police training colleges at Ryton-on-Dunsmore and Hendon; others were seconded to the Metropolitan Police or large county forces where they were exposed to the latest policing techniques. During 1950, for example, seven officers were sent to special CID courses in Britain, and on their return became instructors at the fledgling CID in Nairobi. The Officer-in-Charge of CID was promoted to Assistant Commissioner, and seven more men were dispatched to Britain for further training in December 1950. In April 1951, Commissioner O'Rorke attended the first gathering of Colonial Commissioners of Police at Ryton-on-Dunsmore, while closer collaboration was established with neighbouring Uganda and Tanganyika and other colonies in the region, with the introduction of annual gatherings of police chiefs from East and Central Africa.[24]

From the later part of 1950 until the declaration of the State of Emergency in November 1952, the Kenya Police was thus engaged in a major period of transition. The thrust of these changes was intended to bring to colonial policing in Kenya the standards of county and metropolitan policing in Britain and to improve the abilities of the police in dealing with crime. Yet as these ideas were in the process of being implemented the politics of colonial Kenya were already turning in a direction that placed new demands upon the police, drawing them into political policing. Still coming to terms with their task of criminal investigation on the 'British model' of policing, the Kenya Police did not find it easy to accommodate the demands of political policing.

Although the police were aware of the existence of the Mau Mau movement by 1950, senior officers of Police Headquarters throughout 1951 and for most of 1952 were more concerned by the difficulties of traffic control in Nairobi than they were by the potential political troubles held in store by Mau Mau. Yet there was already evidence by 1950 that new and increasingly prevalent forms of criminal activity in Nairobi were sometimes linked to political activity. Under cover of Kikuyu gangs such as Maina Heron's, which operated from Ziwani controlling prostitution in Ngara, political activists assaulted their opponents, gathered money, and collected weapons as the political situation deteriorated during 1950 and 1951. Gangs like these were preparing for Mau Mau assaults on British rule and African collaborators.[25]

While the police caught only glimpses of this shady world where criminality and African politics merged, the challenges presented by the militant politics of emergent trades unions were more visible. The first serious labour disputes had emerged in Mombasa during the 1940s,[26] but it was the Nairobi General Strike of May 1950 that presented the real test of police authority against the political power of the union movement. Eight months earlier, in October 1949, the introduction by Nairobi City Council of new regulations to control African taxi drivers led to a sixteen-day strike and gave police a taste of what was to come. Tension in the city remained high in the following months as the city authorities attempted to reassert control over the workforce. Taxi drivers, thrown out of business by the new regulations, looked to the Transport and Allied Workers' Union for leadership and played a prominent role in the May 1950 General Strike, clashing with police and strike-breakers. The General Strike became the vehicle for the expression of discontent amongst a wide range of Nairobi's African population: bands of thirty or more unemployed Kikuyu roamed the streets, armed with pangas and knives. Only large bodies of police, operating in military-style formations, were able to assert control and to prevent violence spreading to European areas of the city.[27] For the first time police riot training, introduced after the January 1947 strike in Mombasa, was tested. Armoured vehicles, equipped with tear gas, patrolled the African locations, breaking up crowds of demonstrators and arresting strike leaders. During the months before the strike, the special Emergency Company had been doubled in size to 157 constables, and trained to fire tear gas canisters from armoured Bren vehicles.[28] This was not the sort of operation that Johnson or O'Rorke had in mind when seeking to reform the Kenya Police and improve its capacity as a criminal investigation unit, yet by the end of 1952 the political situation in the Colony had propelled the police back into the paramilitary role that had characterised an earlier phase of colonial policing.

The police, Special Branch and Mau Mau

As the political situation deteriorated in the early 1950s, Special Branch played an increasing role in gathering the intelligence that gave the colonial administration their 'insights' on anti-government groups, and especially the Mau Mau movement. But the reforms implemented by O'Rorke from 1950, combined with a series of promotions for middle-ranking officers to other colonies, undermined the effectiveness of the Special Branch. During the first months of 1947, paid informers had

[137]

infiltrated both the Mombasa and Nairobi branches of the African Workers' Federation, which had taken control of the Mombasa General Strike. John Mungai, one of the leaders of the Nairobi taxi drivers and a close associate of radical African politicians, who became General Secretary of the Transport and Allied Workers' Union and a key figure after 1951 in the militants' take-over of the Nairobi branch of the Kenya African Union, had long acted as a police informant, supplying Special Branch Inspector Ian Henderson with reports on KAU and trade union affairs. Although such reports continued to flow into Special Branch, O'Rorke and his senior colleagues gave them little credence and made little attempt to draw the information to the attention of the Secretariat or John Whyatt, the Attorney General and Member of the Executive Council with responsibility for Law and Order.[29] O'Rorke and his senior officers were more concerned to tackle the crime wave than to suppress trade union and political radicals. Whyatt, for his part, as a lawyer, was reluctant to adopt any measures which encroached upon civil rights, despite mounting pressure from District Commissioners in Kikuyuland and from settler leaders. Percy Wyn Harris (Chief Native Commissioner from 1947 to 1949) and his successors protested several times that the Attorney General's chambers was undermining the influence of 'loyal' chiefs by prosecuting them when they infringed the law in their clashes with local political activists. In short, the Police Commissioner and other senior officers in the Legal Department were not prepared to press for the drastic measures that Special Branch political reports suggested might be warranted.[30]

The lack of influence of Special Branch can perhaps also be attributed to changes in the senior command of the intelligence network. In 1950 Cecil Penfold, who had joined the Kenya Police as a constable in 1930 and had served from 1946 as Director of Intelligence and Security with the rank of Superintendent of Police, was promoted to Assistant Commissioner. His replacement, brought in from the Gold Coast, lacked Penfold's deep knowledge of the intricacies of Kenya, and especially of Kikuyu politics, and was unable either adequately to analyse the material gathered by the network of informers established by Penfold or to present those findings with sufficient vigour to his superiors.[31]

O'Rorke was eager to improve the morale and quality of his force, but he had little interest in Special Branch activities or political policing beyond the preservation of civil order. When protests got out of hand, as in the May 1950 General Strike in Nairobi, or the clash at Kolloa with Pokot religious mystics of the *Dini ya Msambwa* in April 1950, or during the anti-inoculation riots in Murang'a at the end of 1951, police reinforcements were at hand to reassert order. In Murang'a more than 400 women, led by the veteran Kikuyu Central Association activist, James

Beauttah, were convicted of illegal assembly and imprisoned or fined, and a police levy force was stationed in the district. Senior officers underestimated the significance of the intelligence, particularly from Naivasha and Nyeri, about the Mau Mau movement. Until mid-1952, they did not appreciate how widespread oathing had become in the Kikuyu Reserves or how far preparations for armed revolt had gone in Nairobi. Senior policemen, like constables on the beat, were better prepared to deal with normal crime than to infiltrate African political organisations and trades unions.[32]

[Complacency was evident in the Police Annual Report for 1951, in which O'Rorke merely observed that: 'prosecutions against members of the proscribed Mau Mau organization for administering oaths continued and, while there was no marked increase in its activities, it cannot be said that counter-propaganda materially led to their decrease. No subversive action, apart from the actual administration of the oath, could be attributed to its members during the year.'[33] Such a bold assertion seriously misrepresented the reality, but although a few individual policemen – serving in areas such as Nanyuki and Naivasha, where there had been a growing number of arson incidents and attempts to maim cattle on European farms – had become concerned about the movement's growing support, officers in most districts and at Police Headquarters were relatively unperturbed.[Few members of the police understood the extent or sophistication of Mau Mau's chain of command or its radical nationalist ideology, seeing it as merely a squatter protest movement fighting the new regulations imposed by the settler controlled District Councils, as a dissident sect in the Reserves, or as yet another Kikuyu criminal gang in Nairobi. Many believed Mau Mau to be merely another Kikuyu quasi-religious movement, determined to repudiate all European ways.]Even when the bodies of farm night-watchmen were discovered floating in Lake Naivasha in 1951, and the huts of twenty-one agricultural instructors, chiefs' messengers and police informants were burnt in Nyeri within a few days in January 1952, and the bodies of two Africans, slashed by *pangas*, were discovered in a river near Dagoretti on the outskirts of Nairobi, the police had little appreciation of the dimensions of the problem. It was only in May 1952 that a special section of Special Branch was established to concentrate exclusively on Mau Mau, following the murder in Nairobi of an important witness in a case against Mau Mau oath administrators.[34]

By then it was evident that the situation, particularly in Nairobi, was out of control. The new anti-Mau Mau Special Branch detachment reported in June and July that large-scale oath ceremonies had taken place, attended by crowds of up to several thousand people in parts of Murang'a and Nyeri. Accounts of Mau Mau beatings – the forceful administration of oaths and assaults on those who refused to support the movement – were now commonly heard. In July 1952, an African constable who stumbled upon an oathing ceremony in Nairobi was murdered. Even before the formal declaration of the Emergency, there were widespread attacks on European stock and burning of crops on farms in Nanyuki, Laikipia, Naivasha and Nakuru Districts where most of the farm labourers were Kikuyu squatters. In August, the focus of Mau Mau activities switched to European farms in the Thomson's Falls area. In September, the incidence of arson attacks on farms and huts in Nyeri further increased, and on 25 September, four Mau Mau gangs disembowelled 146 European-owned cattle and 380 sheep on farms in Timau.[35] In October, four Africans and a European woman were murdered, and an Asian and another four Europeans seriously injured, despite the government's introduction in late September (under pressure from settler leaders) of draconian measures restricting freedom of assembly and movement by Africans. The assassination of one of the government's main Kikuyu supporters, Senior Chief Waruhiu wa Kungu of Kiambu, on his way home from a meeting at Government House, was the outrage that finally brought the Declaration of Emergency.[36]

The Declaration of Emergency on 20 October 1952 propelled the police force to the centre of the political stage. Despite O'Rorke's reforms the force had remained a small, under-financed arm of the colonial state, the extension of its authority beyond the European settled area in the White Highlands and the cities of Nairobi and Mombasa still only partially complete. Even by 1952 the police presence in many parts of the Kikuyu Reserves was minimal. The situation was worst in Nairobi where the incidence of both offences against the person and against property during the first ten months of 1952 had doubled. More intensive policing following the Declaration of Emergency saw a fall in criminal activity during the last two months of the year, but by the end of 1952 the police had discovered the bodies of 121 'loyal' Africans, including chiefs, agricultural instructors, policemen, and those who had given evidence against suspected Mau Mau members. The violence reached new heights on Christmas Eve, with a series of concerted attacks in Murang'a in which ten prominent African Christians, an Asian trader and two Europeans were murdered.[37]

With the onset of the Emergency, which was in theory a police rather than a military action, the size and operations of the force underwent a far more dramatic transformation than O'Rorke's earlier reforms had ever intended or desired. The Kenya Police, and especially a newly restructured Special Branch, now had to provide the 'framework on which the action of Military Forces can be superimposed'.[38] In order to perform this central role, three decisions were quickly taken. First, it was essential to introduce closer policing in the areas affected by Mau Mau. Whereas in October 1952 there had been only four police stations in the three Kikuyu Reserves, by the end of the year these had been upgraded and twenty-seven new stations built. By December 1953 every Kikuyu location had one, and many had two, police stations. Secondly, special police posts were established in the European settled area and in the suburbs of Nairobi to protect the settler population.[39] Finally, special police units were formed to maintain order in those areas from which the Army had withdrawn to pressure the Mau Mau forest gangs. This programme required a substantial increase in the size of the police force. The manpower crisis was an immediate and serious problem: during the first months of the Emergency there were not enough regular police officers to take control of the expanded network of stations in the Kikuyu Reserves and many had to be staffed by members of the Kenya Regiment (a volunteer force consisting mainly of European settlers).[40]

By December 1952, 14 of the 39 Police Divisions and 65 of the 148 Police Stations were in African areas; the expansion of police authority that the force had been struggling to implement over the previous nine years had been largely achieved in a period of nine weeks.[41] By the end of 1953 the number of regular and auxiliary police on full-time duties had grown from 7,000 to 15,000, while 6,000 more – mainly European settlers – were recruited into the Kenya Police Reserve. While the British organised a campaign to win the support of Kikuyu 'loyalists', and to arm such groups for 'self-defence', it was considered too risky to attempt to recruit Kikuyu into the police: by the end of 1953 the number of Kikuyu policemen was still only 178. During 1953 nearly 2,000 Africans were recruited to serve as Special Police in the operational areas under the

Table 7.1: Expansion of the Kenya Police, 1 October 1952 to 1 December 1953

	1 Oct. 1952			1 Dec. 1953		
	Euro.	Asian	Afrn	Euro.	Asian	Afrn
Kenya Police	384	111	6,640	1,131	185	9,850
Police Reserve	2,054	493	435	4,822	1,090	2,635
(of which full-time)	–	–	–	(601)	(180)	(1,295)
African Specials*	–	–	–	–	–	2,009
Tribal Police	–	–	1,169	–	–	2,195

* African Special Police were an untrained auxiliary force. They were predominantly used for guard duties and were commanded by members of the Kenya Police Reserve.

Sources: *Kenya Police Annual Reports*, 1952, 1953.

[141]

command of European officers. These Kikuyu 'loyalists', mainly recruited from the more prosperous smallholders and traders with close ties to the senior lineages and chiefs, were initially armed only with spears and bows and arrows, but by December nearly 90 per cent had received guns: this had the effect of making them a focus for Mau Mau attacks.[42]

To gain trustworthy men with experience and training, desperate attempts were made to secure officers on short-term contracts from forces in the United Kingdom. The Inspectorate grew by half within two months of the Declaration of Emergency as a result of the recruitment of 31 local officers and 67 men from Britain, while the number of African Inspectors grew from 158 to 267. Between October 1952 and December 1953, the number of European police officers increased from 384 to 1,131, while full-time 'volunteers' in the Kenya Police Reserve more than doubled from 2,054 to 4,822. By April 1954, approximately 600 contracted Assistant Inspectors had been trained. To cope with the new recruits from Britain a second police training school was established at Gilgil, while the Nyeri school was considerably expanded to train African recruits. In addition, police from other parts of the colony were redeployed to the operational areas in Central Province, Nairobi and the eastern Rift Valley.[43] The full dimensions of the expansion can be seen from Table 7.1.

Where the police and the district-level administration had previously operated in parallel, seldom connecting and often with divergent aims and methods, the Emergency forced them to work more closely together. Senior representatives of the police, the army and the administration now met regularly in the District Emergency Committees. Similar co-ordinating groups emerged at Provincial headquarters and in Nairobi. This degree of consultation did not suit all senior police officers, some of whom felt that policing matters were too often subject to the political decisions of the administration. In the Police Commission Report of 1953 Colonel Young, Commissioner of the City of London Police, argued that the police should be given greater independence of action and that their command be separated entirely from the district administration. After talks with General Templer, the Chief of the Imperial General Staff, Governor Sir Evelyn Baring directed that no operations should be undertaken which had not been agreed by the appropriate civil-military-police committees to which experts and officers from the technical departments were seconded.[44] In response, Young tendered his resignation. Young's attitude was partly ideological – he wished to see the Kenya Police established on the same basis as any English force – but it was also partly a matter of operational demands, in that keeping police-men always under the command of their own officers was a surer means of maintaining discipline and practice.[45]

From the very beginning the police were deeply involved in anti-Mau Mau actions, serving as the front line of the colonial state in the Kikuyu Reserves. On 23 November 1952, for example, one of the newly-enlisted European corporals and seven African constables were attacked by a crowd of 2,000 protestors at Kiruara in Murang'a District. Shots were fired before the police could escape and call for reinforcements. Following the arrival of three European Inspectors and another twenty-two constables, the crowd again advanced, throwing stones, and two rounds of shots were fired before the line of protestors broke, leaving twenty dead and thirty wounded. Subsequently, 350 people were arrested. In many other locations police units were attacked. During November and December 1952, and throughout the first months of 1953, Mau Mau fighters continued to operate over wide areas in Murang'a and Nyeri, and in western parts of Kiambu near the forest, even burning down the newly-built but still unoccupied police station at Gaturi in Murang'a.[46]

[The expulsion of Kikuyu squatters from the farms by nervous European settlers increased the flow of recruits into the forest during the first months of 1953, and by March 'gangs' of considerable size were operating in both the Aberdares and Mount Kenya forests and in the neighbouring parts of the Kikuyu Reserves. In this phase Mau Mau attacks against the police intensified. One of Mau Mau's greatest successes was the raid in March 1953 against the police station at Naivasha, when weapons and large quantities of ammunition were captured and several Mau Mau prisoners were freed from the goal.] In another attack, against Othaya police station, the forest fighters broke into the compound and ransacked the local administrative headquarters before being driven back. Throughout 1953 and 1954, the police countered these attacks with the close patrolling of all the locations of the Kikuyu Reserves, working with the army and the Kenya Regiment, in an attempt to establish a buffer between the centres of Kikuyu population and the European farming areas of the lower Rift Valley – the Kinangop and Naivasha – and to prevent Mau Mau forces in the Aberdares forest from infiltrating on to European farms or moving into or out of Nairobi.[47]

These operations, and others like them, tended to militarise the police. The former Emergency Company, which had played such a prominent role in the 1950 Nairobi General Strike, was expanded to a detachment of forty-seven Europeans and more than 1,000 African ranks and renamed the General Service Unit (GSU). This highly trained and well-equipped mobile strike force had an essential role to play in the policing of the Emergency.[48] Six companies were formed; two based in Nairobi, and the others in Nyeri, Rift Valley Province, at the Coast and in Nyanza. The companies were divided into platoons under the control of two Inspectors – one European and one African – containing three sections each with one sergeant, two corporals and ten constables. All platoons were fully mobile and self-sustaining in the field, and armed with Bren guns, Sten guns, rifles and revolvers. Members were transferred from general duties and served for two years, before being sent back to normal police work. This, it was hoped, would ensure that the GSU did not become a small elite unit of 'rather tough soldiers dressed up in police uniform'. Considerable care was taken to keep the unit firmly under Police Headquarters' control. It could only be committed to action by the Commissioner himself, following a request by the Superintendent in Charge of a Provincial Force to the operations room at Police Head-quarters. It operated under the command of the Provincial Police Chief but functioned under the command of its own officers. 'The unit and its capabilities and effectiveness,' Catling recalled, 'had political significance for the government too as it reduced to a minimum the need to commit the Army in support of the civil power, with all the difficult and often biased publicity which that entails.'[49]

Although it was impossible to isolate 'ordinary' crime from Mau Mau-related incidents during the Emergency, it was clear that the political situation affected the types of crime and their distribution. Overall, the incidence of crimes fell during 1953, but the number of murders increased from thirty-two to 159. Early in the year Nairobi was averaging one murder a day, and the Commissioner of Police even spoke of 'a reign of terror in the African areas of the city'.[50] Many of these crimes stemmed from attempts by Mau Mau supporters to secure money and supplies for the forest fighters; others arose from attempts to reduce the amount of information on Mau Mau being passed to the authorities by informers. During the early part of 1953, the police and army found that the supply of information about Mau Mau dried up in both Central Province and Nairobi. Following the spate of attacks and murders of informants during the latter part of 1952, most Kikuyu realised that those Africans who supplied information about Mau Mau to the British could not be effectively protected. This caution was intensified by the attacks on Naivasha police station and the murder of Chief Luka and the members of his lineage at Lari in March 1953. Only after the build-up of security forces and the establishment of a new and extensive intelligence organisation in the Reserves did information begin to trickle in once more.[51]

To achieve this the Special Branch was considerably expanded and its operations extended down to divisional level in all districts where Mau Mau forces or supporters were active. Military Intelligence Officers from the army were also appointed in the three Kikuyu Districts, in Embu, Meru and in several parts of the Rift Valley in order to supply operational intelligence in collaboration with the Special Branch, further improving the integration of the army, the police, the administration and the Kikuyu Guard units. The Special Branch had also to develop the capacity to target and penetrate Mau Mau on a vastly extended and more sophisticated scale than its pre-Emergency attempts to plant informers in the trades unions and the Kenya African Union.[52]

A closer look at the growth of Mau Mau in one district, Embu, can give us some idea of the task confronting Special Branch. Mau Mau activists began to organise oath-taking in this district on the south-eastern foothills of Mount Kenya rather later than in Kiambu, Murang'a, Nyeri and Nairobi. Most early Mau Mau activists were migrant labourers in Nairobi, where many Embu people were employed by the Municipal Council as street-cleaners or as blacksmiths. Once Mau Mau leaders had established a network of activists and administrators, considerable attempts were made to recruit support from workers from Embu, where there was a large Kikuyu population, and from neighbouring Meru and Machakos. Throughout August and September 1952 many people from Embu quietly returned home and began to spread the Mau Mau oath, operating in the mainly Kikuyu-populated areas around Embu township and throughout the locations of Ndia and Gichugu. These activities continued throughout October and November 1952, swamping the attempts of the small force of forty Tribal Police to maintain order. In September, when the deteriorating situation had become clear, a local branch of the Kenya Police Reserve was recruited from the European and Asian residents, and in mid-October – a few days before the Declaration of Emergency – twenty Kenya Police, most of them raw recruits under a European Assistant Inspector, were stationed in Ndia where they were soon joined by two platoons of the King's African Rifles. A third platoon was stationed at nearby Gichugu. The first months of 1953 saw a marked increase in Mau Mau oathing and widespread support for the movement throughout Ndia. Large daylight ceremonies were organised and the administration believed that the vast majority of local people had taken at least the Mau Mau oath of unity. During February 1953, Mau Mau organisers moved into Gichugu, rapidly securing recruits and strengthening the movement's influence in southern Ngandori and in Embu town. Soon afterwards, considerable numbers of young men departed to join gangs operating in the Mount Kenya forest and the Mau Mau forces established a strong presence in many parts of the district, remaining in close contact with Nairobi. Between April and August 1953, an estimated 300 Mau Mau fighters arrived from Nairobi by train, protected by the guards and ticket collectors who belonged to the pro-Mau Mau Transport and Allied Workers' Union.[53]

Intelligence-gathering in Embu was poor. Many chiefs were involved with Mau Mau or feared the consequences of denouncing it, although a few devout African Christians continued to supply valuable anti-Mau Mau information, enabling the security forces to arrest the Kikuyu managers of the Embu Commercial Stores and other local traders, who were clandestinely organising oathing ceremonies under the cover of their business ventures. With no Special Branch officer in the District, the Kenya Police Reserve – largely recruited from members of the administration and Agricultural Department – had established a small intelligence-gathering section. Thus, for the first six months of the Emergency, the security forces largely depended upon reports to the field administration by chiefs, headmen and agricultural instructors, or from loyal African Christians.[54]

Only in March 1953 was a Special Branch officer transferred to Embu, along with three African policemen who had worked with Special Branch in Murang'a – a Kikuyu corporal, who had himself been oathed; a local Embu constable, who proved to be 'an effective interrogator'; and a Kamba constable. The new Special Branch officer worked with a military intelligence staff of six, including the District Military Intelligence Officer (usually a Captain or Major) and five Field Intelligence Officers (who were usually sergeants from the locally-recruited Kenya Regiment). These Field Intelligence Officers were posted to the district's four divisions while one covered Embu township. This unit operated with an annual budget of £1,600, occupying three small, dark offices in Embu township, which soon housed reports on 25,000 suspected Mau Mau adherents. The emphasis was on gathering operational intelligence collected by the police and the administration, assessing it, and passing it on to the army for action as quickly as possible.[55]

Throughout 1953 the restructuring of intelligence-gathering made a significant contribution to the gradually successful campaign to drive the Mau Mau 'gangs' out of the Reserves and into the Aberdares and Mount Kenya forests. The CID and the Criminal Records Office also had a greatly increased workload. Following the Lari massacre, for example, a special CID detachment was dispatched to the area, eventually prosecuting 342 people, including 135 who were convicted of murder. The processing of finger-prints increased to 65,000 during 1953, a 50 per cent increase, and by the end of the year the Office had finger-print slips for 475,884 people – nearly 10 per cent of Kenya's population.[56]

In July 1953 a Commission of Inquiry was appointed to consider the effects of the rapid Emergency expansion of the police, and to make recommendations on the force's organisation and administration, and on recruitment, training and conditions of service. The Commission noted that the reorganisation required by the Emergency had 'created very serious long-term problems for the Police Force', and had 'completely altered the whole pattern of policing in the Colony', transforming the force into a quasi-military organisation and disrupting training and ordinary police operations.[57] The need for sheer numbers had taken precedence over quality. Richard Catling, who arrived in Kenya as Deputy Commissioner direct from the Malayan Emergency, later summed up the immediate priorities of the Emergency: 'The great need was to get these men out on the ground in the required numbers as soon as decently possible. Not surprisingly, the courses were too brief and police stations and posts received only partially trained men and were compelled to supply the balance "on the job".'[58] The Kenya Police in the mid-1950s, he considered, like those in Palestine and Malaya before and Cyprus and Aden subsequently, suffered from becoming too prepared to cope with internal subversion and armed revolt, while normal police work and crime prevention and investigation were neglected.[59]

The Police Commissioner's report highlighted these same points. Inspectors and constables, who had been recruited since October 1952, had neither 'a proper grounding in the elements of their profession' nor 'a proper conception of their duties as guardians of the Queen's peace'. The report acknowledged that 'the overriding need to deploy still more and more police in the troubled areas made it necessary to curtail the training given to such an extent as to deprive it of all semblance of a grounding in normal police duties'. Revised training courses at Nyeri and Gilgil had been reduced to three months, giving new Constables 'only the bare minimum of instruction in police duties proper and went little beyond drill, weapon training, and the instillation of discipline into men who are largely illiterate and who had in many cases little or no experience of life outside their own villages'. These problems, the Commission feared, were bound to have far-reaching effects. The new recruits, for example, had been trained 'to act as squads of men operating in hostile surroundings where their first instinct is to use their rifles. They had to work from police strong-points behind barbed wire and to take part in ambushes and offensive operations against a ruthless enemy.' Consequently, the Commission concluded, many members of the force would have to be retrained.[60] But such refinements would have to await the ending of the Emergency.

The establishment of 'protected villages' in the three Central Province districts during 1954 and 1955, where the rural population could be concentrated and isolated behind barricades with twenty-three-hour curfews, transformed the security situation. Villagisation also improved relations between the police, the administration and the security forces, allowing highly effective joint operations – 'population sweeps' – to be launched in areas where Mau Mau fighters had recently been active.[61] When the police and army interrogated virtually all male Kikuyu living in the capital and detained 20,000 suspects during Operation Anvil in Nairobi during March and April 1954, they fractured the lines of communications between Kikuyu in the city and the Mau Mau forest gangs.[62] For most of 1953, Mau Mau had held the upper hand in the Reserves, being able to operate freely throughout most parts of Nyeri and Murang'a and large parts of Kiambu. But during 1954 the police and military reduced Mau Mau's freedom of operation, gradually driving 'gangs' out of the Reserves. In 1955, villagisation and the effective isolation of fighters in the forests established the clear superiority of the security forces: a series of large-scale military operations during the first three months of 1955 disorganised and scattered the major Mau Mau units, forcing them increasingly on to the defensive. The year was a time of consolidation for the police, bringing to an end the period of rapid expansion of the force. By early 1956 it was estimated that only twenty medium-sized Mau Mau units were still operating into Embu District from the Mount Kenya forest.[63] In theory, at least, the police could now return to more normal duties: in practice, things would never again be as they had been for the Kenya Police.

The difficulties encountered by the police in coping with the Emergency had much to do with the initial failures in intelligence-gathering and analysis. In a series of lectures delivered in 1979, former Police Commissioner Catling reflected that colonial governments – in Palestine and Malaya as well as in Kenya – had been slow to appreciate 'the value of accurate and up-to-date intelligence'. He considered that the Police Forces with their 'close proximity to local populations' were in the best position to provide such information, enabling security measures to be directed at precise targets. Catling, however, believed that the Kenya government had over-reacted in the first stages of the Emergency, detaining large numbers of people who were not clearly implicated in Mau Mau. Instead of using preventive detention to detain only 'the subversive who could not be charged in court for lack of evidence', the Kenyan authorities had devolved responsibility to local District Officers, who frequently detained individuals without reliable information. In Palestine, for example, the number of detainees never rose above 500; when General Templer arrived in Malaya he immediately began to release some of the 1,200 detainees. By contrast, in 1954 when Catling arrived in Kenya, some 78,000 Mau Mau suspects were behind barbed wire. He observed: 'it took a very long time, once the mistake had been recognised and acknowledged, for Special Branch screening teams to sort the wheat from the chaff in the camps and repair some of the damage done to the campaign for Kikuyu hearts and minds by shutting away from society those who were not subversive.'[64]

The police and the transfer of powers

On 15 July 1955, the police and the administration resumed responsibility for law and order in Nairobi and all three Provinces – Southern, Rift Valley and Central – which had been disrupted by Mau Mau operations. Only in Nanyuki District, and in the Aberdares and Mount Kenya forests, did the Army remain in control. More than 1,000 European and 340 Asian members of the Kenya Police Reserve returned to civilian life and the first batch of contract-Inspectors returned to Britain. The CID began to turn its attention to 'regular' crime, and to dealing with a backlog of cases. The end of the Emergency was in sight, although full police control was only established on 18 November 1956, with the cessation of military operations in the Colony. Operation Anvil had, for the present, reduced the incidence of crime in Nairobi, having removed all Africans who could not demonstrate that they had jobs, and many Kikuyu, Embu and Meru who were suspected of supporting Mau Mau. The greatly improved security situation enabled the police to be disarmed, or as Chief Commissioner Catling expressed it, 'the baton replaced the rifle'.[65]

By the end of 1956, the police force was considerably larger than in the pre-Emergency period with 247 gazetted officers, 1,787 inspectors, 1,946 NCOs and 8,876 constables (or in racial terms, 1,341 Europeans, 106 Asians and 11,045 Africans). Expenditure had also risen dramatically, reaching £6,490,500 in the period July 1955 to June 1956, of which £3,137,000 was related to the Emergency.[66] The number of Kikuyu members, however, remained very low, with only 353 members, although the Kamba, who had been implicated to a much lesser extent in Mau Mau, still formed the largest single ethnic source of recruits with 2,285 members. A few Kikuyu were recruited during the year from the Kikuyu Guard and Tribal Police units attached to the administration and the chiefs. With the end of military operations, Catling pressed for more Kikuyu recruits, arguing that 'the tribe could not be effectively policed without the use of at least some of its own people'. He protested that it was illogical for the Kikuyu to be excluded from the police when the Swynnerton agricultural plan was designed to promote economic development in Central Province, consolidating land-holdings and creating a class of Kikuyu yeomen with a vested interest in the survival of the status quo. The Commissioner also suggested that African constables should be permitted to serve in their home districts. Until the late 1950s, no policeman had been permitted to serve in his home locality until he had been in the force for at least six years. The new ruling, which allowed up to 45 per cent of police in any district to be locals, improved relations with local communities, facilitating the recruitment of men from the more developed regions, such as Kikuyuland.[67]

F

No sooner did military operations end than the police, especially in Nairobi, had to begin to cope with renewed African political activity, beginning with the March 1957 campaign for the first elections for African Members of the Legislative Council. As the nationalist movement gathered momentum once more, after five years when all African political gatherings had been banned, the police had to become more politically sensitive. Responsibility for this new task fell on M.K. Akker, who became Senior Assistant Commissioner of Police and Officer-in-Charge of Nairobi in 1957. Catling instructed him to reorganise the whole structure and to separate the Nairobi force from central Police Headquarters. Akker went even further, decentralising police operations and transferring Divisional Commanders within the city to stations in the neighbourhoods they controlled. He also secured the separation of the city from neighbouring southern Kiambu and Thika, redrawing the police command to correspond with Provincial Administration boundaries. The reforms aroused considerable opposition within the force, but enabled Akker to keep a firm grip on political policing in Nairobi.[68]

The new skills of political policing were required to maintain order at the growing number of mass meetings called by Tom Mboya, Nairobi Africans' Legislative Councillor, and other nationalist leaders. Large meetings usually took place on Sundays, held in halls in the Kaloleni and Shauri Moyo locations, on the edge of the industrial area and within easy reach of most of Nairobi's African residents. The meetings were initially closely monitored by the police and attended by two Inspectors, who during the first gatherings actually sat on the platform with the politicians to record the proceedings for Special Branch. Akker, however, lowered the police presence, removing the Inspectors to a Land Rover outside the door. Although only 5,000 people could get into the Makadara Hall, crowds of 30,000 people regularly flocked to these meetings. After a few months the police largely withdrew, concentrating instead upon crowd control and taking precautions to prevent marchers moving towards the city centre.[69]

Serious clashes between nationalists and the police were largely avoided, although matters nearly got out of control following the African Legislative Councillors' return from Lancaster House in 1960, when Mboya attempted to lead a march into the city centre. Political expectations of the London talks fuelled tensions in Nairobi at this time. Only a few weeks earlier, just before Christmas 1959, there had been serious riots in the city, precipitated by a traffic accident when an Asian motorist ran over an African near River Road on the border of the business district and African slums. Police had battled with rioters throwing stones at passing cars throughout the afternoon until 10 o'clock at night. The police were therefore out in force when the African leaders returned from

[150]

London, to be greeted by a crowd of more than 50,000 people who had gathered at the city stadium. The subsequent march to the African locations led close to the city centre. After setting out along the approved route back to the locations, the marchers changed direction and headed for the central business district. Plans had been prepared and, led by Akker and the Commander of the GSU, baton-wielding police squads advanced towards the crowd to stop them entering the Asian part of the city. The crowd was dispersed when the police used tear-gas. By this time the Nairobi force had considerable experience of riot control operations and few people were injured as Akker persuaded Mboya to urge his supporters to turn back.[70]

In the wake of this potentially damaging incident, and with the growing realisation that power would soon be transferred to African nationalist leaders, relations between senior police officers and African politicians improved. Mboya was even invited to speak to the Police Officers' Mess. After his release from confinement in 1962, reasonable working relations were also established with Kenyatta, then President of the Kenya African National Union.[71]

The Commissioner of Police, Richard Catling, who had served in Palestine and Malaya before arriving in Kenya in April 1954, presided over the Kenya Police from December 1954 until January 1965. It fell to Catling to supervise the transition of the force from its struggles against Mau Mau to the preparations for African majority rule and the establishment of an independent African state. He was conscious of the sensitive political, racial and ethnic questions that confronted him, but was confident that earlier reforms in the force had in fact anticipated the need for a change of attitude as well as new patterns of recruitment. Under Catling, training programmes and promotion procedures were reshaped to encourage better African and Asian applicants and to prepare the best officers for the most senior positions in the force. By 1960, these men were already rising through the Inspectorate, occupying responsible positions, but the Colonial Office's 1960 decision to transfer power to an African government within less than four years 'made it impossible to maintain the thoughtful, careful preparation and testing of locals for more senior work'. The discussions at Lancaster House in January 1960 certainly transformed expectations of timing. Soon terms were announced for the retirement of expatriate officers, requiring a rapid acceleration of training programmes for African and Asian officers and an attempt to entice direct entry recruits from Makerere and University College, Nairobi (though few came forward).[72]

On Catling's own admission, the speed of decolonisation meant that the police were 'overtaken by events and had to scramble ... The only regret was that after years of watching it move at snail's pace the run-up

[151]

to Kenya's independence was to be helter-skelter for political reasons which seemed to have little to do with the Territory's ability suddenly to stand on its own feet.'[73] One Asian officer, for example, in the eighteen months before independence, attended three courses, including one in Britain, was promoted three times, and during that period did only six weeks' police work.[74]

By the early 1960s, it was evident that major changes would also have to take place in the ethnic composition of the constabulary, altering 'the tribal composition of the lower ranks of the Force to fit the tribal content of the African population so that in every locality there would be a carefully calculated number – not too many, not too few – of local men who would not only speak the local dialect but act as a link between population and police'.[75] By casting suspicion upon all Kikuyu-speaking peoples in Kenya, the Emergency had retarded a long-overdue ethnic reconstruction and the recruitment of constables, NCOs and officers from the more developed regions. Mervyn Manby, who was a Superintendent in Mombasa during the Emergency, recalled that Police Headquarters in Mombasa had carefully identified 'our precious literates', essential to the 'effective running of the Division', so that they would not be transferred to operational areas.[76]

Senior officers like Manby, the last colonial Director of Intelligence, were convinced that the final stages of the transfer of powers were being rushed, and that carefully-devised plans to train senior African officers had to be reformulated to meet the foreshortened deadline. For Commissioner Catling the critical problem was that they did not have sufficient time to allow newly-promoted African officers to learn the skills of exercising 'command at the higher levels'.[77] As a result, able African officers, 'young intelligent men', were 'pitch-forked into senior positions after only a couple of years in the Police Force'.[78]

Despite the sense that senior officers expressed of the police force being caught up in currents from which it could not escape, they did have some influence over events. Most notably, recommendations from the Special Branch helped to bring about the most important step along the road to independence – Kenyatta's release. By the time of the 1961 elections, the Special Branch, unlike the field administration in Kikuyuland, had become convinced that 'African politics would not, indeed could not, settle down until the unknown factor of his [Kenyatta's] influence had been tested in the world outside detention'. Some officers considered that Kenyatta would prove to have little political influence, and that his continued restriction was exaggerating his authority and disrupting the evolution of Kenyan politics. They suggested that after ten years in detention, Kenyatta might find the political climate uncongenial and rapidly disappear from the scene, replaced by a new generation of more educated African politicians. Even if he thrived, they argued, it was better to deal with a tangible, proven political force, rather than an intangible background presence.[79] Catling, the Commissioner of Police, concurred, emphasising the need for Special Branch reports to analyse Africans' expectations from independence, to be free from the vested interests of the district administration and to provide accurate judgements and forecasts. It ought to act 'as a counter to any wishful thinking or cover-up by administrators concerned to deny the prospect of trouble'.[80] Catling was, indeed, shaping a new police force for a new era.

The imminent transfer of powers affected the Special Branch perhaps even more than other sections of the police force. Operating on the basis that Kenya would become independent early in 1963 – the date was actually to be 12 December 1963 – the Special Branch abandoned the training of European officers in 1960, designing a new course that would prepare African officers for senior positions, although there was then only one African of gazetted rank. Most African members of Special Branch were deemed unsuitable for senior office, being either insufficiently educated to hold senior positions or too young and inexperienced; twelve, nevertheless, were earmarked for rapid promotion. 'Hitherto', Manby reflected with frank if patronising honesty, 'we had taught them what to do; now they were to start to learn not only the reasons but also the reasoning behind our practice.' But the first training scheme failed, and a new system had to be devised which cut the amount of paper-work required of district and provincial level officers. 'We were too sophisticated,' recalled Manby:

> We discussed it anxiously and came to the conclusion that since in the short term – and we only had a short term – we could not raise our senior Africans we would have to change our system of work. So I took my two excellent deputies on a week's tour of our district offices in one province and spent the following weekend making decisions in the seclusion of a country hotel. One deputy still wanted a Rolls Royce of a Special Branch, but the other one and I settled for a Ford. We drastically simplified the paper work at district level, saw it worked well in that province and then introduced it into others, and were prepared to impose the same ideas at provincial level ... Training programmes were revised to suit the new method ...[81]

In particular, during the last months an attempt was made to distance the production of intelligence from the taint of colonialism and racialism, seeking to justify Special Branch work in terms of the security intelligence needs of the Kenyan state, and enlisting 'the specific knowledge and approval of Kenyatta' after he became Prime Minister on 1 June 1963. It was ultimately the growing threat from Somali *shifta* incursions in north-eastern Kenya that persuaded Kenyatte not to disrupt the Special

Branch, despite the new Cabinet's decision in October 1963 that Colonial Service Permanent Secretaries and the Director of Intelligence should be replaced by Africans before independence.[82]

Despite the speeding-up of the hand-over to African rule, by 12 December 1963 the force had trained a substantial number of senior African officers fully capable of supervising the complex range of police duties from crime detection to the maintenance of civil order. With the support of Kenyatta and his conservative Attorney-General, senior colonial policemen such as Catling and Akker (who remained in post for some months after independence) were able to resist the attempts of the Minister for Home Affairs, Vice-President Oginga Odinga, to politicise the police force. In his memoirs, Catling favourably reflected upon the support that Kenyatta had given to the force, preserving its independence through the Police Service Commission and ensuring that senior officers remained of a high standard. Certainly, the police showed little inclination in January 1964 to join the mutinous soldiers, instead being deployed to guard public buildings and emerging from the crisis with an enhanced reputation. Throughout his fifteen years in office, Kenyatta's personal guard was provided by a Kikuyu detachment from the General Service Unit rather than the army. The police force under Catling's command negotiated the immediate transfer of power relatively smoothly, adapting with little outward signs of disruption or strain to the process of Africanisation in the higher ranks.[83]

Individuals such as Ben Gethi, a Kikuyu, who became Commissioner of Police in 1978, and his deputy Michael Arrum, a Luo, were among the first Africans promoted to gazetted rank in the early 1960s. Both successfully navigated the gradual politicisation of the force that took place during Kenyatta's presidency. The police force they served during the 1960s was not so very different from its colonial predecessors: the extension of authority into the remoter rural areas and the anxieties over levels of urban crime remained the dominant concerns of daily policing, while the political intelligence previously demanded by the colonial state continued to be gathered, though now for the service of new masters. The Mau Mau revolt had profoundly affected the development of policing in Kenya, accelerating processes of reform, introducing new methods and bringing about a more pragmatic response to the difficulties of organising and maintaining a reliable police force: independent Kenya's police force was undeniably not the 'Rolls Royce' service that an earlier generation of senior colonial police officers had hoped to create, but it at least had the advantage of dependability.

Notes

The author wishes to acknowledge the invaluable assistance of David Anderson in preparing the final version of this paper for publication.

1 For the best of the contemporary works, see Carl G. Rosberg and John Nottingham, *The Myth of 'Mau Mau': nationalism in Kenya* (New York, 1966), and F. D. Corfield, *Historical Survey of the Origins and Growth of Mau Mau*, Cmd. 1030 (London, 1960) for the official history. Amongst recent scholarship the most important works include Tabitha Kanogo, *Squatters and the Roots of Mau Mau* (London, Nairobi and Athens, Ohio, 1987); David W. Throup, *Economic and Social Origins of Mau Mau 1945–53* (London, Nairobi and Athens, Ohio, 1987) and Frank Furedi, *The Mau Mau War in Perspective* (London, Nairobi and Athens, Ohio, 1989).

2 The crucial work here is that by John Lonsdale, 'Mau Maus of the mind: making Mau Mau and the remaking of Kenya', *Journal of African History*, 31 (1990), pp. 393–422, and 'Wealth, poverty and civic virtue in Kikuyu political thought', in Bruce Berman and John M. Lonsdale, *Unhappy Valley: clans, class and state in colonial Kenya* (London, Nairobi and Athens, Ohio, 1991), pp. 167–280. See also E. S. Atieno Odhiambo, 'Kenya from protest to decolonisation', in W. R. Ochieng (ed.), *New History of Kenya* (Nairobi, in press).

3 See David M. Anderson, 'Policing the settler state: colonial hegemony in Kenya, 1900–52', in Dagmar Engels and Shula Marks (eds.), *Contesting Colonial Hegemony: state and society in Africa and Asia, 1858 until independence* (forthcoming); David M. Anderson, 'Policing, prosecution and the law in colonial Kenya', in D. M. Anderson and D. Killingray (eds.), *Policing the Empire: government, authority and control, c. 1830–1940* (Manchester, 1991).

4 *Kenya Police Annual Report* [*KPAR*], *1949* (Nairobi, 1950), pp. 2–3. All Kenya Police Annual Reports were published, but copies are also available at the Public Records Office [PRO], Kew, under classification CO 544.

5 *KPAR, 1945*, pp. 8–9; *KPAR, 1946*, p. 8.

6 *KPAR, 1945*, pp. 8–12; *Legislative Council Debates, Hansard (Kenya)*, second series, vol. XX (1944–5), third session, 9 January 1945, cols. 612–49, and 10 January, cols. 651–75.

7 For a detailed discussion of Nairobi's social problems, see Throup, *Economic and Social Origins*, pp. 171–96.

8 Such minor offences had dominated police work since the early 1930s. See Anderson, 'Policing, prosecution and the law', *passim*.

9 The above paragraph is drawn from *Legislative Council Debates, Hansard (Kenya)*, second series, vol. XX (1944–5), third session, 4 January 1945, Archdeacon J. J. Beecher, col. 505; 'Legislation: Urban Pass Laws, 1946', Kenya National Archive [KNA] MAA 7/377; Minutes of meetings to discuss Vagrancy Bye-laws, 29 June, 8 August, 8 September and 12 October 1948, 'City African Affairs Officer: Correspondence, 1947–50', KNA MAA 8/22; Minutes of African Advisory Council, 21 and 22 January 1946, and Crime Committee, 19 and 26 June, and 15 August 1947, 'Nairobi Advisory Council, 1946–49', KNA MAA 2/5/223.

10 *KPAR, 1948*, p. 8; *KPAR, 1949*, p. 1.

11 See T. G. Askwith, Annual Report on African Affairs in Nairobi, December 1947, in 'African Housing: General 1946–51', KNA Lab 9/1751; and 'Legislation: Urban Pass Laws, 1946', KNA MAA 7/377. For a recent account of one aspect of 'criminal' African life in Nairobi, see Luise White, *Comforts of Home: prostitution in colonial Nairobi* (Chicago, 1991).

12 *KPAR, 1950*, p. 21. See also *KPAR, 1951*, pp. 3 and 7–9.

13 *KPAR, 1951*, p. 8.

14 *KPAR, 1951*, pp. 7–8 and 22–3.

15 *KPAR, 1952*, pp. 1, 10–12. See also, Throup, *Economic and Social Origins*, ch. 10.

16 James B. Wolf, 'Asian and African recruitment in the Kenya Police, 1920–1950', *International Journal of African Historical Studies*, VI (1973), pp. 401–12.

[155]

17 *KPAR, 1949*, pp. 2–3.

18 *KPAR, 1949*, pp. 4–5; *KPAR, 1950*, pp. 2–3.

19 W. C. Johnson, Inspector General of Colonial Police to Acting Governor J. D. Rankine, 10 June 1950, 'Review of Police and Security Forces in relation to Communist infiltration: Kenya', PRO CO 537/542.

20 *Ibid.*

21 *Ibid.*

22 *Ibid.*

23 *KPAR, 1951*, pp. 3–5.

24 *Ibid.*, pp. 2–3.

25 Throup, *Economic and Social Origins*, pp. 188–95.

26 On the Mombasa strike, and more generally on labour and unions in that city, see Frederick Cooper, *On the African Waterfront: Urban Disorder and the Transformation of Work in Colonial Mombasa* (New Haven and London, 1987), esp. pp. 78–113.

27 *East African Standard*, 23 and 24 May 1950.

28 Markan Singh, *History of Kenya's Trade Union Movement* (Nairobi, 1980), vol. 1, pp. 240–50; *East African Standard*, 23 and 24 May 1950; *KPAR, 1950*, pp. 10–11, 17; Throup, *Economic and Social Origins*, pp. 194–5.

29 Throup, *Economic and Social Origins*, pp. 227–8.

30 See especially, P. Wyn Harris to Basil Hobson, 30 July 1949, 'Chief Waruhiu, 1948–52', KNA MAA 8/68.

31 Throup, *Economic and Social Origins*, pp. 227–8, 280.

32 *KPAR, 1950*, pp. 9–10, and W. R. Foran, *The Kenya Police, 1887–1960* (London, 1962), pp. 161–71, for details of the Kolloa incident, and *KPAR, 1951*, p. 9, for O'Rorke's comments on the disturbances in Murang'a.

33 *KPAR, 1951*, p. 9.

34 *KPAR, 1952*, pp. 11–12.

35 *KPAR, 1952*, pp. 1–12; Corfield, *Historical Survey*, pp. 125–6; *East African Standard*, 26 February 1952; Foran, *Kenya Police*, pp. 177–84.

36 For detailed discussion of the events of this period, see Throup, *Economic and Social Origins*, ch. 10.

37 *KPAR, 1952*, p. 11.

38 See the comments of S. J. Baker and W. A. Muller, *Report of the Kenya Police Commission, 1953* (Nairobi, 1953), pp. 2–3, 6–7.

39 On earlier attitudes to the policing of the settler farms, see Anderson, 'Policing the settler state', *passim*.

40 For a survey of the impact of these changes and the difficulties encountered, see Foran, *Kenya Police*, pp. 184–94. Also, Anthony Clayton and David Killingray, *Khaki and Blue: military and police in British colonial Africa* (Athens, Ohio, 1989), pp. 109–36, for a short account of the history of the Kenya Police, based upon oral histories drawn from former officers, much of which deals with discussion of the effects of the Emergency.

41 *KPAR, 1952*, pp. 2–3.

42 *KPAR, 1953*, p. 20; 'History of the Kikuyu Guard', Mss. Afr. S 1915(2), Rhodes House, Oxford.

43 *KPAR, 1952*, pp. 2–4; *KPAR, 1953*, pp. 2–3, 18–21; Baker and Muller, *Kenya Police Commission*, p. 6. For a detailed discussion of the expansion of the force, see Foran, *Kenya Police*, pp. 188–94.

44 *KPAR, 1953*, pp. 2–3; Papers of Sir Richard Catling [Catling Papers], ff. 9–10, 18–19, Box X, Mss. Afr. S 1784, Rhodes House, Oxford. For discussion of the operation of these committees, see Papers of M. K. Akker [Akker Papers], ff. 14–16, Box VIII, Mss.Afr. S 1784, Rhodes House, Oxford.

45 'Reorganisation of Kenya Police Force, February 1954 – January 1956', PRO CO 1037/36, various papers. Young resigned in February 1955.

46 *KPAR, 1952*, p. 12.

47 Gen. C. Nicholson to Lt. Gen. H. Redman, 18 May 1953, 'Report of C-in-C Middle East Land Forces' visit to Kenya, 11–16 May 1953', PRO WO 216/852; Gen. Erskine to

CIGS, 11 June 1953, 'First impressions of General Erskine on the situation in Kenya', PRO WO 216/853.

48 *KPAR*, *1953*, p. 18.

49 Catling Papers, ff. 9–10.

50 *KPAR*, *1953*, pp. 7–10.

51 *Ibid.*, p. 10; Embu District Intelligence Reports, in possession of author.

52 Catling Papers, ff. 18–19; *KPAR*, *1953*, p. 2.

53 For fuller details, see David W. Throup, 'Mau Mau in Embu', paper presented at the conference on 'The Construction of Colonial Terror', Trinity College, Cambridge, March 1991.

54 *Ibid.*, and interviews with former District Intelligence Officer, Embu, dd. Nairobi, September 1985.

55 Embu District Intelligence Reports.

56 *KPAR*, *1953*, pp. 11, 19.

57 Baker and Muller, *Kenya Police Commission*, p. 4.

58 Catling Papers, ff. 4–6.

59 Catling Papers, f. 7.

60 This, and the above quotations, from Baker and Muller, *Kenya Police Commission*, pp. 6–8.

61 Akker Papers, f. 16.

62 'Anvil Vol. 2', PRO WO 276/187, contains details of the preparations for Operation Anvil. For a more critical view of the effect of the operation upon the military situation in Central Province, see Foran, *Kenya Police*, pp. 205–13.

63 Summary drawn from Furedi, *Mau Mau War*, pp. 120–5; Rosberg and Nottingham, *Myth of Mau Mau*, pp. 292–303; Embu District Intelligence Reports.

64 Catling Papers, 'Lecture at The University of New Brunswick, 14 February 1979', ff. 22–3.

65 *KPAR*, *1955*, p. 9; Catling Papers, ff. 18–19.

66 *KPAR*, *1956*, pp. 2–3, 16–17.

67 Catling Papers, f. 17.

68 Akker Papers, ff. 17–18.

69 *Ibid.*, ff. 18–21.

70 *Ibid.*

71 *Ibid.*, ff. 22–3. See also Catling Papers, 'Lecture at the University of New Brunswick, 14 February 1979', ff. 13–15.

72 Catling Papers, ff. 14–15.

73 *Ibid.*, f. 12.

74 *Ibid.*, ff. 12–15, 26–32.

75 Papers of Mervyn Colet Manby [Manby Papers], ff. 10–11, Box X, Mss.Afr.S 1764, Rhodes House, Oxford.

76 *Ibid.*, ff. 10–11 and 15.

77 Catling Papers, f. 12.

78 Manby Papers, f. 15.

79 *Ibid.*, *passim*, but esp. ff. 10–12.

80 Catling Papers, f. 29.

81 Manby Papers, f. 10.

82 *Ibid.*, ff. 11, 14.

83 Catling Papers, ff. 15, 26–7, and 'Lecture at the University of New Brunswick, 14 February 1979', ff. 12–15.

CHAPTER EIGHT

Authority and legitimacy in Malawi: policing and politics in a colonial state

John McCracken

Among the various attempts made over the last two decades to provide an explanation for the maintenance and ultimate dissolution of colonial authority in Africa, one stands out above all others. Ronald Robinson's 'sketch for a theory of collaboration' may no longer be accepted as helpful in explaining why Africa was partitioned, but on the larger question of how colonial rule was maintained, his analysis has been accepted virtually unchallenged by a variety of historians of widely differing ideological persuasions.[1] Disputes may exist about such arcane issues as the validity of 'collaboration' as a term[2] but there has been little disagreement with Robinson's basic propositions: that 'The amount of force at the disposal of colonial rulers locally seemed tiny in comparison with the possibility of disaffection and revolt'; that, in consequence, 'the official agents of imperialism ... still had to work through indigenous collaborators and political processes'; and that 'when the colonial rulers had run out of indigenous collaborators, they either chose to leave or were compelled to go'.[3]

The strength of Robinson's analysis, however, should not blind historians to certain limitations contained within it. In the first place, as A. E. Atmore has noted, the theory does little to identify and define collaborators in the context of their own societies.[4] Beneath the exotic images conjured up by Robinson in his list of potential collaborators – 'zamindars and taluqdars, Hindu bhadralok and Muslim jihad leaders, African clan heads, paramount chiefs and kings' – there lies an absence of serious social analysis. Secondly, by concentrating on the construction of elaborate networks of collaborative alliance – 'tacit agreements for mutual non-interference and mutual support between colonial government and indigenous society' – Robinson loses sight of the priority accorded by all colonial regimes to the instruments of coercion used in upholding colonial authority and in furthering the economic interests of the colonisers. There can be no dispute that the emphasis placed by colonial governments on the use of armed force to maintain internal and external security varied substantially from one period to another. But, as the regular updating of colonial defence schemes demonstrate, at no times were such matters regarded as being other than important. Finally, Robinson's theory throws little light on the central problem, illuminatingly discussed in a pioneer article by Low, of how colonial regimes sought to make themselves legitimate in the eyes of those whom they had conquered.[5] From the perspective of the 1990s, the rituals of loyalty patched together by colonial governments seeking the acquiescence of their subjects may appear threadbare and unconvincing when compared with the much more elaborate strategies devised by their successors. Nevertheless, it was as much through their ability to capture the imagination of particular groups of local allies as it was through their capacity to strike up favourable bargains that colonial regimes succeeded in sustaining authority. By the same token, the loss of ideological conviction could presage the collapse of a collaborative alliance.

In this chapter the focus of investigation is shifted from the grand vistas sketched by Robinson to the narrower horizons viewed in a single colony. The central aim is to chart the changing character of colonial authority in Nyasaland (colonial Malawi), giving due weight to the collaborative mechanisms employed in the recruitment of rural elites, but also taking account of the role of force in maintaining internal security and of the ideological strategies pursued by the colonialists. Four major periods in the evolution of authority are suggested: the era of coercion beginning in 1891, the era of control reaching its peak in the years immediately following the First World War; the era of collaboration lasting through the 1930s into the Second World War, and the crisis of authority which came to a head in the 1950s with profound consequences for Britain's decolonisation strategy. In each period a variety of stratagems was utilised, but it is the contention of this chapter that the relation between them dramatically altered as a consequence of changes in the priorities and assumptions of leading decision-makers and the context in which they operated.

The era of coercion

The manner in which British rule was established had a profound effect on the subsequent character of colonial authority in Nyasaland. Hardly had he arrived in the Protectorate in 1891 as the first Commissioner than Harry Johnston set out to make the colonial state a reality by establishing territorial hegemony, creating a revenue base through the imposition of hut tax and unlocking supplies of labour hitherto immobilised by the slave trade.[6] In other parts of Central Africa where few white settlers

[159]

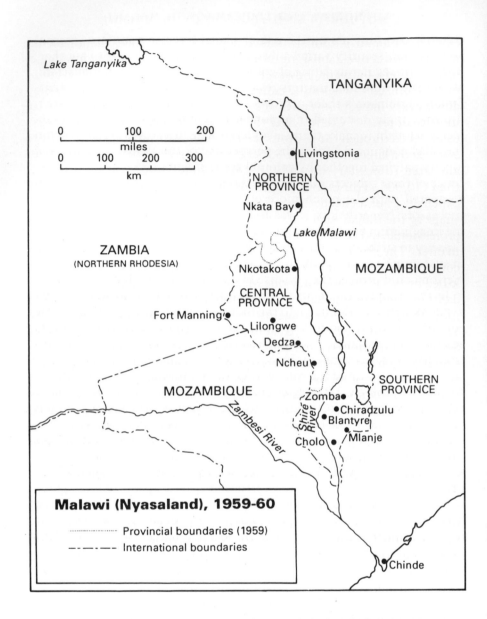

Malawi (Nyasaland) 1959–60

existed, colonial administrators tended to make good their lack of military power by establishing formal alliances with the more formidable of local rulers. Johnston, however, after a brief flurry of diplomacy, committed himself to a 'spoiling policy of weakening, dividing and wearing down every indigenous political system that possessed any capacity to menace or resist'.[7] Control over the balance of power was painstakingly established through the rigorous restriction of African ownership of firearms, and a large slice – over 50 per cent – of government revenues was allocated to military expenditure. With funds limited to little more than £10,000 a year in the early 1890s, British troops were prohibitively expensive, but a cheaper imperial alternative was close at hand in the shape of the Indian Army, reorganised during the 1860s and at least as professional and certainly more experienced than anything Britain had to offer.[8] The first contingent of Indian troops – seventy-one men in all, consisting of thirty unmounted cavalrymen whose horses were swiftly killed by tsetse fly, and forty-one Mazhabai Sikhs (unconsidered descendants of Hindu untouchables) – was too small and disorganised to have more than limited success against the tenacious resistance mounted by Yao chiefs. But, with the arrival in 1893 of a fresh contingent of 200 Jat Sikhs recruited from the most prestigious Punjabi regiments and conventionally regarded as the best troops in the Indian Army, the balance tilted in favour of Johnston's tiny army.[9] Commanded by a handful of white officers attracted to Central Africa by the exceptional opportunities for promotion that service with Johnson provided,[10] the Sikhs combined an accuracy of marksmanship with a steadiness under fire that their opponents could not match.[11] By 1898 they had effectively established British dominance, not just in Nyasaland, but also in North Eastern Rhodesia. Only in 1912 was the last contingent of Indian troops withdrawn.[12]

The employment of Indian troops was combined with a concerted and ultimately successful attempt to recruit an indigenous army. As Isaacman has noted, the dual impact of the Ngoni invasion and the extension of the slave trade in the second half of the nineteenth century resulted in the creation not only of divisions between new Yao and Ngoni conquest states and older Chewa and Tumbuka agricultural societies, but also of friction between different social strata within Central African states.[13] Chewa, Tonga and Tumbuka incorporated in Ngoni kingdoms attempted through a variety of stratagems to preserve their cultural identity. The uses to which such divisions could be put was first demonstrated by Frederick Lugard in 1888 when he persuaded Tonga headmen, harassed by their Ngoni neighbours, to supply him with nearly 400 mercenaries to fight on behalf of the African Lakes Company against Swahili traders at the north end of Lake Malawi.[14] Although this ill-managed expedition was repulsed, the Tonga irregulars, buoyed up with Lugard's promise of loot, performed sufficiently well to persuade Johnston of the merits of repeating the experiment. The Indian troops in 1891–2 were supplemented by some 170 Swahili and Makua mercenaries from Zanzibar and Mozambique, products of a coastal culture which Europeans were beginning to dominate. They in turn were supplemented from February 1892 by increasingly large contingents of local troops, some of them occasional levies provided by African rulers; among them were the Yao chief Mponda and the Ngoni leader Chifisi whose readiness to ally themselves militarily with the British was a reflection on the extent to which they were challenged by political rivals.[15] Further contingents of predominantly Tonga mercenaries were recruited by Johnston in January 1893 from labourers employed by the leading planting and commercial firms in the country – Buchanan Brothers and the African Lakes Company.[16] These formed the nucleus of a contingent of up to 250 Tonga irregulars, actively employed in a number of campaigns between 1893 and 1895. Paid wages of five to six shillings a month, the irregulars were no more disciplined or less ruthless than the fearsome bands of *ruga ruga* utilised by Johnston's Swahili opponents. Under the personal leadership of Sergeant Bandawe, their brutal commander, they 'shot children and women and babes indiscriminately', according to one observer, and indulged in wild drunken celebrations following their raids, according to another, at which the heads of opponents were occasionally displayed.[17]

The transition of those irregulars into valued instruments of imperial authority had its origins in the construction in June 1895 of a military camp at Zomba on the site still used as the headquarters of the First Battalion Malawi Rifles.[18] Military depots are at once the most open and the most mysterious of total institutions, more embracing in their controls and more draconian in their punishments than the harshest mining compound, yet at the same time the source of a pervading ideology that can imbue soldiers with loyalty to their comrades and sustain their courage under stress. The Zomba depot of what in 1896 became officially known as the Central African Rifles was no exception to this comment. Staffed by a nucleus of Sikh sepoys under the command of a small group of British officers, virtually none of whom had any knowledge of African languages, the depot must have been a place of quite exceptional disorientation for the first generation of recruits, who were regularly worked from dawn to dusk, clouted over the head when they asked a reasonable question of a British officer, and periodically flogged for trivial breaches of discipline.[19] All the same, even in these unpromising conditions, a strange alchemy was at work, transforming freelance combatants into disciplined soldiers of the Crown. The number of troops increased from a bare handful in 1893 to 720 in 1896–7. On 1 January 1899 a second battalion, over a thousand strong, was raised; later that year it was shipped to Mauritius, where the troops, provoked beyond endurance by the taunts of the local population, broke out of barracks on a two-hour rampage that resulted in their ignominious removal to the sands of bleak Somaliland and settler calls for the disbandment of the regiment.[20]

The turning-point came in 1900 following the outbreak of the Ashanti War at a time when British troops were already fully extended by the Anglo-Boer War in South Africa and by the Boxer Rising in China. Four companies of Malawian soldiers were despatched to the tropical forests of West Africa, where they performed with an effectiveness that convinced military observers of 'the extraordinary value of the black regiments' for the defence of the empire, particularly in tropical conditions where wagon transport could not be used.[21] In the next two years, Nyasa contingents were successfully employed in the gruelling campaign against Muhammed Abdille Hassan in Somaliland and to put down a rising in the Gambia. It is not surprising, therefore, that when the King's African Rifles was established as the regional army for Britain's East African possessions in 1902, the two Nyasa battalions should be prominently involved; thereafter soldiers from Nyasaland were recruited in disproportionately large numbers for service in the regiment, with at least one battalion being permanently stationed abroad. During the First World War almost half the KAR troops – between 15,000 and 19,000 men – were recruited in Nyasaland, though its population was little more than a third of that of either Kenya or Uganda.[22] In the 1920s and 1930s Nyasa troops provided garrisons for Tanganyika and British Somaliland as well as for Nyasaland itself.[23]

It is by no means easy to classify those Malawians who joined the colonial army. Up to the late 1890s a majority of the irregulars were conscripts – levies hastily recruited by African chiefs seeking short-term alliances with the British, who tended to disperse as quickly as they had gathered. Few of the 3,000 men placed at the disposal of Captain Keane by chiefs Mponda and Chifisi in March 1892 were still active in the service of the administration a fortnight later. No sooner had the Chewa chief, Mwasi Kasungu, been defeated in December 1895, than the 5,000 men who had joined the campaign from Nkotakota, 2,300 with guns, returned to the town with their spoils.[24] Of greater utility to the administration at this period were the small gangs of young mercenaries, rarely numbering more than 100, following a personal leader and attracted by the lure of loot. 'To watch the Atonga looting the houses and pursuing Mkukus (chickens) was very good fun,' wrote Dr Wordsworth Pole in 1895 of such a party. 'The Atonga go through a village like a dose of salts ... They know all the likely places for treasure trove.'[25] Some pioneer soldiers were wage labourers committed by their European employers to military service as an extension of their civilian duties; others, like the unfortunate Private Naso, were press-ganged for service overseas. Seized by soldiers on the road to Chikwawa in 1900, Naso was carried in irons aboard the steamer at Chinde which was to take him to the Gold Coast and service in the Ashanti campaign.[26]

Very differently treated were the small group of mercenary leaders, almost the only active collaborators in Robinson's sense, who committed themselves positively to the British alliance. The legendary Sergeant Bandawe, captor of the Swahili trader Mlozi, was paid 33 shillings a month in the early 1890s, wages which rose to £40 a year after he had led his gang into service with the Crown.[27] Even in retirement he was not forgotten by his benefactors. On the instructions of Alfred Sharpe, Johnston's successor, he received a pension of £40 a year up to his death in 1931, along with a substantial land grant and the right to keep his own gun. He was also expressly exempted from the authority of the local chief, an indication of the preference shown by the administration before 1914 for military as opposed to political alliances.[28]

For most soldiers the inducements supplied to Bandawe must have appeared impossibly remote. No doubt the recruits who flocked in increasingly large numbers to join the army from the mid-1890s were attracted by the relatively generous wages on offer, rising from five shillings a month to ten shillings in 1902, over twice the normal monthly rate on estates. But if above-average wages provided the 'pull' to military recruitment, it was the 'push' of a disintegrating domestic economy that explains why some communities produced so many more soldiers than others. The remarkable increase in the number of Yao recruits in the years after 1894 can be used to illustrate the point. Up to the late 1880s Yao communities around the south end of the lake had prospered from their involvement in the slave and ivory trades. But following the colonial occupation and the imposition of high tariffs on the export of ivory, long-distance trade collapsed, as did subsequent attempts by Yao peasants to grow cotton in an area only marginally suitable for cash-crop farming.[29] Required to find the wherewithal for hut tax, many young Yao men were therefore forced into migrant labour, some as unskilled porters but more as policemen and soldiers with the KAR, for whom by 1914 they normally provided half of Nyasaland's two-battalion strength.[30] Savings from military wages thus became an important part of the Yao domestic economy, particularly from the 1920s when an increasing number of soldiers with nine years' service obtained exemption from hut tax. In contrast to the situation in the Punjab, land grants were not used to cement the burgeoning military alliance. But from 1932 a system of gratuities was in operation providing lump sums of between £7 10s and £10 for those who had served nine or twelve years with the colours.[31]

As these figures suggest, a particular attraction of Nyasa troops to the military authorities was the cheapness of this form of labour. Because wages in Nyasaland were significantly lower than in other East and Central African countries, the KAR could pay Nyasa soldiers twice the average wages pertaining in their homeland while still making significant savings on what it could cost to attract Kenyan or Ugandan recruits.[32] Whereas East Africans serving in the army automatically received exemption from hut tax, Nyasas had to wait for nine years in order to qualify.[33]

If Yao involvement in the colonial army was in part a consequence of the impoverished character of their domestic economy under the British, it was also a result of certain stereotyped assumptions made by the colonialists and accepted by some Yao themselves. No imperial regime has ever been more active in the construction of 'ethnic security maps' designed to ensure that military power was located only in the hands of those 'martial races' specially trusted by the authorities than the British in India in the half-century after the Mutiny of 1857.[34] It was therefore of significance that Indian Army officers played a major role in founding the Central African and King's African Rifles. At first their attention focused on imagined differences between the lakeside Tonga, 'faithful servants of the white man ... plucky and reliable', and the 'wily skulking' Yao, 'the essence of cowardice and laziness and never will be any good'.[35] But the readiness of some defeated Yao chiefs to throw in their lot with the British from the mid-1890s was mirrored by as remarkable a change in colonial ethnic stereotypes. As early as 1896 Harry Johnston had come to the conclusion that the Yao 'make excellent soldiers, better than any other race in the Protectorate', and within a decade this view had hardened into dogma.[36] By 1922 the Nyasaland Military Handbook was solemnly listing the 'Military Value of Tribes', starting with the Yao who were considered 'Excellent. Good physically, intelligent and amenable to discipline' and ending with the Chewa whose military value was considered 'only slight'.[37] Efforts were made to ensure that half of all Nyasa troops were Yao and their identity was reinforced by the insistence of the Inspector General that all companies should be recruited on tribal lines: 'Throughout my service with the King's African Rifles I have urged the advisability of tribal classification by companies or sub-units. It makes for safety in case of unrest, tends to greater military efficiency by producing a spirit of rivalry and com-petition and makes for mutual respect in times of trial in action.'[38] The aim of military recruitment in Nyasaland, the Governor Sir Shenton Thomas noted in December 1930, 'is that the Battalion should be 50 per cent Yao, 25 per cent Atonga and 25 per cent Angoni, and in a country such as this, where the tribal distinctions are more marked than is usual in East Africa, it is important that the policy should be followed as closely as possible.'[39] As late as 1939, 58 per cent of all soldiers called themselves Yao.[40]

The era of control

The defeat of the Swahili trader, Mlozi, in 1895 marked at once the high point in the era of coercion and the beginning of its rapid decline. With the colonial state victorious over its local adversaries, concern over the extension of military authority diminished and official attention switched to the creation of a civilian police force (the Boma askari), armed with rifles, recruited almost entirely from the military askari and occupied in 'the checking of hut taxes and obtaining of labour and the carrying of orders from the Resident to the Chiefs and information from the Chiefs to the Resident'.[41] The military became increasingly identified as an instrument of broad imperial strategy, and internal unrest was confidently discounted on the grounds, so a senior colonial official confided in December 1912, 'that, being good fighting men, the natives of Nyasaland suffered more severely than those in other countries at the beginning of British administration. At all events I always understood that the possibility of a native insurrection in the country might be neglected because "they had learnt the lesson once for all".'[42] The number of troops stationed in Nyasaland was reduced from over a thousand in the late 1890s to 286 on the eve of the First World War and the artillery available to the military dwindled to almost nothing. Surveying his resources in 1914, the senior military officer in Nyasaland noted 'that the only guns available for service in the field with infantry are the six 7-pounder RML guns, and these would probably be more of a hindrance than use'. Only one gunner was serving with the KAR and he was about to be posted to East Africa, leaving no other officer with a knowledge of guns. There were only two Maxim guns in the whole of the country. Nyasaland, so a Colonial Office official minuted on a despatch from the Governor, 'is the last country in Africa where there is likely to be any native trouble: the natives are peacefully disposed and very well content with British administration'.[43]

The transformation of this mood of complacency into the almost hysterical concern with internal security that characterised official attitudes in the early 1920s must be ascribed principally to events arising from the First World War. The first and most dramatic of these was the sudden eruption of the Chilembwe Rising in January 1915, an event which revealed to the administration the ineffectiveness of the Boma askari as information-gatherers, as well as the profound discontent felt by sections of the tenant population of the Shire Highlands, several of whose members had become active proponents of quasi-millenarian doctrines.[44] Officials were further worried in the aftermath of the war at the potential threat posed by 'large numbers of men who have been trained in the King's African Rifles and now disbanded', and they also feared that labour migrants returning from the Transvaal and Southern Rhodesia might have been welded into a 'dangerous class', prone to acts of lawlessness and particularly susceptible to revolutionary doctrines.[45]

With his confidence shattered, the Governor, Sir George Smith became increasingly obsessed by the precarious state of white rule in Nyasaland, placed, so he believed, 'on the edge of the wave of Mohammedanism progressing southwards and where the southern counterflow of Ethiopianism is running north' and liable to be swept away if these two dangerous currents were to mingle.[46] His first step in the aftermath of the rising was to strip the local population even of the small collection of firearms allowed to local notables, while at the same time enforcing collective punishments on a number of villages believed to be involved. This was followed in 1920 by the establishment of a professional, European-officered police force in the Southern Province, partly based on the paramilitary Rhodesian model and equipped with a Criminal Investigation Department designed to investigate serious crimes and political activities threatening to the state.[47] New regulations were introduced on the suppression of riots and civil disturbances: the reading of the Riot Act would no longer be required before firing; policemen were instructed not to fire over the heads of rioters, but rather to shoot to kill.[48]

Particularly controversial was Smith's proposal to reduce dependence on African troops by forming a European Defence Force 'for what may be regarded as purely defensive purposes as against native risings and revolt'.[49] Dismissing the Nyasaland Volunteer Reserve into which the majority of European settlers had been previously recruited as 'little more than a loosely organised rifle club', Smith and his principal ally, Major C. S. Phillips of the KAR, put forward detailed proposals in April 1920 whose effects, had they been implemented, would have been to extend to Nyasaland the same structure of white military control that existed south of the Zambesi.[50] A Defence Force was to be created, 'in which, with few exceptions, service will be compulsory for all non-native males between the ages of 16 and 60 years', organised by districts under district commanders. All members would be required to attend annual training camps for at least three years. Two well-trained mobile units would be formed with the capacity to strike hard in the case of civil insurrection.[51]

However, the publication of the draft ordinance provoked an angry response. Protestant missionaries, led by Drs Laws and Hetherwick, the two main pillars of the Scottish Presbyterian establishment, denounced the scheme as placing them in an impossible position in relation to their African parishioners.[52] Some white settlers complained at the introduction of conscription in peacetime; others protested that their prestige would suffer if they were observed by Africans being ordered about on the drill-square or performing fatigue duties in camp.[53]

The crucial blow came in 1922 after Smith, in the face of widespread opposition, had used his official majority to steer the ordinance through the Executive and Legislative councils. Concerned at the high cost of the scheme and unimpressed by the Governor's warnings, the Colonial Office in April took the unusual step of declaring the ordinance invalid.[54] Henceforth, military training for the European community was virtually abandoned, with the Nyasaland Volunteer Reserve reverting to its former role as an undemanding rifle club.[55] It had been made clear that while the white settlers wanted security, they were not prepared to provide it for themselves. Elsewhere in southern Africa, settlers might function as ideal 'prefabricated collaborators' in sustaining white authority; in Nyasaland from the 1920s onwards this option was essentially foreclosed. Some local whites, it is true, were subsequently recruited as special constables during the two popular challenges to colonial authority of 1953 and 1959, but in neither instance did they contribute much of significance to the ultimate suppression of the disturbances.

The era of collaboration

The disallowance of the Defence Force Ordinance in 1922, followed by Sir George Smith's departure from Nyasaland, marked a new stage in the evolution of colonial authority. As memories of the Chilembwe Rising faded in the 1920s and 1930s, official concern over internal security once more slackened and the colonial government embarked on a variety of new strategies in which the use of coercion took second place to the construction of collaborative alliances. Through the efforts of the new Governor, Sir Charles Bowring and his successor, Sir Shenton Thomas, the number of troops stationed in Nyasaland was reduced from 1,125 in 1921 to 250 (the battalion headquarters, one company and a machine-gun platoon) in 1930.[56] Major reforms were carried out in the financing of the Southern Brigade of the KAR, with the result that from the mid-1930s, five-sixths of the annual expenditure was paid by Tanganyika, though two-thirds of the troops were recruited in Nyasaland.[57] The proportion of government revenues spent on the police and the military was reduced to 9·5 per cent in 1937 as compared to 53·8 per cent forty years earlier. The collection of military intelligence was virtually abandoned, though the police Criminal Investigation Department continued its surveillance of potential troublemakers when it could spare the time from all its other duties, including the investigation of serious and complicated crimes.[58] The KAR still made occasional patrols in order 'to remind natives who might forget it that the Government have effective means of enforcing their orders if necessary'.[59] But over much of the country, colonial authority was very thinly spread. The provincial administration in the late 1930s consisted of two provincial commissioners and forty-four district officers, one quarters of whom were always on leave. No European officer and fewer than sixty African policemen served in the Northern Province.[60] Only in the neighbourhood of Blantyre and Zomba did the prevention and detection of crime form a significant part of the duties of policemen. More commonly, they were employed in supervising the collection of hut tax and in certain more marginal economic activities, such as keeping order at tobacco markets and patrolling European estates.

The decline in military expenditure was accompanied by the forging of collaborative alliances. Even in the days of Sir Harry Johnston, the need to form favourable alliances with selected African chiefs had never been far from the minds of colonial administrators, and this concern was heightened in the aftermath of the Chilembwe Rising when Yao chiefs in the Shire Highlands received considerable inducements to become members of the colonial bureaucracy.[61] It was only with the official implementation of indirect rule in 1933, however, that chiefs in Nyasaland became exposed to the wide range of ideological and institutional inducements utilised by the British elsewhere to sustain colonial rule. Bestowed with the legal power to issue their own rules, control their own finances and manipulate 'customary law' so as to gain control of labour, particularly the labour of women and the young, those chiefs designated Native Authorities had access to significant privileges designed to bind them to the colonial connection.[62] What they lacked however, were the basic instruments of coercion – tribal policemen and personal tax-collectors – used by indigenous authorities in other areas, for example rural Kenya or Northern Nigeria. They also suffered from the fact that the introduction of indirect rule coincided with the impact of the 1930s Depression which undermined confidence in the newly-established alliance and rendered its influence negligible. With tax receipts falling as a consequence of the collapse of markets and the growth of unemployment, the administration in 1934 initiated a coercive 'Grow More Groups' campaign designed to enforce an increase in peasant cash-cropping irrespective of the prices obtained.[63] As opposition arose, Native Authorities were bypassed and increased responsibility was given to newly-appointed European agricultural supervisors, many of them tobacco farmers bankrupted by the Depression.

The appointment of a full-time soil erosion officer in 1937 further

[169]

exacerbated the problem. Ambitious schemes for the construction of bunds on hill slopes and the cultivation of ridges met with widespread opposition, particularly on the Cholo escarpment and in the Lower Shire valley, where Native Authorities either refused or were unable to enforce agricultural orders.[64] The fundamental dilemma of the colonial state was beginning to emerge, though it was not till the 1950s that the collaborative structure finally collapsed under the economic demands that the government placed upon it.

Indirect rule was associated with the articulation of an official imperial cult. As Ranger has noted, the idea that colonial rule could be legitimised in the eyes of a subject people through an emphasis on the monarch as the personification of imperial authority was widely held in both British and German Africa prior to the First World War.[65] In official circles, however, annual celebrations of the King's Birthday were frequently haphazard and racially divisive affairs, more concerned with re-emphasising the culturally distinct qualities of the European community than in affirming a common multi-ethnic loyalty to the Crown. If some Africans became reconciled in this period to the colonial presence, they were more likely to be influenced by optimistic assumptions concerning the beneficial impact of 'Commerce and Christianity' than they were by an official ideology. Only among the Christian mission elite was an effective cult of royalty propagated, for only among teachers, pastors and clerks could the idea of progress through Christianity be reconciled with loyalty to the Crown. 'We expected him to train African boys and girls for the development of Central African civilization as well as for the extension of Christ's Kingdom and also for the extension of our King George V's Kingdom,' wrote Edward Bote Manda, one of the most independent-minded of Livingstonia pastors, in 1919 bemoaning the death of P. S. Kirkwood, headmaster of the Overtoun Institution school. 'He was bound to open the eyes of the Central African people so that they may be able to see ... that they are one in God one in King George V and one in humanity.'[66]

The extension of indirect rule, and perhaps the collapse of the modernising Christian ethic, was accompanied by a much more systematic approach to the projection of rituals of royalty. In 1930 standard procedures were laid down for that most mystical of ceremonies, the Royal Salute on the King's Birthday, to be delivered to an empty chair symbolising the absent monarch rather than to the Governor, his corporal representative.[67] Loyal chiefs were rewarded at King's Birthday parades with King's Medals; potential troublemakers were awed into submission (so some officers believed) through impressive demonstrations by planes of the Royal Air Force Flight, 'the swift agents of government' as they were enthusiastically described by a Governor-General of the Sudan.[68] Even in remote Fort Manning (now Mchinji), King George V's Silver Jubilee in 1935 was celebrated with a wealth of calculated symbolism:

> Crowd estimated at 6,000. No Bugler. Flagstaff ceremony at 11 a.m. First, Father Rouviere, White Fathers Mission; second, Reverend Eybers, Dutch Reformed Church Mission. Jubilee Medal presented to Native Authority Zulu. Adjourn to Football Ground. Ambitious drill display by over 1000 Kachabere (White Fathers) children, followed by a play depicting ancient conditions in Nyasaland – warfare, slavery, etc. and peace and content-ment of today – ending with an epilogue delivered by the three chief actors aged 10 in each case – entirely unselfconscious. Mganda dancing judged by three Native Authorities, head teachers of each Mission and Head Clerk. 1.30 p.m., after European lunch, native sports till 3.0 followed by football match Mcinji v. Boma – Boma won 7–0. 3.30 Distribution of meat, flour and beer at prison. 6.00 Fireworks.[69]

Church and state, black and white, Afrikaner and Frenchman had been brought together in mutual tribute to the Crown. Material progress had been suitably celebrated, though with unfortunate timing at the peak of the Depression. An invented tradition of the younger generation – the Mganda dance, stemming in Malawi from the First World War – had been adjudicated upon by representatives of the three main sources of rural privilege: Native Authorities embodying 'traditional' legitimacy, teachers representing the modernising, Christian road to advancement, and the Head Clerk, a symbol of the power of the Boma. All that was lacking was a demonstration by the Royal Air Force such as had taken place at Fort Manning in 1933, of 'mammoth "Ndeges" diving from the sky' with the aim of convincing the most hardened conspirator of 'the extreme folly of another "chilembweism" '.[70]

It is questionable whether Malawians in general were impressed by such activities, but for some at least the impact was genuine enough. On the death of George V in 1936, Native Authority Kawinga, anxious 'to dry the tears of the Queen', collected money for the purchase of a wreath which was later placed with ceremony on the King's tomb at Windsor.[71] The abdication of Edward VIII a few months later thus came as a serious embarrassment to the government requiring careful handling at the highest levels. When the *Nyasaland Times* reprinted an article from the *New York Woman* entitled 'Mrs. Wallis Simpson', the editor was fiercely rebuked by the Chief Secretary and all copies of the offend-ing edition were withdrawn.[72] District Officers were informed that in explaining the abdication to Africans they should lay 'particular stress ... on the fact that Kind Edward felt that in the present circumstances his health was not strong enough to allow him to continue to discharge the very heavy duties of Kingship to his own satisfaction'.[73] The cult of royalty had the particular attraction to administrators that it did not

[171]

involve the automatic granting of rights of citizenship to subjects within colonial states. By the same token, it assumed the moral integrity of the monarch to whom allegiance was due.

The crisis of authority

The loss of British control over the countryside in Malawi was associated with the new burdens placed on colonial collaborative structures. Up to the Second World War, state involvement in peasant agriculture had been confined largely to control over the marketing of major African cash crops and, to a lesser extent, to the encouragement of soil conservation through non-coercive measures. However, from the mid-1940s the drive to combat what was perceived as a major ecological crisis transformed the role of the state. As Beinart has noted, 'Conservationist imperatives began to win out against administrative concern to maintain social order'.[74] New comprehensive Natural Resources Ordinances were promulgated in 1946 and in 1949 with the aim of enforcing ridge cultivation and the construction of contour bunds. Land-usage schemes were introduced in almost every district in the country and the staff of the Agricultural Department was substantially increased. Funds were made available on a much larger scale than previously for the enactment of soil conservation measures, and the resources of the District Administration were committed to the task of agricultural extension. The question raised by one senior agricultural officer as to whether it was possible to force cultivators through legislation into altering their productive techniques was set aside;[75] instead, a highly coercive regime was introduced involving the closest co-operation between district commissioners and agricultural instructors in imposing a host of onerous and frequently socially disruptive regulations on an increasingly hostile peasantry.[76]

Faced by the spread of discontent among tenants on the large estates of the Shire Highlands, the Nyasaland government also took measures to reform landlord–tenant relations. Acting on the recommendations of the 1946 Abrahams Commission, it embarked on an ambitious programme of land purchase that resulted in it buying up some 460,000 acres of largely undeveloped land from European landowners between 1948 and 1956. Large-scale land settlement schemes were introduced and thousands of Malawians were moved on to new areas of land where they were compelled to practise improved methods of land husbandry and accept the consolidation of holdings.

The crisis of control that resulted from this attempt to transform the character of peasant agriculture affected strategies pursued by the colonial authorities in a number of ways. As late as 1943 the Nyasaland government had seriously contemplated replacing the small number of policemen employed in rural areas by tribal policemen under the control of native authorities.[77] But with the growth of unrest in the Shire Highlands associated with the introduction of resettlement, the policy was reversed and instead the new Governor, Sir Geoffrey Colby, sanctioned a substantial increase in expenditure on the police force. In the next few years, new equipment and housing were provided for policemen, the training programme was overhauled, and instruction was provided in riot control by Geoffrey Morton, a former member of the Palestine Police. At the behest of the Colonial Office, alarmed at what it saw as the growth of communist infiltration throughout the dependent empire, a Special Branch, responsible for the collection of political intelligence and distinct from the CID, was established in 1949.[78] And a significant expansion in the strength of the police force also took place with the number of European officers rising from nineteen in 1948 to fifty-one in 1952. The number of African policemen was increased from 500 to 743, though as the Commissioner, Apthorpe, noted in his annual report in 1952, 'Police cover in the Protectorate is (still) very thin.'[79] 'The Nyasaland Police Force has neither the numbers nor the organisation to meet the need in the rural areas,' a senior official reported.[80]

No attempt, therefore, was made to involve policemen in enforcing the extensive soil conservation drive launched by the government in the late 1940s, despite the fact that in 1955 there were over 10,000 prosecutions in the Southern Province alone for breaches of the new Natural Resources legislation. Against the wishes of their superiors, agricultural instructors were increasingly compelled to act as agricultural police with predictably disastrous results. 'We have now finished checking bunds ... [and] we have caught many cases', Agricultural Instructor Hoda reported from near Dedza in 1955. 'But what I can also report is that people are not happy with capitaos, they say: We are troubling them, and also they say we are stealing their money ... They speak bad words to us, saying we trouble them, and why do we agree with Azungu [Europeans]'.[81] So widespread was the opposition that the government significantly relaxed the policy of compulsion in 1956 and virtually abandoned it as unenforceable in 1959.

The disturbances that took place over the greater part of the Southern Province between August and October 1953 demonstrated in a particularly vivid manner the decline in colonial chiefly authority.[82] In the previous half-century thousands of Lomwe from Mozambique had settled under the jurisdiction of Yao chiefs in the Chiradzulu and Mlanje Districts. These chiefs in turn had formed collaborative alliances with the Nyasaland government and Shire Highlands' estate owners to whom they provided labour in exchange for official recognition. As the responsibilities heaped upon the shoulders of the chiefs were increased, their legitimacy in the eyes of their subjects dwindled, leading in July 1953 to a concerted assault on the Yao chief Mpama, who was only saved from being deposed by the intervention of the district officer. A month later violence erupted near Luchenza, to be followed over the next fortnight by sporadic outbreaks of rioting throughout six districts of the Southern Province. For several weeks, 'Native Authority Administration in large parts of the District virtually ceased, in some cases Native Authority buildings were destroyed and lawful Native Authorities were "deposed" by rioters.'[83] Chiefs' courts, extensively used for the enforcement of soil conservation and land settlement measures, were a particular focus of hostility. Several were burnt to the ground and the records of the courts were scattered.

Some chiefs, in the aftermath of the disturbances, sustained a measure of credibility with their subjects by following the example of Chief Gomani at Ncheu in publicly denouncing agricultural rules. Others, like Chief Tengani in the Lower Shire valley, put their trust in an intensified alliance with the British only to be abandoned as the crisis deepened. For most, the loss of control resulted in the puncturing of their confidence in the ideological underpinning of the state. As late as the Second World War, thousands of Malawians had demonstrated their 'true loyalty and attachment to the King and British Empire' by enlisting for service in the KAR or making voluntary contributions to the cause.[84] But by the 1950s, rituals of loyalty were being re-interpreted by the political elite in a manner that challenged the legitimacy of imperial-directed constitutional change. In opposing the imposition of the Federation of Rhodesia and Nyasaland, Congress politicians repeatedly argued that treaties sanctioned by Queen Victoria specifically prohibited such an action.[85] When their protests were ignored, they organised a highly successful boycott of the coronation celebrations in 1953, thus demonstrating their rejection of the imperial tradition.[86] A few radical politicians attempted to found an African Republican League,[87] though the majority were content to adopt the concept of monarchy to their own political purposes. In January 1953, for example, the British government was embarrassed by the attempt of a visiting delegation of chiefs, advised by Dr Banda, to present a petition against the Federation directly to the Queen.[88] Boy Scouts were required to sing the British National Anthem at the beginning of their campfire meetings, but in the 1950s they normally concluded by singing the nationalist hymn, 'Nkosi Sikelele Afrika'.[89]

As the informal mechanisms of control collapsed in the 1950s, increased efforts were made to strengthen the coercive arm of the state. The creation of the Central African Federation in August 1953 had profound implications for the exercise of authority in Nyasaland. Responsibility for defence was vested in the Federal government, with the result that the two Nyasa battalions of the KAR were transferred from the East African Command to the Federal Defence Force with its headquarters at Salisbury. But law and order, and hence the police, remained a territorial responsibility, despite the energetic attempts of Sir Godfrey Huggins to persuade the northern governors of the value of a Federal police force.[90] It was therefore Colby rather than Huggins who was the architect of police expansion. In December 1953 he persuaded the Colonial Office to approve a plan to improve police cover throughout the Protectorate, and in the next few months he saw to it that the initial stages were put into effect. Priority was given to the creation of the Police Mobile Force (PMF), a paramilitary organisation founded in direct response to the troubles of 1953 and designed 'to provide a striking force for use in disturbed areas'.[91] Led by John Mesurier, for seventeen years a regular soldier, the Force consisted in 1954 of fourteen European officers, several of them battle-hardened veterans of the Palestine Police Force, and 200 mainly illiterate recruits with a minimum of five years' military service behind them, many of them veterans of the Burma or Malaya campaigns, chosen for their toughness in combat and excused the normal five months' training at the Zomba depot. Trained mainly in riot control and dressed in distinctive black jerseys, these men were proud of their status as members of an elite unit, feared by the civilian population but utilised with increasing frequence by a harassed colonial government. By 1958 nine platoons of the Force, 330 men in all, had been recruited, and the next year, shortly before the state of emergency was declared, a further three platoons were formed. Most of these were based at Zomba from where they were rushed in blue-painted, purpose-built Bedford trucks, protected by canopies of wire mesh, to wherever their services were required. In 1954 two platoons of the PMF spent several weeks patrolling extensively in the Nkotakota district. Later the Force was used as a blunt weapon in the enforcement of agricultural rules and as the spearhead in the government's struggle against an increasingly assertive Nyasaland African Congress. During 1958, platoons, usually travelling at night, were constantly on the move to wherever trouble threatened.[92]

The creation and expansion of the Police Mobile Force was only one aspect of the wide-ranging changes in the character of the Nyasaland Police that took place in the 1950s. In an attempt to improve the quality of political intelligence, about which Colby had complained to the Colonial Office,[93] Assistant-Inspector Lodge was given responsibility for reforming and enlarging the Special Branch, a body only 'in the process of formation' in 1950, according to the Inspector General of Colonial

Police, but ninety-eight strong in 1959, and linked to a network of paid informers.[94] The mobility of the Force was increased following the formation of a Communications Branch which purchased several motor cycles and Land Rovers. And radio communications with vehicles was also improved as a consequence of the installation of an elaborate network of VHF radio stations. Several officers were appointed on secondment from the United Kingdom and Southern Rhodesia and rates of pay for all ranks were made more attractive. Total numbers rose by 1959 to over 130 European officers and 2,200 African other ranks, an increase of over 300 per cent in just six years. Expenditure on the force, excluding housing, rose to £540,000 as compared with only £22,000 twenty years earlier.

Yet despite all the efforts of the government to strengthen the forces of internal security, its work proved unavailing. This is not the place to consider the widespread disturbances (part peasant revolt, part nationalist rising) that took place in 1959 except to say that within days of the first clashes in February, the Commissioner concluded that the police force, over two-thirds of whose members were inexperienced recruits, 'were obviously insufficiently strong to deal with a rapidly deteriorating situation'.[95] Initially the Governor, Sir Robert Armitage, was reluctant to accept the assistance eagerly offered by the Federal Prime Minister, Welensky. But faced by a deteriorating security situation, he changed his mind and on 20 February requested reinforcements. The next day detachments of the King's African Rifles and the Royal Rhodesian Regiment were dispatched from Salisbury to Nyasaland. A week later they were reinforced by platoons from the Tanganyika and Northern Rhodesian police forces. By the beginning of March, well over 2,500 additional troops had been ferried to the Protectorate, nearly five times as many as were normally stationed in the territory.[96]

No discussion of law and order in Africa can fail to ignore the fact that, whereas political control in independent states is normally dependent on the support and effectiveness of those armies and police forces directly controlled by the indigenous regime, political control in a colony can be sustained through the employment of imperial reinforcements. Indeed, it was a crucial aspect of colonial defence schemes from the 1930s that it was considered necessary to locate in Nyasaland only a part of the military forces required to suppress internal disturbances, the rest being available for rapid mobilisation in neighbouring British colonies.[97] The central dilemma facing administrators in the 1950s, however, was that the most accessible external forces, those under the control of the Federal government in Salisbury, were also those most politically damaging to use. By calling on Federal reinforcements, Armitage ensured the successful imposition of a state of emergency in March and the arrest of the

[176]

Congress leaders. But in the view of senior officials he also undermined the credibility of his government with the local population and with the many external critics of federation, particularly after the events at Nkata Bay on 3 March when white territorial troops of the Royal Rhodesian regiment opened fire on an unarmed crowd, killing twenty and wounding twenty-nine.[98] Thereafter the colonial government became 'naturally extremely anxious to avoid the use of white troops in Nyasaland again from whatever quarter they may come' – a shift of opinion of considerable significance in view of the fact that territorials constituted nearly half the Federal Army.[99] Armitage's comments in July 1960, rejecting the arguments of the Federal High Command that substantial number of Federal troops should be re-introduced into Nyasaland, captures the tone of the new British policy with remarkable effect:

> His Excellency continued by asking at what stage it would be possible to end the enforcement of authority by the use of military forces. Clearly bayonets would achieve no compromise with African nationalism and they could not be held ever present. Forces would have to be withdrawn in the face of United Kingdom and world opinion, or following the Monckton Commission Report, or the Review of the Federal Constitution.[100]

It is a measure of the strategic importance of Nyasaland in the late 1950s and early 1960s that whereas previously questions concerning the size and composition of the police force had been matters for the Governor to discuss with the Police Commissioner, now the Prime Ministers of both Britain and the Federation became intimately involved. By 1960 Roy Welensky and Harold Macmillan had both become convinced of the need to re-establish political security, but they differed fundamentally on how this was to be achieved. Welensky's line, made clear in secret correspondence only recently released by the Zimbabwe Archives, was to downgrade the role of African intermediaries (seen as suspect in the light of the army mutiny in the Congo) while strengthening the coercive base of white, particularly settler, authority. Under his proposals, three new regular European battalions would take their place in the Federal Army as an insurance against possible unrest among African troops, while an extra 200 British policemen were to be recruited to Nyasaland, appointed on short-term contracts, paid by the United Kingdom government, drawn in part from the ranks of former soldiers and employed predominantly on internal security duties.[101] He actively worked for the transfer of Federal troops to Nyasaland in July 1960, no doubt hoping that the resultant wave of unrest would scupper the constitutional talks held in Lancaster House that month, thus bringing British negotiations with Dr Banda to an end.[102]

Macmillan's strategy was at once more cautious than Welensky's and had a different end in view. Starkly aware of the metropolitan constraints that limited Britain's options in Central Africa, he was yet anxious to prevent any further descent into disorder while negotiations with the nationalists continued. He therefore sanctioned an expensive programme, to which Britain promised to contribute the unprecedented sum of £1,523,000, aimed at increasing the strength of the police force from 1,820 at the beginning of 1959 to 3,190 by June 1961.[103] However, he vetoed the large-scale secondment of British policemen to Nyasaland, recognising that their ignorance of the language and conditions of the country would prevent them operating effectively, and forcefully rejected the idea of recruiting semi-trained 'Black and Tan' irregulars, the employment of whom would be likely to undermine the morale and loyalty of the force as a whole. The logic of his argument led step by step towards acceptance of the dissolution of the Federation. 'I wish this were not so, but we just cannot see any practicable way of reinforcing the Nyasaland Police which could make it any less likely, in the event of serious trouble in the near future, that troops would have to be introduced,' he informed Welensky on 1 July 1960.[104] Yet he also rejected Welensky's calls for the re-introduction of Federal troops to stem the revived tide of popular nationalism, arguing in a message dated 20 July, 'I am sure we must not contemplate moving any troops to Nyasaland before the [Lancaster House] Conference or even to make overt preparations for moving them afterwards.'[105] The aim was the achievement of 'political stability'. And if it could be obtained only through repeated concessions to Dr Banda and the Malawi Congress Party, then that was the price Macmillan was now prepared to pay.

From one perspective, decolonisation in Nyasaland was indeed a consequence of 'changing conditions *within* the metropole', as Holland has eloquently argued.[106] From another, however, it was the outcome of a crisis of control, the recognition by British ministers and officials that authority could be retained in the protectorate only through the employment of forces that it was no longer politically expedient to use.

Conclusion

It is ironic that one of the most successful challenges to colonial authority in southern Africa in the 1950s took place in a territory described by the Devlin Commission in 1959 as 'no doubt only temporarily – a police state'.[107] Certainly the constant patrolling of over 4,500 soldiers and policemen, the great majority non-Nyasa, making arrests, burning houses, seizing possessions and enforcing the payment of collective fines, involved an assertion of state power more brutal and direct than anything witnessed in Nyasaland since the dark days of the First World War. During the sixteen months of the emergency, 1,339 persons were detained without trial and a further 2,160 were convicted of political offences. Government handouts were widely circulated among villagers calling on them to denounce their neighbours as Congress sympathisers.[108]

Yet if, for a limited period, British rule in Nyasaland took on some of the characteristics of the totalitarian regimes of Eastern Europe, for most of the time, as David Arnold has written of India, 'it fell short of being a police state in the conventional sense. It was not a society ruled through fear of a secret police that pursued, terrorized and eliminated all who dared speak out against the government.'[109] Rather, for most of its existence, the edifice of colonial control in Nyasaland was flimsily constructed, making the colonial state peculiarly vulnerable to popular unrest. As we have seen, no strong network of 'traditional' rulers supported by their own 'Native Authority' police was ever coaxed into existence in the territory, but neither was there a stable cohort of 'prefabricated collaborators', armed settlers sufficiently numerous or confident to fill the vacuum of authority. In these circumstances, the role played by soldiers and policemen took on a special importance. Here the paradox of Nyasaland was that a richly fertile harvest ground for military recruits remained starved of military resources. Because wage levels in the Protectorate were low, many thousands of Malawians were attracted into the KAR, but because government income was equally small, the expedient was followed from 1900 onwards of stationing the majority of Nyasa soldiers in other territories and at the expense of other governments. As late as the 1950s one of the two Nyasa battalions was normally stationed in Malaya defending the British Empire against Chinese Communist guerrillas.

More important for the maintenance of internal security was the role of the Nyasaland Police. Armed with guns and often experienced as soldiers, policemen were commonly regarded as alien oppressors 'strutting about the villages terrorizing the people demanding fowls, food, eggs, ufa [maize flour], beer and … even women', so Dr Banda recollects.[110] But if police coercion was pervasive, the extent of their control was not. As has been demonstrated by this author in a previous article, there were many issues, extending from the attempt to eliminate *kachasu* [maize spirit] distilling to the campaigns launched against witchcraft eradication movements, where the police lacked the moral authority to act effectively, and many districts outside the area of European settlement where their remit hardly extended.[111] As late as 1939, so the Commissioner noted, 'The vast majority of the Protectorate is from a police aspect unexplored, and it would perhaps be more correct if the nomenclature of this Force were "the Southern Province Police".'[112]

[179]

Any attempt to evaluate the significance of the attempt to change the character of the police force from 1953 must start with the acknowledgement that, superficially at least, policemen were largely untouched by the crisis of confidence in the colonial order that swept through the ranks of African intermediaries from the late 1930s onwards. Helped by a combination of improved wages and the growth of unemployment in Nyasaland from 1957, local recruitment to the enlarged force remained buoyant right up to the eve of self-government, with many potential recruits being turned away. Some nationalist sympathisers were dismissed or moved into bureaucratic jobs, but the rate of desertion remained low with most policemen, whatever their sympathies, carrying out the duties demanded of them.[113] Even in 1959 at the height of the disturbances, only one policeman deserted and sixty-five were dismissed out of a force of over 2,000 – figures not materially different from those of earlier years.[114] Men posted to isolated stations or working in plainclothes for the Special Branch were subjected to considerable pressures, but as most policemen were segregated in police lines it was difficult for the nationalists to make contact with them.[115]

Yet if the police force remained largely unresponsive to nationalist blandishments during its greatest period of growth, this did not make it strikingly more effective. Quadrupling its numbers in less than a decade increased the coercive capacity available to the government, but did nothing to improve the standing of the force with the community at large. As the Devlin Commission judiciously reported: 'We have not received enough evidence to suggest that the Nyasaland police force, despite the devotion of many of its officers, has succeeded in making itself a thoroughly acceptable part of the population of the Protectorate.'[116] Furthermore, the composition of the force militated against its effective deployment. Because a substantial proportion of the new recruits were posted to the PMF, the uniformed police remained overstretched and undermanned, 'too weak to deal with anything but the slightest disturbance' and hence reliant 'on the special branch to anticipate trouble, so that a unit of the PMF can be moved to the spot to crush it'.[117] A related problem was that, despite the undoubted improvements made in the collection of intelligence from the early 1950s, the Special Branch at the time of the emergency remained a highly fallible body: understaffed (only twenty-two plainclothes detectives and fourteen paid informers in the Northern Province), unreliable in the evidence it supplied (as witness the lurid reports of a 'Murder Plot'), and crucially lacking in all but the vaguest information on peasant protest in the greater part of the territory.[118] 'In our recent operations which were of course on a pretty large scale, it was borne on us that the security forces were hampered by lack of intelligence ... [caused largely] ... by lack of staff', Armitage confessed to Welensky in April 1959. No radical changes in the organisation of intelligence were contemplated, 'but we shall have to build up our Special Branch staff in order to obtain better coverage'.[119] In his final months in Nyasaland prior to his retirement, Armitage committed the government to a further dramatic phase of expansion involving the recruitment of yet another 1,100 policemen and the expenditure of an additional £1,500,000 on the construction of new stations and quarters.[120]

It is the final irony that changes introduced unsuccessfully as a means of reinforcing colonial authority had their greatest long-term effects on the structure of post-colonial power. This is not the place to analyse the means employed by Dr Banda in sustaining his authority in Malawi over the past twenty-five years. What one can say is that the institutional legacies which he inherited have contributed significantly to his success. By 1962 on the eve of self-government, Nyasaland at long last possessed a substantial police force, 3,220 strong, adequately equipped, reasonably well housed, boasting a brand new training school opened at Kanjedza, a suburb of Blantyre, in 1960, and with an infinitely more effective Special Branch than at any previous time in the force's existence. It was a far cry from the late 1940s when there were little more than 500 demoralised policemen dressed in rags, mainly barefooted and subjected at the Zomba depot to a training which largely consisted of 'cutting thatching grass and patching up the roofs of their mud huts'.[121] Few Malawian officers were promoted to positions of responsibility prior to the late 1950s, a potential source of weakness, but as a result of a belated programme of accelerated promotion introduced in 1960, more than one in three inspectors were Malawians by 1961.[122] Typical of these in his apparent detachment from the gusts of political nationalism was Mc. J. Kamwana, a stalwart of the Presbyterian Church, who entered the force in 1953 at the time of the Cholo disturbances, attended a course at the Hendon Police Training School on the eve of independence, and became the first Malawian Commissioner of Police in July 1971, going on to hold the post for more than fifteen years.

To return to the starting point of this chapter, such institutional competence provided a necessary, but by no means a sufficient, basis for the maintenance of political authority. As articulated by policemen and soldiers, state coercion played an important role in suppressing political opponents and in the ordering of Malawian society. But it did so in a context where a variety of alternative strategies had also to be employed to ensure the continuity of the regime. The events in Nyasaland from the 1950s through to 1962 provide a demonstration of how quickly authority can be undermined when these strategies start to fail.

[181]

G

Notes

I am grateful to Richard Hodder-Williams for his detailed comments on an earlier draft of this paper. I would also like to acknowledge the financial support of the British Academy and the Carnegie Trust for the Universities of Scotland for my research in Malawi and London.

1 Ronald Robinson, 'Non-European foundations of European imperialism: sketch for a theory of collaboration', in Roger Owen and Bob Sutcliffe, *Studies in the Theory of Imperialism* (London, 1972). For an important reconsideration of this issue see John Lonsdale, 'The European scramble and conquest in African history', in Roland Oliver and G. H. Sanderson (eds.), *The Cambridge History of Africa*, vol. 6, 1870–1905 (Cambridge, 1985), esp. pp. 722–60. A good factual account of how authority was maintained is David Killingray, 'The maintenance of law and order in British colonial Africa', *African Affairs*, 85 (1986), pp. 411–37.

2 For a vigorous denunciation of the term see A. Adu Boahen, 'Africa and the colonial challenge', in Boahen (ed.), *Africa under Colonial Domination 1880–1935: Unesco General History of Africa*, vol. VII (London, 1985), pp. 10–13.

3 Robinson, 'Non-European foundations', pp. 133, 139.

4 A. E. Atmore, 'The extra-European foundations of British imperialism: towards a reassessment', in C. C. Eldridge (ed.), *British Imperialism in the Nineteenth Century* (London, 1984), p. 123.

5 D. A. Low, *Lion Rampant: essays in the study of British imperialism* (London, 1973), pp. 8–33.

6 A. J. Hanna, *The Beginnings of Nyasaland and North-Eastern Rhodesia 1859–95* (Oxford, 1956), pp. 173–265; Roland Oliver, *Sir Harry Johnston and the Scramble for Africa* (London, 1959), pp. 197–271; L. H. Gann, 'The end of the slave trade in British Central Africa, 1889–1912', *Rhodes-Livingstone Journal: Human Problems on British Central Africa*, 16 (1954), pp. 27–51.

7 Eric Stokes, 'Malawi political systems and the introduction of colonial rule, 1891–1896', in Eric Stokes and Richard Brown (eds.), *The Zambesian Past* (Manchester, 1966), p. 360.

8 Philip Mason, *A Matter of Honour: an account of the Indian Army, its officers and men* (Harmondsworth, 1976, 2nd edition), pp. 313–40.

9 See Mason, *A Matter of Honour*, pp. 352–5. 'Jat Sikhs' were descendants of Hindus who were Jats by caste before conversion.

10 See W. Poole to his mother, 14 June 1895, Malawi National Archives [MNA] PO 1/1. Lieutenant C. A. Edwardes of the 35th Sikhs arrived in Nyasaland in 1892. By the time of his death at the age of 33, four-and-a-half years later, he had risen to be the youngest lieutenant colonel in the British Army. (See obituary contained in Francis Poole papers, MNA PO 1/5/1.)

11 For the role of the Indian troops see Sir Harry H. Johnston, *British Central Africa* (London, 1897), pp. 97–151; *Report by Commissioner Johnston of the First Three Years' Administration of the Eastern Portion of British Central Africa, 1893*, Cmd. 7504.

12 *Annual Report on the Nyasaland Protectorate for 1912–13*, Cmd. 7050.

13 Allen and Barbara Isaacman, 'Resistance and collaboration in Southern and Central Africa, c. 1850–1920', *International Journal of African Historical Studies*, 10, 1 (1977), pp. 31–62. See also A. J. Dachs, 'Politics of collaboration: imperialism in practice', in B. Pachai (ed.), *The Early History of Malawi* (London, 1972), pp. 283–9.

14 John McCracken, *Politics and Christianity in Malawi 1875–1940* (Cambridge, 1977), pp. 82–3.

15 H. H. Johnston to Lord Salisbury, 24 November 1891, in *Papers relative to the Suppression of Slave-raiding in Nyasaland* (1892), Cmd. 6699.

16 H. H. Johnston to Lord Rosebery, 19 March 1893, in *Papers relative to the Suppression of Slave-raiding in British Central Africa*, 1893–4, Confidential Print, 75.

17 Journal of Dr Wordsworth Poole, entry for 23 September 1895, MNA PO 1/2; Diary of Edward Alston, 9–10 April, 1895, MNA.

18 Wordsworth Poole to his mother, 14 June and 9 October, 1895, MNA, PO 1/1.
19 Diary of Captain Edward Alston, 2, 16, 19 July, 1895, MNA. For a pioneer analysis of military ideology see George Shepperson, 'The military history of British Central Africa', *Rhodes-Livingstone Journal*, 26 (1960), pp. 23–33.
20 *Central African Times*, 14 April 1900; H. Moyse-Bartlett, *The King's African Rifles* (Aldershot, 1956), pp. 27–31.
21 Article in the *Scotsman*, 7 November 1900, quoted in *Central African Times*, 12 January 1901.
22 For a discussion of the numbers involved see G. W. T. Hodges, 'African manpower statistics for the British forces in East Africa, 1914–1918', *Journal of African History*, XIX, 1 (1978), p. 103: C. P. Lucas, *The Empire at War*, vol. IV (London, 1921), p. 270.
23 Moyse-Bartlett, *The King's African Rifles*, pp. 453–62.
24 Johnston to Salisbury, 8 April 1892, in *Papers relative to the Suppression of Slave-raiding in Nyasaland* (1892), Cmd. 6699; Edward Alston, Account of the Mlozi Campaign, 1895, Alston Diaries, MNA.
25 Journal of Wordsworth Poole, entry for 23 September 1895, MNA PO 1/2.
26 For a brief autobiography see 'History of the Ashanti Campaign by a Native of the West Shire District, 1900', MNA KAR 2/1/4. See also Moyse-Bartlett, *The King's African Rifles*, pp. 125–6 which documents the division between Lt. Col. Brake who used press-gang methods of recruiting and Commissioner Sharpe who recruited men through their headmen.
27 Johnston, *First Three Years' Administration*; Alfred Sharpe to Sir Clement Hill, 31 January 1902, Public Record Office, Kew [PRO] FO 2/605.
28 Dowa District Book.
29 Megan Vaughan, 'Social and economic change in Southern Malawi: a study of rural communities in the Shire Highlands and Upper Shire Valley from the mid-nineteenth century to 1915' (Ph.D. thesis, London, 1981): Violet Jhala, 'The Yao in the Shire Highlands, 1861–1915: the establishment of their authority and adjustment to changing socio-economic conditions' (BA Honours research paper, University of Malawi, 1980).
30 Moyse-Bartlett, *The King's African Rifles*, p. 159.
31 See files on 'Hut tax exemptions for long service KAR natives', MNA S1/897/21; S1/1709/23; S1/475/26.
32 Memorandum on Defence presented to the East African Governors' Conference, 1926, Evidence to the Hilton-Young Commission, Foreign and Commonwealth Office Library, London.
33 Shenton Thomas, Governor of Nyasaland to Secretary of State for Colonies, 12 September 1931, MNA S1/1709/23.
34 See Cynthia H. Enloe, *Ethnic Soldiers: state security in a divided society* (Harmondsworth, 1980); Mason, *A Matter of Honour*, pp. 341–61.
35 Wordsworth Poole to his mother, 21 August 1895, MNA POL 1/1; Johnston, *First Three Years' Administration*.
36 *Report by Commissioner Sir Harry Johnston on the Trade and General Condition of the British Central African Protectorate*, 1895–1896, Cmd. 8254.
37 'Information for Military Handbook of Nyasaland', 1922, MNA S2/6/27.
38 Report by Inspector-General KAR embodying further details of the Reorganization Scheme, 14 January 1930, MNA S2/11/29.
39 Note by T. S. W. Thomas to Inspector-General KAR, 17 December 1930, MNA S2/11/29.
40 Half Yearly Additions to Nyasaland Intelligence Report, June 1939, MNA KAR 3/3/2.
41 Resident Fort Johnston to Chief Secretary, Zomba, 16 March 1921, MNA S1/850/20. For further information on the evolution of the police force see John McCracken, 'Coercion and control in Nyasaland: aspects of the history of a colonial police force', *Journal of African History*, 27 (1986), pp. 127–48.
42 Note by W. C. Bottomley, 17 December 1912, PRO CO 525/43.
43 Note by Lt. Col. R. W. Baldwin, OC Nyasaland, June 1913, MNA KAR 1/1/1. Minute on G. Smith to Harcourt, 14 August 1914, PRO CO 417/57.

44 See George Shepperson and Thomas Price, *Independent Africa* (Edinburgh, 1958); Ian and Jane Linden, 'John Chilembwe and the "New Jerusalem"', *Journal of African History*, 12 (1971), pp. 629–51.

45 Minute by Hector Duff, 12 May 1919, MNA S1/152/19; Sir George Smith to Secretary of State for Colonies, 24 January 1921, MNA S2/10/20.

46 Sir George Smith to Secretary of State for Colonies, Secret, 18 February 1918, PRO CO 525/78.

47 McCracken, 'Coercion and control', pp. 129–130.

48 'Report of a Committee appointed ... to consider and report upon available means and desirable methods of dealing with riots and civil disturbances, Blantyre, 14 May 1919', contained in Hector Duff, Acting Governor, to Secretary of State for Colonies, Secret, 22 May 1919, PRO CO 537/845.

49 Sir George Smith to Secretary of State for Colonies, 24 January 1921, MNA S2/10/20.

50 W. K. Hancock, *Survey of British Commonwealth Affairs*, vol. 2. *Problems of economic policy 1918–1939* (London, 1942), Part 2, ch. 1.

51 Hancock, *Survey*; C. S. Phillips, Major O. C. troops Nyasaland, 'Memorandum on the Establishment of a European Defence Force for the Nyasaland Protectorate', MNA S2/10/20.

52 Minutes of the Livingstonia Mission Council, 15 July 1921, October 1922, MNA.

53 Minutes of meetings of Cholo Planters Association, March 1921, and of European inhabitants of Fort Johnston, 27 March 1921, MNA S2/10/20 and S1/1379/22.

54 Colonial Office minutes on Smith to Secretary of State for Colonies, 7 November 1922, and Secretary of State to Smith, 28 March 1923, PRO CO 525/102.

55 Half Yearly Intelligence Report for the Nyasaland Protectorate to 31 December 1936, MNA S2/6/27.

56 Governor, T. S. W. Thomas to Secretary of State for Colonies, 8 February 1930, MNA S2/11/29. Report of the Nyasaland census for 1930, MNA S1/1309/30.

57 Memo on Reorganisation of the KAR by O.C. 1 KAR, Zomba, July 1930, MNA S2/11/29. The special attraction of Nyasa troops, apart from their cheapness, was that they could serve wherever they were required, while troops from Tanganyika, under an agreement with the League of Nations, could only serve in their own country.

58 Following the retirement of the Intelligence Officer, Major H. E. Green in 1935, his duties were performed by the Adjutant, 2nd Bn. KAR. 'At present no very efficient system of supplying him with information is in force, and some difficulty is experienced in obtaining anything of interest or value.' Half Yearly Intelligence Report from period ending 30 June 1936, MNA S2/6/27.

59 Reports on KAR patrols, January 1920, MNA S2/8/20. See also Francis De Guingand, *African Assignment* (London, 1953), pp. 60–4.

60 McCracken, 'Coercion and control', pp. 130–1.

61 Landeg White, 'Tribes and the aftermath of the Chilembwe rising', *African Affairs*, 83 (1984), pp. 526–33.

62 Martin Chanock, *Law, Custom and Social Order* (Cambridge, 1985), pp. 145–216.

63 See file entitled 'The development of native economic agriculture', MNA NS 1/2/4.

64 John McCracken, 'Experts and expertise in colonial Malawi', *African Affairs*, 81 (1982), pp. 110–14. For a comprehensive survey see William Beinart, 'Soil erosion, conservationism and ideas about development: a southern African exploration, 1900–1960', *Journal of Southern African Studies*, 11 (1984), pp. 52–83.

65 Terence Ranger, 'The invention of tradition in colonial Africa', in Eric Hobsbawm and Terence Ranger (eds.), *The Invention of Tradition* (Cambridge, 1983), pp. 229–36. See also T. O. Ranger, 'Making Northern Rhodesia imperial: variations on a royal theme, 1924–1938', *African Affairs*, 79 (1980), pp. 349–73.

66 Edward Bote Manda to Mrs P. S. Kirkwood, 7 February 1919, private collection.

67 Lord Passfield to Officer Commanding Nyasaland, 30 April 1930, MNA S1/840/30.

68 Fort Manning District Report for 1933, MNA S1/112 A–E/34. David Killingray, ' "A swift agent of government": air power in British colonial Africa, 1916–1939', *Journal of African History*, 25 (1984), pp. 429–44.

69 Annual Report for the Northern Province, 1935, MNA S1/80/36.
70 Fort Manning District Report for 1933.
71 Annual Report for the Southern Province, 1936, MNA NS 3/1/6. Of course, as Killingray has noted, the fact that some traditional rulers actively participated in rituals of monarchy does not mean that their views were automatically shared by their subjects. Killingray, 'The maintenance of law and order in British colonial Africa', p. 435.
72 Acting Provincial Commissioner, Blantyre to Chief Secretary, 15 December 1936, MNA S1/287/36.
73 Chief Secretary to all PCs and DCs, 12 December 1936, MNA 51/287/36.
74 Beinart, 'Soil erosion, conservationism and ideas about development', p. 75. See also Beinart, 'Agricultural planning and the late colonial technical imagination: the Lower Shire Valley in Malawi, 1940–1960', Centre of African Studies, *Malawi: an alternative pattern of development* (Edinburgh, 1985).
75 P. B. Garnett, Acting Director of Agriculture to Senior Agricultural Officer, Lilongwe, 16 October 1947, MNA NCL 1/30/1.
76 D. W. Saunders-Jones, Provincial Commissioner, Central Province, to DCs and Provincial Agricultural Officers, 13 October 1947, MNA NC 1/30/1.
77 See file on 'Reduction of Nyasaland Police Force and appointment of tribal police', 1943–50, MNA NC 1/29/1.
78 P. L. Brown to C. E. Lambert, Colonial Office, 22 December 1949, PRO CO 537/4413.
79 Quoted in McCracken, 'Coercion and control', p. 138.
80 Provincial Commissioner Central Province to Chief Secretary, 23 August 1950, MNA NC 1/29/1.
81 Report for Agricultural Duty by Agricultural Instructor Hoda, 20 January 1955, MNA 15/1/4F 7325.
82 The best account of these disturbances is contained in Robin Palmer, 'Working conditions and worker responses on Nyasaland tea estates, 1930–1953', *Journal of African History*, 27 (1986), pp. 121–6. See also White, 'Tribes and the aftermath of the Chilembwe rising', and McCracken, 'Coercion and control'.
83 Quoted in Palmer, 'Working conditions', p. 124.
84 Southern Province Annual Report for 1939, MNA NS 3/1/8.
85 Nyasaland Monthly Political Intelligence Report, October 1949 and January 1951, PRO CO 537/4725 and 723.
86 Political Intelligence Report, June 1953, PRO CO 1015/464.
87 Political Intelligence Report, July 1952, PRO CO 1015/464.
88 'Visit of delegation of Nyasa chiefs to the UK', 1952–3, PRO CO 1015/159.
89 Ida Ndovie, 'The origins, growth and decline of the Boy Scout Association of Nyasaland 1946–1952', History Seminar Paper, Chancellor College, University of Malawi, 1981.
90 'Proposals for the unification of the police services of Central Africa, 1952', PRO CO 1015/370; *Annual Report of the Ministry of Defence, Federation of Rhodesia and Nyasaland* (Salisbury, 1954).
91 *Annual Report of the Nyasaland Police* (Blantyre, 1953).
92 *Annual Report of the Nyasaland Police* (Blantyre, 1954). See also memoirs by Malcolm C. P. Llewellyn and John M. le Mesurier, Rhodes House, Oxford, Mss. Afr. S. 1784, pp. 45 and 46.
93 Colonial Office minute, 1 May 1953, PRO CO 1015/243.
94 W. C. Johnson, Inspector General of Colonial Police, to The Governor, Nyasaland, 23 August 1950, PRO CO 537/5427; *Report of the Nyasaland Commission of Inquiry* (HMSO, London, 1959), Cmd. 814, p. 37.
95 *Annual Report of the Nyasaland Police* (Blantyre, 1959), p. 5.
96 *Report of the Nyasaland Commission of Enquiry*, 1959, p. 38.
97 See for example, 'Co-ordination of defence schemes in Central and East Africa', Memo. by Overseas Defence Sub-Committee of the Committee of Imperial Defence, August 1933, MNA KAR 1/1/2; Minutes of a meeting of the Nyasaland Defence Committee, 5 April 1939, S2/17/35.
98 Author's interview with Sir Glyn Jones, 21–2 August 1982. Because many relevant primary sources have not yet been released, no adequate analysis of the impact of the

Nyasaland disturbances on the process of decolonisation in Central Africa has yet been published. There is much useful material, not very well presented, in J. R. T. Wood, *The Welensky Papers: a history of the federation of Rhodesia and Nyasaland* (Durban, 1983). See also Philip Short, *Banda* (London, 1984), pp. 89–154. Less reliable personal accounts are provided by Lord Butler, *The Art of the Possible* (London, 1971), pp. 214–15, and by Harold Macmillan: *Riding the Storm* (London, 1977), pp. 736–8; *Pointing the Way* (London, 1972), pp. 131–50, 164–6.

99 Armitage to Secretary of State for Colonies, 6 June 1960, Zimbabwe National Archives [ZNA], F236 CX27/2. In 1958, the Federal Army consisted of 3,211 African other ranks, 802 European regulars (officers and ORs) and 3,020 territorials, almost all European. *Annual Report of the Ministry of Defence, Federation of Rhodesia and Nyasaland* (Salisbury, 1958).

100 Notes of a meeting held at Government House, Zomba, 14 July 1960, ZNA F236 CX 27/2.

101 Welensky to Macmillan, 3 June 1960; statement by J. M. Caldicott in notes of a meeting held at Government House, Zomba, 14 July 1960, ZNA F236 CX 27/2.

102 Welensky to Macmillan, 21 July 1960, Top Secret, ZNA F236 CX 27/2.

103 Macmillan to Welensky, 1 July 1960, ZNA F236 CX 27/2.

104 Macmillan to Welensky, 1 July 1960, ZNA F236 CX 27/2.

105 M. R. Metcalf to Welensky, 20 July 1960, ZNA F236 CX 27/2.

106 R. F. Holland, *European Decolonization 1918–1981: an introductory survey* (London, 1985), pp. 191, 220–30.

107 *Report of the Nyasaland Commission of Inquiry*, 1959, p. 6; Armitage to Secretary of State for Colonies, 6 June 1960, ZNA F236 CX 27/2.

108 *Report of the Nyasaland Commission of Inquiry*, pp. 90–142; *Annual Report of the Nyasaland Police* (Blantyre, 1959), p. 6; Armitage to Secretary of State for Colonies, 6 June 1960, ZNA F236 CX 27/2.

109 David Arnold, *Police Power and Colonial Rule: Madras 1859–1947* (Delhi, 1986), p. 230.

110 Introduction by H. Kamuzu Banda to C. Marlow, *A History of the Malawi Police Force* (Zomba, 1971).

111 McCracken, 'Coercion and control', pp. 135–7.

112 Memo by W. G. Bithrey enclosed in Bithrey to Chief Secretary, Zomba, 16 May 1939, MNA POL 2/17/3.

113 Author's interview with Mr Brian Burgess, Zomba, 22 January 1983.

114 *Annual Report of the Nyasaland Police* (Blantyre, 1959).

115 Memoirs by M. C. P. Llewelyn and A. R. Lodge, Rhodes House, Oxford, Mss. Afr. S. 1784, pp. 45 and 48.

116 *Report of the Nyasaland Commission of Inquiry*, p. 38.

117 *Report of the Nyasaland Commission of Inquiry*, p. 36.

118 *Report of the Nyasaland Commission of Inquiry*, pp. 37, 74–89.

119 Armitage of Welensky, 29 April 1959, ZNA F236 CX 27/2.

120 *Annual Report of the Nyasaland Police* (Blantyre, 1959).

121 Geoffrey J. Morton, *Just the Job: some experiences of a colonial policeman* (London, 1957), p. 242.

122 *Annual Report of the Nyasaland Police* (Blantyre, 1961), p. 12. Africans were first appointed to the rank of Assistant Inspector in 1956.

CHAPTER NINE

Policing and communal conflict: the Cyprus Emergency, 1954 – 60

David M. Anderson

On 25 January 1955 a Greek caique named the *Aghios Georghios* (St George) slipped quietly into the remote Khlorakas bay on the shore of Paphos, in western Cyprus, under the cover of darkness. The engines of the boat had been adjusted so that, to anyone listening from the shore, it might sound like another of the many small fishing vessels that commonly took shelter in this bay, and others like it, along the coastline. The Greek skipper and his crew had good reason to disguise their intentions: the hold of their vessel contained arms, ammunition and explosives purchased in and shipped from Greece and intended for the establishment of an underground movement in Cyprus, whose aim was to be the overthrow of British rule and the unification of Cyprus with Greece – *Enosis*. But the arrival of the *Aghios Georghios* had been anticipated by the British authorities. The caique was intercepted by the Royal Navy frigate HMS *Comet*, and its Greek crew taken into custody. On the shore a party of Cyprus Police, headed by Assistant Superintendent Alexis Ioannou, effected the arrest of the Greek Cypriot reception committee as they were taking charge of the first part of the disembarked cargo. Among them was Socrates Loizides, a senior aide to Colonel George Grivas (alias Dighenis), the right-wing and staunchly anti-communist Greek leader of the organisation that planned to use the arms shipment, soon to be well known to the British as EOKA (Ethniki Organosis Kyrion Agoniston – The National Organisation of Cypriot Fighters).[1]

Although the State of Emergency was not to be declared in Cyprus until 26 November 1955, the interception of the *Aghios Georghios* and its cargo marked the beginning of the full-scale guerrilla campaign mounted by Greek Cypriots against the British administration. The intensity of that campaign, as it unfolded during 1955, took the colonial administration by surprise. Senior officers in the Cyprus Police had remained largely ignorant of the extent of the clandestine activities of the supporters of *Enosis* until 1954, when British Military Intelligence gathered substantial

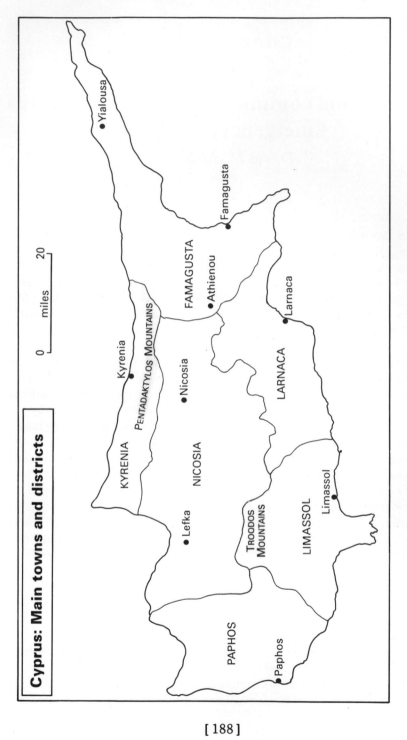

Cyprus: Main towns and districts

evidence regarding arms smuggling from mainland Greece. In November 1954 an earlier shipment of arms and explosives had been jettisoned at sea by the captain of the caique on which it was being carried on realising that his mission was under British surveillance.[2] To the British, the discovery of arms-smuggling to Cyprus posed a threat of greater significance than the smooth administration of a small island colony: with the retreat from Palestine in 1947 and then from the Suez Canal zone in the summer of 1954, Cyprus had become the base for the General Headquarters of Military Intelligence for the Middle East – an intelligence 'listening post' and military garrison of immense strategic and political importance for Britain and the NATO. Moreover, the presence of both Greek and Turkish communities in Cyprus and the historical claims that Greece might make to the island made the issue of Cyprus's future an international question, and one that involved wider British interests than those of the Colonial Office alone.[3]

The Emergency which followed upon the capture of the *Aghios Georghios* has most commonly been viewed through the lens of international affairs, with the strategic considerations of British imperialism and NATO holding centre stage and the story continuing after the independence of Cyprus through the debates in the United Nations, culminating in the Turkish occupation of the island. It is a saga on which emotions run high. Much of the literature on the history of the conflict is polemical, written with self-conscious advocacy.[4] In all of this the colonial nature of the Cyprus emergency of the 1950s tends to be overlooked, or at best given scant attention. Cyprus was a colonial possession within the British Empire, administered through the Colonial Office, and subject to many of the same policy directives, fiscal constraints and administrative peculiarities as other colonies of a similar status. In certain important senses the Cypriot experience was unique, but in others it bore a close relation to a more general colonial experience after 1945. The focus of this chapter is on the policing of the Cyprus Emergency in its colonial context, with the aim of establishing the basis upon which to compare the events on Cyprus during the 1950s more readily with those in other colonies where the British were confronted by an armed guerrilla insurrection, notably Palestine, Malaya and Kenya.[5]

Although the Colonial Office long persisted in the view that the Cyprus Emergency had erupted without warning, the British government were aware from the middle of 1954 (and probably earlier) that they faced a serious problem, with the potential for armed uprising. They were also evidently aware of shortcomings in security. Their mistake was a persistent belief that the only real threat to law and order came from Greece and not from within Cyprus. As a result they had little appreciation of how acute the failings of internal security were or how serious the armed insurrection would be: the potential threat was understood, but its form misconceived and its scale seriously underestimated.

Policing and politics to 1954

The close relationship between the economic poverty of Cyprus and the agitation among Greek Cypriots to be rid of British rule was of long standing. Most Greek Cypriots felt themselves to be worse off under the British government than they had been under the rule of Turkey in the nineteenth century. Early resentment against the British derived most directly from the annual payments of 'tribute' to Turkey – a sum amounting to more than £90,000, raised by additional taxation – which were not abolished until 1927. The bitter legacy of this oppressive tax was still deeply felt in the island when the cold winds of the 1930s Depression prompted Governor Storrs to present a series of stringent economy measures before the Legislative Council: viewing this as yet another example of colonial exploitation, Greek Cypriot members of the island's Legislative Council resigned their seats *en masse* in October 1931, sparking two days of rioting in Nicosia during which Government House was razed to the ground.[6] The extent of the rising and its violence shocked the British into sharp reaction: the Legislative Council was abolished, martial law declared, and the Bishop of Kition and nine other church leaders were deported for their involvement in 'inciting' the rebellion.[7]

The overt role of the clergy in these events led the government to lay the blame for the uprising squarely on the shoulders of the bishops, who articulated economic grievances whilst tying these complaints to demands for political reform and especially union with Greece (*Enosis*).[8] *Enosis* had been a political rallying-cry of Greek Cypriots throughout the years of British administration, usually associated with church leaders. In a rather heavy-handed and dangerously interventionist measure, the government tried to restrict the involvement of church leaders in politics through legislation, imposed in 1937, which allowed them to disqualify troublesome clergy from office. This ill-considered and unpopular measure was repealed by 1946, but the damage inflicted upon relations between church and state on the island in the wake of the 1931 troubles was never to be repaired during the British administration. This reduced the scope for 'legitimate protest' and seriously deepened the rift between the Greek Cypriot clergy, who were the effective leaders of Greek political opinion on the island, and the British administration: Britain was not ignorant of local opinion after 1931, merely 'disinclined to heed it', especially with regard to any call for *Enosis*, which they viewed as emanating from the politics of Greece rather than from any true desire on the part of the majority of the Greek Cypriot population.[9] In many important senses the British response to the events of 1931 set the tone for political discourse between the British and the Greek Cypriot community that was to culminate in the EOKA campaign of the 1950s.

The 1931 'rebellion' led directly to the first attempt to modernise and reform policing on the island. At the time of the British occupation in 1878 the island had been policed by a force of some 275 men recruited entirely from amongst the Turkish community. The 'Turkish Police', as this force was known, had dealt with tax collection and revenue matters rather than crime. In 1880 the British established a new police with wider powers, appropriately named the Cyprus Military Police, with eight British officers and over 700 other ranks drawn from all sections of the community. This force was a *gendarmerie* of mounted and dismounted infantry, trained to some extent in police duties but with a strongly military character. The scope of the training and duties of this force remained largely unchanged from 1880 until after the riots of 1931. In 1935 the police force was reorganised: with a change of title to the Cyprus Police Force, the army officers who had previously filled the senior ranks were replaced by trained police officers recruited from other colonies, and the force took on the pattern closer to the model of civilian policing by then becoming familiar in other colonial forces in Africa and Asia.[10] With this 'modernisation' achieved, the Cyprus government made no further attempt to improve policing methods until 1954.[11]

The Cyprus Police were inadequately trained, equipped or staffed to cope with the political difficulties that began to come to the fore in Cyprus during the later 1940s. Political demands from the Greek Cypriot community for *Enosis* intensified after 1945. Among the catalysts of this campaign were undoubtedly factors lying beyond the shores of Cyprus – the politics of the government of Greece, the influence of the new international order taking shape in the wake of the Second World War, and the example of emergent nationalisms in other parts of the colonial world; but socio-economic and political developments specific to the island had a more direct impact. There was a dramatic rise in urbanisation on Cyprus between 1940 and 1947, allied to increases in the cost of living. Between 1939 and 1951, prices of basic foodstuffs increased four-fold, leaving wage rises far behind.[12] In the towns these pressures were felt most acutely, and the politics of the left took a hold, with the Communist Party of Cyprus, AKEL, winning control of virtually every major town during the 1940s (except Kyrenia). This threatened the dominant and previously unchallenged conservative and right-wing political position of the Orthodox Church. In response to the left, which sought to build support across the communal divide, the church could be nothing other than communal in its appeal. The challenge from the left thus forced

[191]

the church into an increasingly militant role on the *Enosis* issue in order to regain political control, and in the process contributed to the emergence of a communal polarity in Cypriot politics.[13]

The leading bishops, and most importantly after 1950 Archbishop Makarios III, readily emerged as leaders of the *Enosis* movement. The British were inclined to dismiss Makarios and his churchmen as the puppets of Greece, but this was to disregard the very real demands for political representation being expressed through *Enosis*. The British also rested on the complacent belief that church leaders would never sanction a violent campaign against government, whatever the issue: this was to misjudge Makarios and the politics of the island. The expectation of some form of constitutional reform in the wake of the Second World War undoubtedly fuelled the popularity of the *Enosis* campaign, as did the contest between left and right in local politics.[14]

When political reforms were offered, the proposals had more to do with Britain's awareness of the rapidly evolving strategic position in the Middle East and Eastern Mediterranean than with any genuine desire to advance Cyprus towards a process of self-determination. From the British point of view, Cyprus became too important after 1945 to let go. No concessions were made on the issues of *Enosis* or immediate self-government in the detailed proposals for a new constitution unveiled by the British in May 1948, which would have allowed communal rolls for elections to the Legislative Council. Such proposals were already being outpaced by the politics of *Enosis*.[15] Moreover, the proposals of May 1948 were thrown upon the fire of AKEL–Greek church rivalry. Between July and December 1948 violence erupted in several clashes between left- and right-wing political groups on the island. This was a presage of what was to come: over six months, twenty-nine incidents involving the use of dynamite were reported, along with seventy-four cases of assault that were thought to be linked to political quarrels.[16] After these events, the church increasingly vocalised its support for *Enosis* as a means of staving off pressures from AKEL, and in this it was largely successful in politicising its own position and bolstering the right. In the elections of 1949 right-wing candidates took 60 per cent of the vote, although AKEL still retained control over Limassol, Famagusta and Larnaca.[17] The balance of power on the island had swung back to the church and its communally-based politics: *Enosis* was now the only aim that could satisfy the majority of Greek Cypriots, whether politically radical or conservative. After 1950 the politics of left and right gave way to the politics of communalism: AKEL became closely associated with the Turkish community and declared its opposition to *Enosis*, whilst the involvement of the Orthodox Church in the *Enosis* movement unified the Greek Cypriot communities.

British attitudes hardened in the early 1950s with the shifting geo-politics of their position in the Eastern Mediterranean. The retreat from the Canal Zone in 1954 was crucial here, leaving Cyprus as Britain's final base in the region and prompting Conservative MPs to press their government for assurances that there would be no similar retreat from Cyprus. The key statement on the future of Cyprus was made in the House of Commons on 29 July 1954 by Henry Hopkinson (Minister of State for the Colonies), who assured his anxious back-benchers that the British position in Cyprus was secure: self-determination for Cyprus was an issue that Britain would 'never' concede, asserted Hopkinson.[18] With this declaration the rug was pulled from under the Greek Cypriot moderates, and the likelihood of violence increased as the militants took the initiative and church leaders were propelled towards condoning an armed struggle for *Enosis*.[19] By the close of 1954 Archbishop Makarios, now convinced that Britain could only be made to negotiate reforms under threat of civil disorder, had committed his church to the support of an armed struggle in Cyprus.[20]

Despite the emergence of a sharper and more confrontational form of politics on the island after 1945, the government was slow to respond to the new challenges this created for the maintenance of law and order. The Commissioners sent to report on the Cyprus Police in 1956, in the midst of the Emergency, lamented the lack of progress that had been made in policing the island from the mid-1930s, and were severely critical of the shortsightedness of the administration in failing properly to monitor the changing political situation. The long-serving Commissioner of Police, Ashmore, was singled out for his failure to highlight the need to modernise the police force.[21] All of this was echoed by Commissioner Robbins on his arrival from Tanganyika to take command of the Cyprus Police in November 1954. The force then comprised a staff of 1,386, of whom 37 per cent were Turkish Cypriots.[22] The general quality of local recruits was low, a factor attributed to the low prestige of the force and especially the poor levels of pay. A police constable earned a wage of only £21 per month, whilst an unskilled labourer might expect to earn £26 or more. There was therefore little incentive for men with better educational qualifications to offer themselves for police service. Poor conditions of service similarly affected the quality of officers recruited on transfer from other colonial police forces, with the result that the standard of leadership among senior officers was not high.[23] Reporting on the Cyprus Police in 1950, the Colonial Office Police Adviser, W. C. Johnson, had opined that the Police Department had been treated as the cinderella service in a cinderella colony: expenditure on the force was minimal, efficiency was in decline and morale was low.[24]

In the period preceding the Emergency of 1955 the police were therefore in no position to respond to the development of underground political activity. The British persisted in the belief that the real threat came from *Enosis* sympathisers in Greece, and that if the supply of arms and personnel from outside the island could be staunched then there would be no prospect of a rising led and organised by the Greek Cypriots themselves. In this the British misjudged the depth of Greek Cypriot feelings and overestimated their own success in sealing off the island.[25] With the advantage of hindsight, the Police Commissioners' Report of 1956 reflected that 'a vicious circle developed in that the government neglected the police force because there was no evidence of unrest in the island, and the force failed to get any inkling of unrest because the government neglected it'.[26]

The crisis of 1955

The complacency of both the Cyprus administration and the Colonial Office was glaringly apparent. 'We can assume,' minuted a Colonial official at the end of January 1955, '... that Sir Robert Armitage [the Governor] is satisfied that the police and military available in the island are sufficient to quell any riots on a scale that can at present be considered even remotely possible. He would, I am sure, let us know at once if he had any doubt on that score.'[27] This confidence was grossly misplaced. The Cyprus Police were simply overwhelmed in the months between April and November 1955.

In the early hours of 1 April the terrorist campaign of EOKA began in earnest.[28] Among the first targets was the transmitter of the Cyprus Broadcasting Station, blown up by well-placed bombs after the watchmen had been overpowered by four EOKA members; all over the island the pattern of attacks on army and navy bases, administrative posts and especially police stations quickly became apparent. Bombs thrown at the Secretariat building and at Wolseley Barracks hit their targets, and although they did rather less damage than the assailants may have hoped for, the success demonstrated the vulnerability of important colonial buildings. The attacks caught the British administration unawares: most installations were unguarded. What immediate successes the police had were due to a mixture of their own good fortune and the incompetence of the inexperienced and poorly-trained terrorists. A car loaded with EOKA leaflets and containing explosives was apprehended by police in Famagusta and traced to Afxentiou, EOKA commander in that town and second-in-command to Grivas himself. The raid on his home revealed a Greek Army handbook on sabotage and other documents linking him to EOKA and to 'Dighenis'. Afxentiou was fortunate to escape.[29] Several other group leaders had been arrested shortly after the attacks: in Larnaca

[194]

the EOKA group had damaged the court house and police station with bombs, but all the perpetrators had been arrested by daybreak; while in Limassol two police stations and a power plant had been bombed but an EOKA group had been caught. Moreover, due to the carelessness of the terrorists, the police had stumbled across the entire arsenal of the Limassol EOKA section.[30] These enthusiastic, if amateurish, attacks continued until 10 April, with bombs thrown at the homes of British military personnel and even an attempt on the life of Governor Armitage.

The next burst of violence came in June and marked the beginnings of EOKA's concentrated compaign against the police force. On 10 June bombs exploded at the Commissioner's Office in Larnaca, and at the Income Tax Office in Nicosia. Police stations in Nicosia and Kyrenia were attacked on 19 June, and on 21 June a bomb exploded outside Nicosia Central Police Station, killing a Greek bystander and injuring thirteen Turks. The following day Renos Kyriakides led an EOKA attack on Amiandos Police Station, killing a police sergeant and wounding a constable. The raiders stole three rifles and ammunition.[31] Makarios's earlier somewhat naive insistence that every effort should be made by EOKA to avoid loss of life was now of little significance: with violence directed against the police, the Archbishop gave up the centre stage to Grivas.[32]

The disruption of policing was obviously a shrewd and necessary political tactic on the part of EOKA aimed primarily at drawing the army into the conflict and thereby 'militarising' the struggle, but it was also apparent that isolated police posts offered opportunities to acquire much-needed arms with which to carry the struggle forward.[33] The attacks had a very profound effect upon the morale and efficiency of the Cyprus Police. At the time of the April bombings EOKA warnings were sent to many Greek Cypriot policemen, threatening them with execution should they do anything to interfere with the terror campaign. From the very beginnings of the insurgency the police were exposed to pressure and influence. It was clear that some policemen were providing EOKA with information and probably helping to target their colleagues for intimidation and attack. During the early months of 1955 Grivas had instructed Polycarpos Georgadjis, a clerk at the government Chamber of Commerce, to organise the EOKA intelligence team in Nicosia, charging him specifically with recruiting Cypriots from the police and administration who would provide EOKA with information. The network of police informers was kept relatively small – numbering twenty by June 1955 – but they were carefully scattered throughout every department of the force. Many other policemen assisted EOKA agents to escape detection, and some even sheltered them in their own homes.[34]

By the summer of 1955 Commissioner of Police Robbins was admitting the success of EOKA in their infiltration of the force and in their campaign of intimidation against the police: with police connivance at EOKA activities becoming more apparent and with Greek Cypriots beginning to resign from the force, the effectiveness of the EOKA campaign was difficult to disguise.[35] It was the matter of police pay which brought the crisis to a head. Compelled to work longer hours, yet without bonus payments, and with levels of pay falling rapidly behind the ever-increasing cost of living, police dissatisfaction was channelled into economic grievances. In June, and again in July, many Greek Cypriot policemen refused to draw their pay on the grounds that it was 'inadequate'. This protest became more concrete in August, when 'a large number' of Greek Cypriot police tendered their resignations. Already short-staffed, and with recruitment tailing away, Robbins refused to accept the resignations and threatened his men with disciplinary action on 'charges of disobedience to the force' should they refuse to draw their pay again. Seven officers were placed on disciplinary charges and five others were suspended from the force in August as a result of the protests over pay, but Robbins' intimidatory tactics succeeded in preventing mass resignations.[36] Robbins had retained his Greek Cypriot men within the force, and the pay increases announced during June went some way toward improving their morale: his problem remained how to make efficient and reliable policemen in a situation where to carry out their duties properly would almost certainly have been to risk assassination.

EOKA attempts to 'terrorise' the police into inaction also became a matter of open public debate in Cyprus during August, after the murder of Michael Zavros, a 21-year-old Greek Cypriot Special Constable. A letter written by the brother of the murdered constable, condemning EOKA and accusing them of spreading terror among the police, was carried on the front page of *The Times of Cyprus*, the English-language newspaper. *Enosis* was a widely supported aim, but the tactics of EOKA were not admired by all Greek Cypriots. As in other anti-colonial insurgency movements, fear of reprisals conditioned silent acquiescence more often than active support.[37] The British valued the favourable propaganda of a Greek Cypriot publicly criticising EOKA, but this had no impact upon EOKA tactics. Other murders of policemen soon followed, most notably the shooting of Special Branch officer Herodotus Poullis, murdered in front of several hundred 'witnesses' at a political rally, none of whom 'saw' anything. The police had been singled out by EOKA as primary targets, and without public support there was no prospect of offering them effective protection.[38]

Street disturbances, mostly involving schoolchildren, presented the police with yet another serious difficulty in their dealings with the public. The vulnerability of the police when confronted by such disturbances had been graphically exposed in December 1954, when a demonstration in reaction to the decision of the United Nations to postpone discussion of the Cyprus question required the army to be sent to assist the police in Nicosia after a crowd of 2,000 (mostly young) protesters overwhelmed a contingent of twenty constables.[39] An instruction to recruit and encourage 'demonstrators' was subsequently issued by Grivas in May. This type of protest was seen as an easy way of tying down the police and exposing them to criticism for their actions against 'mere schoolchildren'.[40] It proved an effective tactic. In the early days of July serious rioting erupted in Nicosia, rumbling on periodically throughout the year but becoming ever more pervasive and serious after the failure of the London talks on Cyprus in September.[41]

Faced with a rapidly deteriorating situation, with the police now unreliable in any incident of civil disorder, and with the political negotiations ended in deadlock, the British swiftly moved into a much harsher phase in their reactions to EOKA. On 7 September the police joined the army in Nicosia in their first joint cordon-and-search operation, and one week later EOKA was declared an unlawful organisation. Curfews were enforced and collective punishments imposed.[42] On 20 September the creation of the Police Mobile Reserve was announced, a force that was intended for use in the dispersal of urban demonstrations and which would comprise only Turkish recruits: here was the direct response to EOKA's intimidation of Greek Cypriot police.[43]

At the end of the month the 'softly, softly' approach of Governor Armitage gave way to a new and sterner regime headed by Field-Marshal Sir John Harding, a man already experienced in colonial counter-insurgency campaigning and a military governor appointed for what was now recognised as a military job. His intentions were quickly apparent. To cope with the number and scale of instances of disturbance, the army were already regularly being called in to assist the police, and by mid-October Governor Harding informed the Colonial Office that he wished formally to enlist the army in the aid of the civil power:

> I have had to give definite orders that troops will carry out police duties by providing patrols, riot squads and other appropriate assistance. In doing so they will use police methods, e.g. baton charges and other non-lethal methods of dispersing crowds and maintaining order. The troops are being equipped and trained accordingly. I would like to announce what is being done in this respect as it is becoming obvious.[44]

The Colonial Office granted powers to the Governor to deploy the military in civilian policing roles without the enactment of a specific bill. On 28 October 1955 a Royal Instruction was issued from the office of

H

the Governor giving soldiers the same legal status as the police. The British could no longer rely on the Cyprus Police to keep order: EOKA had succeeded in undermining the basis of civilian government and in pushing the British into an overtly military response. On 26 November 1955 the State of Emergency was declared.[45]

Policing the Emergency

Harding identified the reform of the police as the first priority in the campaign to defeat EOKA.[46] This judgement was informed by a frank report furnished by Robbins on 3 October 1955, much of which amplified the welter of reports and opinions that had emanated from the politicians, senior police officers and counter-insurgency experts who visited Cyprus during 1955.[47] With Palestine, Malaya and Kenya still fresh in the collective memory, the British did not lack for senior officers with relevant experience: by 1955 clearer policies for dealing with colonial guerrilla insurgencies of this type were beginning to emerge.[48] General Templer was the first 'expert' visitor, arriving only two weeks after the beginning of the April bombing campaign. He examined the entire security system, and made recommendations on the structures of command, account-ability and the relationships of the various arms of government: he was particularly struck by the plight of the Cyprus Police, and advocated a thorough overhaul of the force.[49] He was followed a month later by Stourton, the Colonial Office Police Adviser, who made an assessment of the policing position to estimate the likely needs of an expanded force to deal with the Emergency. In July the Secretary of State for the Colonies, Alan Lennox-Boyd, visited the island and met with all the heads of the security services. In October came the logistics expert, Col. D. V. Henchley, who advised on the supply position of the police. Finally, on 9 December came the Inspector General of Colonial Police, W. R. Muller, to review the dramatic changes in policing that had by then already been forced upon the British administration, and to consult with Harding on his future plans for the police.[50]

The full extent of the reforms required in the Cyprus Police were elaborated in the report of the Cyprus Police Commission, produced in the Spring of 1956, after the visit to the island by the three Commissioners in March.[51] The difficulties confronting the police fell into two broad categories. Firstly, conditions of service were so poor as to discourage suitably qualified recruits and to depress general standards. This was a matter which the Commissioners felt could be restored with additional resources, better training and especially improvements in pay. Such items dominated the thirty recommendations of their report. Secondly, there was the more abstract question of the relationship of the police with the local population: how could the police win the trust, and ultimately the consent and support, of Cypriots? In the light of the *Enosis* campaign, this was perhaps a naive question: Cyprus was in revolt *because* it was ruled by Britain, not because of the *way* it was ruled by Britain. Nonetheless, the Police Commissioners asserted the importance of establishing a police force which would function with the consent of the community, and offered the English County Constabulary as the most appropriate model.[52] Given that each of the Commissioners was the head of a County force – Lt. Col. G. C. White and Sir Henry Studdy were Chief Constables of Warwickshire and West Riding respectively, whilst F. J. Armstrong was the Home Office Inspector of Constabulary and a former Chief Constable of Northumberland – this may show nothing more than a lack of imagination. Yet it was plain that without the co-operation of the population, the Cyprus Police simply could not perform their duties.

The police had wide powers under the Emergency regulations of 1955, but very poor relations with the local people. In the years before the Emergency the police had not enjoyed the respect of large portions of the island community. Vendettas were common in the rural areas, and local opinion held that these were private matters into which the authorities should not probe. Even in murder cases the police frequently had difficulty in obtaining information. Commissioner of Police Ashmore reported in 1950 that 'witnesses have withheld vital information and guilty parties have left no stone unturned to bribe, threaten and intimidate potential witnesses'. In 'certain notorious areas', he continued, 'a situation approaching anarchy prevails'.[53] Armed, paramilitary style, in response to the terrorist threat, the police became even further alienated from the public in 1955 and came to be 'bitterly disliked'.[54] Without a measure of public support the police could not win in the struggle to restore law and order: at the same time it was clear that the British could not allow the police to lose. Without a definite programme for the creation of consensual policing, argued the Police Commissioners, there was a danger that policing methods would become dependent upon coercion, with a detrimental effect upon the longer-term pattern of civil authority on the island.[55]

But it was not easy to reconcile the immediate needs of the Emergency with the longer-term ideals of consensual policing. To defeat EOKA the expansion of the police was the only action possible. This implied much greater degrees of policing, surveillance and control and would inevitably be very expensive. Harding quickly recognised that this could be nothing more than a holding operation while the government sought a political solution.[56] The model of the County Constabulary was therefore a distant goal rather than a practical policy during the Emergency, but it did have implications for the way in which the Emergency was policed.

By the time that Colonel G. C. White (fresh from duty on the Cyprus Police Commission) replaced Robbins as Commissioner of the Cyprus Police in June 1956,[57] the pattern of policing for the Emergency had already taken shape. This had three main elements. Firstly, unable to rely upon Greek Cypriot police the British were compelled to place greater trust in Turkish recruits: this was recognised in the deliberate recruitment of Auxiliary and Mobile Reserve Police from among the Turkish community. Secondly, the British needed a reliable and efficient body of police to carry out critical operations and to serve as an example to Cypriot recruits: this was to be achieved by the creation of a unit of police seconded from Britain. Thirdly, effective policing in the Emergency depended upon good intelligence, an area in which the Cyprus Police were woefully deficient: strenuous efforts were made to improve police intelligence, surveillance techniques and police record-keeping. Each of these three aspects of the policing of the Emergency must be examined in detail.

Communal politics and policing

In policing the Emergency the ethnic balance of the security forces became a crucial issue, in political as well as practical terms. The combination of the EOKA campaign directed against Greek Cypriots in the police and the need to expand rapidly the police services to cope with the Emergency had a dramatic effect upon recruitment. By 1958 the size of the Cyprus Police Force had increased to 3,014 men, from a pre-emergency (1954) figure of 1,397 (see Table 9.1). This increase was

Table 9.1:   Police numbers, Cyprus, 1954–9

	1954	1955	1956	1957	1958	1959
Cyprus Police*	1,397	1,838	2,417	2,692	3,014	2,278
Greeks	62·0%	54·6%	28·8%	30·0%	30·5%	49·0%
Turks	37·0%	39·9%	46·9%	51·0%	47·4%	36·5%
Expatriates	0·5%	4·5%	23·0%	18·0%	21·0%	12·5%
Auxiliary Police	–	1,084	1,417	1,362	1,594	+
Mobile Reserve	–	165	569	580	523	+
Special Constables	154	750	1,475	560	304	+
Totals	1,551	3,837	5,878	5,194	5,435	2,278

* These figures include the UK Police Unit. For a brief period in 1958 this force included 53 women police constables, seconded from the UK.

+ The Auxiliary Police, Mobile Reserve Police and Special Constable Forces were disbanded and allowed to run down during 1959.

Sources: Cyprus Police Annual Reports, 1954–1959

achieved by the secondment of over 600 British and colonial police officers and by the recruitment of more than 900 Turkish Cypriots. Over the same period the actual numbers of Greek Cypriots in the force only increased by fifty-three. By 1958 Turkish Cypriots in the Cyprus Police therefore outnumbered Greek Cypriots by a ratio of 5 to 3 and only 30 per cent of the force were Greek Cypriots, as compared with 62 per cent in 1954.[58]

The British were entirely dependent upon the support of the Turkish community to police the island from the summer of 1955. Even prior to 1955 the ethnic balance in the Cyprus Police had not accurately reflected that of the island as a whole. Although in 1954 less than 20 per cent of the Cypriot population were Turkish, 37 per cent of the Cyprus Police were drawn from the Turkish community.[59] This partly reflected a historic pattern of recruitment, but was more immediately the result of the poor pay and low prestige of the police. A career in the police was relatively less attractive to Greek Cypriots, who were generally more prosperous and enjoyed better access to education than did Turkish Cypriots, and who often had a wider range of employment opportunities. By 1958 the Cyprus Police were boldly proclaiming their desire to give preference to Greek applicants 'in an attempt to rectify the racial balance'. All the same, Turkish recruits were undoubtedly felt to be more trustworthy and reliable, even though they were often less well qualified. In these circumstances it proved impossible for the British to maintain any notion of an ethnic balance within the force, or to maintain previous standards of recruitment.[60]

The problem of the quality of local recruits was partly tackled through the creation of separate branches of police to take on the more mundane and less skilled policing duties. To some extent this was achieved by the expansion of the numbers of Special Constables. The Special Constables had been established for duty in the major towns in 1953, all members being provided with a short course of basic training. Their numbers increased from 154 in 1954 to 1,475 in 1956. The majority of the new recruits were Turkish, but the force as a whole was drawn from all communities. During the Emergency the Special Constables were divided into two units, the Ordinary Specials and the Emergency Specials. The latter comprised mainly Cypriot government officials and expatriate volunteers and were assigned beat duties in the urban areas in the hope of reducing the incidence of crime rather than having any direct involvement in the anti-terrorist campaign.[61] Experienced Special Constables were commonly encouraged to join the Cyprus Police, and between 1955 and 1958 more than 300 recruits were secured from their ranks.[62]

The Auxiliary Police, created in August 1955, and the Mobile Reserve Unit established one month later, each had a more significant anti-terrorist role. The principal function of the Auxiliary Police was to guard government buildings and take on escort duties, relieving the Cyprus Police of the many routine labours that Grivas had hoped the EOKA campaign would tie them to.[63] Virtually all the recruits were Turkish Cypriots, many being farmers who worked as Auxiliary Police only during the slack part of their agricultural year.[64] They received no formal training and their quality was widely acknowledged to be very poor. Though considered essential during the Emergency, the Police Commissioners urged that the force be disbanded at the earliest opportunity once civil order was restored.[65] The Mobile Reserve Unit was a more professional body. Consisting entirely of Turkish recruits, but officered by Colonial Police with experience of disturbances in Palestine, Kenya and Malaya,[66] it was initially formed to reduce the role of the army in policing urban disorder. Recruits were given specific training in riot control and the unit was extensively used during the urban riots of late 1955 and 1956. During 1956 the Mobile Reserve was greatly expanded, with two further units being recruited, these being used for cordon-and-search operations in Greek Cypriot villages, an activity that was entirely satisfactory from the security point of view but which engendered much resentment among Greek Cypriot villagers.[67]

Taking all forces into consideration, the policing services consisted of 5,878 men by 1956, of whom more than 70 per cent were Turkish and fewer than 15 per cent were Greek. It has been argued that the recruitment of Turkish Cypriots represented a deliberate policy by the British to place them in the front line of the EOKA attack,[68] but it is difficult to see what alternatives were open to Harding. However, the British were well aware of the vulnerability of Greek Cypriot police to the intimidation of EOKA, and following the capture of Grivas's diaries and other EOKA documents in 1956 they knew of the explicit instructions issued by Grivas to avoid inflicting casualties upon Turkish members of the security forces: Grivas feared the damage that might be done to the aims of EOKA if the terrorist campaign were to be perceived as an inter-communal struggle. The targets of EOKA were accordingly Greek Cypriot 'traitors' and British members of the security forces.[69] The recruiting of Turkish policemen may therefore have been only a pragmatic response on the part of the British, but it brought very tangible political benefits. The casualty figures for the years 1955 to 1958 reveal that EOKA failed to restrict its targets as effectively as might have been wished. Of a total of 49 police killed by EOKA, 15 were Greek, 12 British and 22 Turkish; of those police wounded, 43 were Greek, 34 were British and 108 Turkish.[70]

The deaths of Turkish policemen were commonly followed by demonstrations or retaliations against the Greek Cypriot community. From

1955 an underground Turkish political organisation, initially known as Volkan but later as TMT, had threatened reprisals against Greek Cypriots should Turks be killed by EOKA terrorism. Ali Riza was the first Turkish policeman to be killed, murdered in Paphos on 11 January 1956. His death was followed by widespread attacks on Greek Cypriot properties. Riots in Nicosia in April 1956 followed the murder of Constable Nihiat Vassif, and in May the murder of Irfan Ali led to further rioting in which one Greek Cypriot was killed and eighteen others injured. In the next month the funeral party of a murdered Turkish Special Constable rioted, attacking Greek property.[71]

From at least the summer of 1956 the activities of Volkan/TMT members were well known to the British authorities, yet the organisation was not formally banned until July 1958, as the worst communal riots spread through the island, when Governor Foot ordered the arrest of fifty of its members (to coincide with the round-up of a much larger number of EOKA suspects). Even on this occasion, Foot's vacillation over the wisdom of acting against the Turkish organisation is apparent from his anxious correspondence with the Colonial Office.[72] It is difficult to dismiss the view that the British consciously permitted TMT to operate as a counter-foil to EOKA. Such a strategy may have been viewed as a means of affording some protection to members of the police, whilst also deflecting the energies of EOKA: by the latter months of 1957 EOKA was having to expend resources in defending Greek Cypriot villages from the threat of TMT attack.[73]

Not all communal disturbances were directly linked to attacks on Turkish police. The first serious communal riots broke out in March 1956 amid the escalation of EOKA activities following the deportation of Makarios, when clashes in the village of Vasilia led to an attack on the Greek area of Nicosia by more than 500 Turks.[74] More widespread clashes occurred in December 1956 and again in January and February 1957. The worst and most sustained outbreak of all occurred between June and August 1958. Over four weeks of almost daily disturbances between 7 June and 15 July, 524 Greek Cypriots and 164 Turkish Cypriots were arrested, and during the entire three months of inter-communal fighting 107 civilians were killed, 56 Greek Cypriot and 51 Turkish Cypriot. These events starkly revealed the full extent of the British dependence upon Turkish police, who proved to be unreliable in the policing of the Turkish community. The Turkish Mobile Reserve were withdrawn from the worst trouble spots, and the British were compelled to bring in more troops. To cope with the investigation of crimes committed during the disturbances, the CID had to be augmented by twenty-six British detective officers brought in on a short-term basis: neither Turkish nor Greek Cypriot police could be trusted to effect prosecutions.[75]

A flurry of accusation and counter-accusation invariably swirled around in the aftermath of such incidents. Greek Cypriots complained that Turkish police 'stood by' while Turkish rioters ransacked Greek properties and assaulted Greek Cypriots, claims which tended to be supported by newspaper reports.[76] Turkish leaders, in return, accused Greek Cypriots of incitement and provocation. The British authorities were disinclined to accept any criticism of the police, promoting the view that accusations were part of a well-orchestrated EOKA campaign to discredit the security services.[77] There was undoubtedly some truth in this, but officials who felt that it was important to support publicly the actions of the police were more inclined to admit their doubts in private. When members of the Auxiliary Police were accused of thefts during house searches in Famagusta, the District Commissioner observed of these and similar allegations that 'many recruits come from the lowest stratum of Cypriot Turkish society and are known not to have been beyond criminal activities in the past ... I myself have little doubt that there is substance in a fair proportion of them.'[78]

The Auxiliary and Mobile Reserve Police provided essential manpower for the maintenance of civil government, but they were as much a symptom of as a solution to the problems confronting the British in their effort to police the island. At the outset of the Emergency 'The police were led by outsiders,' writes Clark, 'who expected the local policemen to choose loyalty to the force before the demands of his community.'[79] The reality in Cyprus was that such loyalties were divided: the British therefore gradually came to the conclusion that they could not afford to trust Greek or Turkish policemen with any anti-terrorist activities nor in the policing of communal disturbances. In August 1955 ten colonial policemen with experience of anti-terrorism in Palestine came in to 'stiffen the ranks' of the police, and were put in charge of the Mobile Reserve. Further Colonial Police with experience from Kenya, Palestine and Malaya were transferred to Cyprus during the Emergency, but the numbers of men available on such transfers was limited.[80] Harding wished to minimise the use of troops for political as well as economic reasons:[81] within a few days of his arrival in Cyprus the new Governor had decided that it would be necessary to bring in police from the UK.

The UK Police Unit

A formal request was made to the Colonial Office during October for a special force of 150 British police. The UK Police Unit would be 'a self-contained contingent', ideally suited to a mobile role and able to be deployed for 'special operations'.[82] The force Harding wanted to establish was to be a 'model' to Cypriot policemen, setting an example of discipline and efficiency which the Cyprus Police would observe, learn from and (he hoped) seek to emulate. With no direct experience of policing, Harding's notion of the qualities of the 'British bobby' was somewhat idealised, but his concern was more to improve the morale and attitude of the local police than to impose any particular methods of operations.[83] In their private debriefings to the Colonial Office on their return from Cyprus in March 1956, the Police Commissioners echoed this need: 'the Cyprus rank and file, and particularly the Greeks among them, are at present suffering seriously in morale, not only from political circumstances and bad conditions of service, but also from unimaginative leadership and poor example.' The UK Police Unit would, it was hoped, help to solve these problems.[84]

Despite a general shortage of manpower in England and Wales, the Home Office agreed to co-operate in recruiting men from the Metropolitan Police and a specified group of County Constabularies – Lancashire, West Riding, Staffordshire and Kent – as well as all the Scottish forces.[85] Harding and Robbins placed much faith in the supposed superior quality of the individual recruits. The unmarried policeman, with several years' experience and a good disciplinary record, was the most desired type, but men in this position did not readily come forward. Most volunteers for the first UK Police Unit were older men, many of them close to retirement, who viewed the enhanced pension provisions offered in the terms of service as a significant 'pep' at the end of their often undistinguished careers. Robbins accepted such men as the best he could get.[86]

Despite the difficulties in securing UK police suitable for service in Cyprus, the Police Commission Report of 1956 recommended that the unit be enlarged with the recruitment of a further 100 men for a two-year period of service. The Commissioners wanted this unit to be specifically deployed in Nicosia and other larger towns: 'This force would be invaluable in re-establishing the principle that the police are primarily responsible for law and order and in relieving the military of their present commitments in aid of the civil power.'[87] Senior police officers and army commanders alike shared an abhorrence for the blurring of distinctions between policing and military roles, but this was a powerful argument aimed at the Treasury as much as it was an expression of the desire of the police to distance themselves from the military. Policemen recruited from the UK were considerably more expensive than local recruits, but considerably cheaper than soldiers. Moreover, by the summer of 1956 the Colonial Office had given up any pretence that the Emergency would be swiftly dealt with. To persuade the Treasury of the severity of the situation, the Colonial officials painted a grim scenario: 'we cannot ignore the possibility (though we hope that the presence of

UK police will itself help to prevent it) that a time may come when only the UK and Turkish Cypriot police are really reliable.'[88] In truth, that time had already come, several months previously, during August 1955.

The first contingent of the UK Police Unit took up duties in Nicosia on 10 January 1956. The contradictions in seeking to combine the function of a 'hit squad', to be used against EOKA in the towns, and a 'model force', setting an example of disciplined modern policing, quickly became evident. Following precedents set in Malaya, it had been agreed that the force would be created as a special unit with its own terms of service, and not be integrated within the main body of the Cyprus Police. This reduced the direct influence the UK policemen might have on their Cypriot colleagues, and tended to isolate the unit from the community: in many senses, it became just like another military-style regiment. Though undoubtedly reliable and efficient, the unit was not particularly well suited to its task. None of these policemen had any experience of the island and they had little knowledge of its peoples, culture or geography. British police were often intolerant of the difficulties confronting their Cypriot colleagues, and their establishment as an armed 'elite corps' distanced them from the normal routines of police work.[89]

In the second contingent of the UK Police Unit a greater effort was made to select younger and better recruits, and the net was widened to include all the County Constabularies. Some favoured recruiting from the Royal Ulster Constabulary, among whose ranks it was believed there might be many willing volunteers. Harding vetoed the idea: the RUC had the wrong image – their 'heavy-handed reputation' was 'unsuitable' for the political situation in Cyprus, he argued.[90] But the political realities of policing Cyprus made it difficult for any police unit to perform to the standards that Harding may have expected, and by the summer of 1956 the UK Police Unit was already gaining a reputation not so very different from that of the RUC. Discipline proved to be a serious problem. In June 1956 the officer commanding the first UK Police Unit, Lockley, confessed his 'mixed feelings' about the record of the unit. He was reported to have been 'ashamed of the behaviour and attitude of a certain element', expressing the opinion that 'some of the Home Forces had dumped their unwanted personnel on to Cyprus'.[91] The speed with which the unit had been recruited and the relatively low numbers of applicants – virtually all who applied were taken – left little scope for finding the higher-calibre constables that Harding had hoped for.

Despite its many shortcomings, the UK Police Unit was crucial to the British during the Emergency. Without the unit, and the other police staff seconded to Cyprus from Britain and various colonial forces, it is doubtful that the security forces would have been able to contain the violence to the extent they did. Before the Emergency, fewer than ten serving police officers were non-Cypriot. During 1955 than figure rose to above eighty. With the arrival of the first contingent of the UK Police Unit and a variety of other specialists (notably in intelligence and communications) in 1956 there were more than 550 non-Cypriot police serving on the island. This figure climbed to over 600 in 1958, but towards the end of the year all recruiting for the UK Police Unit ceased, as did all other secondments to the Cyprus Police.[92] Through 1959 the unit was allowed to run down very rapidly, and by the end of the year the number of British and colonial police on secondment to Cyprus had been reduced to 274.[93]

Special Branch, intelligence and EOKA

British Military Intelligence had taken care to monitor the activities of *Enosis* supporters in Greece from at least the early months of 1954. In this they were conspicuously more successful than the Cyprus Police, whose Greek Cypriot inspectors were an unreliable source of information and whose recently-formed Special Branch was believed to be a source of intelligence leaks. In November 1954 the long-serving, conservative and 'notoriously unprogressive' J. H. Ashmore was replaced as Commissioner of Police for Cyprus by G. H. Robbins, transferred from the Tanganyika Police. Along with Robbins' new broom came Mr P. B. Ray, an intelligence officer seconded to Cyprus for six months at the insistence of Military Intelligence and charged with reforming Special Branch and re-establishing it along lines that would allow it to fulfil a proper security role. Ray began by weeding out his office staff – transferring them to other arms of the service – and bringing in new officers for key areas of investigation. It was the work of Ray and his newly refurbished Special Branch, ably assisted by British Military Intelligence, which led to the capture of the *Aghios Georghios* in January 1955.[94] But even in this 'successful' operation, British intelligence of arms shipments from Greece and plans for the surveillance of the beaches along the Paphos coast was passed on to the *Enosis* activists by a Greek Cypriot member of Special Branch, Police Constable Pavlos Stokkos: had the insurgents been able to contact the caique on its journey from Athens they would have been able to avert its capture.[95]

The success of Special Branch in January 1955 was therefore notable if somewhat fortunate, and it was not to be repeated in any significant measure for many months. Even under the guidance of Ray, Special Branch was still an agency more used to dealing with immigration matters than with gathering political intelligence. He was able to bring in better techniques and to improve efficiency, but the security of the office was soon breached again as EOKA deliberately targeted Special Branch officers with intimidation, assault and even assassination.

[207]

Many officers, faced by death threats, became virtually inactive. In the summer of 1955 EOKA effectively won the intelligence battle with these tactics, successfully infiltrating Special Branch, the CID and even the police communications headquarters.[96] By contrast, the police failed to penetrate EOKA and had only a hazy picture of the organisation's membership and structure. This failure of intelligence presented the British with their most serious problem. 'Without intelligence we fight blind,' Robbins reported to Harding in October 1955:

> The volume of intelligence is neglible though there is still some high grade material coming in. Caches of arms and explosives remain unrecovered. The majority of the Special Branch and CID staffs will not in present circumstances go out in search of information. The reluctance must be overcome, hence the urgent need ... for expatriate officers for divisional Special Branches.[97]

Had it not been for the addition of staff from the UK, so urgently requested by Robbins, neither Special Branch nor the CID would have been able to function at all throughout 1956.

With the intelligence centre for British operations in the entire Middle East sector based in Cyprus, breaches of security had implications that went far beyond the colonial administration of the island. In October the War Office sent the Director of Military Intelligence to Cyprus to make recommendations for the complete reorganisation of intelligence at the General Headquarters, Middle East. His report was scathingly critical of the Colonial Office's mishandling of the situation up to the appointment of Harding, describing the history of the island's administration as 'deplorable'. He reserved his most condemnatory passages for the neglect of local policing services:

> it was not until the late head of police retired ... that the decision to establish a Special Branch was implemented even though this had been advocated for a number of years by the Security Service here and strongly pressed in September 1954. By that time it was too late and EOKA has virtually managed to break up the Special Branch by terrorism. The ordinary police are powerless and the fear of EOKA means that almost all the Greek villages in the island are now 100 per cent against the administration and pro-*Enosis*.[98]

The infiltration of EOKA by the Special Branch was the primary intelligence goal identified by the Director of Military Intelligence. The structure of EOKA made this very difficult to achieve. EOKA groups were invariably small, town and village units often numbering as few as half a dozen men and guerrilla bands in the mountains never larger than ten. Members of one unit seldom knew the details of other units, and information was carried by an elaborate network of messengers who committed everything to memory. The amount of information available to any single member of EOKA was therefore very limited. Grivas had devised this highly fragmented structure anticipating that security would be difficult to maintain and that betrayal would be likely. On his own estimation, by February 1956 EOKA consisted of only 1,033 men, organised in seven mountain gangs, seventy-five village groups and forty-seven town units.[99] Aside from these activists, EOKA sympathisers acted as informants within all sections of the administration, as 'shadows' to observe the movements of particular policemen (especially within Special Branch), and as 'demonstrators' within the towns. It was Grivas' intention that youths who began by hurling stones at soldiers in Nicosia and Famagusta would eventually become members of the active terrorist units. In this way EOKA would never lack for a supply of fighters.[100]

The British gained a clearer understanding of this structure in May and June 1956 with the capture of Grivas' diaries, along with other documents, during the army offensive (Operation Pepperpot) against EOKA mountain gangs.[101] The publication of these documents in September dealt a savage blow to EOKA morale, but the private use to which Special Branch was able to put the information gathered from these sources was even more significant. By the end of the year, even after a resurgence of EOKA activity in November following the withdrawal from Cyprus of 6,000 British troops because of the Suez crisis, improved intelligence had contributed to major successes against EOKA: thirty EOKA units had been broken up, twenty-two of the most wanted terrorist killed or arrested, and in a major operation against arms smugglers in Limassol forty-four EOKA members had been apprehended, including the leader of the smuggling ring, Lefteris Chrysohou. In January and early February 1957 Special Branch succeeded in breaking into the EOKA organisation in Nicosia. Two prominent Nicosia policemen, Andreas Rigas and Andreas Houvartas, were arrested for their membership of EOKA, and Andreas Chartas, the EOKA leader in the city, was captured with his chief courier and another substantial cache of documents uncovered in the raid on his house.[102] From the grim failures of the summer of 1955, it had taken the British more than eighteen months to gain the initiative in the intelligence war.

The capture of the Grivas diaries was an important element in this turn-around, but the structures and operations of British intelligence-gathering had also been significantly improved from October 1955. All the senior posts in Special Branch were filled by British officers, and even at Divisional level Greek Cypriot officers were kept at a distance from the organisation of anti-terrorist operations. Liaison with the military was greatly improved. From November 1955 army officers and police officers attended a joint staff school.[103] In the senior command structures both services were represented on the Intelligence Committee, the body which collated and analysed the information gathered by the District Security Committees. It was at the District level where the regular meetings between the Army Area Commander, the divisional Super-intendent of Police and the senior political officer (usually the District Commissioner) effectively integrated the British counter-insurgency campaign.[104] The day-to-day work of Special Branch was co-ordinated with the other security services under the office of the Chief of Intelli-gence. The first incumbent of this post was Ray, transferred in April 1955 from his advisory role with Special Branch.[105] In theory the officer in charge of Special Branch, who carried the rank of Assistant Chief Constable, was responsible to the Chief Constable: but in practice this officer more commonly dealt directly with the Chief of Intelligence, who reported directly to the Governor. This had the effect of separating Special Branch operations from the mainstream of the Cyprus Police: it functioned as a discrete unit, often more closely allied to military than to police operations. The 'separateness' of Special Branch became even more pronounced in 1958, when J. B. Prendergast was brought in from Kenya to take over in the combined role of Chief of Intelligence and Head of Special Branch. In a very real sense, Special Branch was more directly accountable to the Governor than to the Chief Constable of the Cyprus Police.[106]

If the British managed to establish a better intelligence-gathering system, they were not always well equipped to put it to good use. Throughout the Emergency the British struggled to find an adequate number of trained interrogators who spoke Greek.[107] Men brought in from other areas for their 'professionalism' lacked the local expertise that might allow a thorough interpretation of any intelligence gathered. There remained weaknesses which blunted the effectiveness of the intelligence-gathering of the security forces. Without proper information, police measures were too often indiscriminate: they could not avoid harming the innocent and thereby alienating potential supporters. Cordon-and-search operations, curfews and collective punishments yielded only small benefits yet were deeply detested by the local popu-lation. The methods of Special Branch, like other units of the security services, were sometimes heavy-handed rather than sophisticated and their successes were accumulated amongst frequent allegations of torture and brutality. In adopting coercive methods, the British laid themselves open to the same charges of intimidation as were levelled at EOKA.[108] The Cyprus Emergency was a dirty war: the police units which fought it bore little resemblance to the image of the 'model' English County Constabulary that Harding had hoped to see developed on the island.

The police and the transfer of power

The communal fighting during the summer of 1958 can be seen to have effectively reshaped the politics of the Cyprus Emergency in two important respects, each of which contributed to the settlement which brought Cyprus to independence in August 1960. Firstly, Macmillan had come to the decision that control of Cyprus could be sacrificed in exchange for guarantees regarding the security of British bases on Cyprus: [109] British strategic assessments had been modified in the light of the experience at Suez, while the burdens (political and financial) of controlling what appeared likely to be an escalating pattern of inter-communal violence was calculated to be much greater than the already considerable burden of dealing with EOKA. Secondly, Makarios had become alarmed that the communal fighting of the summer of 1958, followed by the EOKA campaign against British civilians in October and November, had combined to alienate international support for the notion of *Enosis* and that this had increased the possibility of Britain being able to impose a partition upon the island. Faced with the prospect of partition, Makarios choose independence as 'the better of two bad things'.[110]

In December 1958 Makarios asked Grivas to suspend EOKA activities to allow for discussions at the UN, and then in January and February he continued negotiations in Paris and London. The agreement to grant independence to Cyprus, free from the control of either Greece or Turkey and with the maintenance of British bases on the island, was signed on 19 February by the Prime Ministers of Greece, Turkey and Britain, and by Archbishop Makarios.[111]

The British security services had not defeated EOKA, but nor had EOKA successfully achieved the goal of *Enosis*. This can at least partly be attributed to the common purpose and mutual support that the EOKA campaign generated between the British administration and the Turkish minority. Political events had overtaken Grivas and his EOKA fighters, who were not directly represented in any of the meetings leading up to the February agreements. Grivas accepted the settlement with reluctance. Far from being the broken organisation that some had thought, EOKA had rebuilt during 1958 and had secured new supplies of arms, as the sheer quantity of EOKA weapons handed in at the amnesty of 1959 demonstrated.[112] EOKA was defeated politically, not militarily: but the impact of the campaign against the terrorists had a profound and long-term impact upon government and civil authority in Cyprus.

The changes in policing brought by the Emergency could not easily be undone. During the Emergency the police had been both politicised and militarised. To Greek Cypriots the changed ethnic composition of the Cyprus Police had been a clear sign of the favouritism shown by the

British toward the Turkish minority, who in turn saw their role in the police as a guarantee of their future security in an independent Cyprus. The increased use of the police in a directly political role, especially in surveillance of political activists, also posed a potential threat to both communities for the future. The ethnic make-up of the police (along with that of the civil service and municipal government) was therefore a central element in the negotiations that brought the political settlement of the Cyprus question during 1959. It was agreed that Cyprus was to have a police force and a *gendarmerie* with a combined strength of 2,000, with the ethnic composition of this force to be 70 per cent Greek and 30 per cent Turkish, thus roughly conforming to the pre-Emergency pattern of recruitment. To allow for the difficulties in making this adjustment in the limited time available prior to independence, an interim target of 60 per cent Greek to 40 per cent Turkish was accepted. A police sub-committee was formed to decide how this force should be dispersed: the police force, with a strength of 1,158, would be responsible for the urban areas, while the *gendarmerie* would police the rural areas.[113]

With only 1,770 Cypriots in the Cyprus Police at the beginning of 1959, additional recruitment was therefore urgently required. The initial British plan to transfer the better Turkish constables from the Mobile Reserve to the Cyprus Police went ahead but did not solve the more urgent problems of recruiting Greek Cypriots. By the end of 1959, 120 Greeks had been recruited and placed under training at the police college, and more than 900 applications were under consideration. However, many of these applicants failed to fulfil the basic educational requirements of literacy and a good knowledge of English.[114] Faced with the prospect of recruiting and training such a large proportion of the new force, the British took the more radical step of inviting seventy members of the force who were discharged or interdicted for political reasons during the Emergency to attend a refresher course 'with a view to their reinstatement after the independence of Cyprus'. The new Cyprus Police thus contained both the EOKA 'infiltrators' who had so successfully crippled police operations during the Emergency, and the Turkish recruits from the Mobile Reserve who had been brought in to replace them.[115]

Leadership and senior postings also presented difficulties for the reorganised police force. The British had deliberately removed Greek Cypriots from all senior positions and very few Turkish police had progressed through the ranks. Promotions of Cypriots had therefore to be dramatically accelerated between March 1959 and independence in August 1960 as British officers were transferred out of the colony. Over this period a force of 200 British police remained in the service of the Cyprus Police to assist in 'the smooth transfer of powers', and many of these officers supervised the 'training' of their successors.[116]

Even as these preparations for the transfer of powers moved ahead in 1959, two further policemen were murdered for their actions against terrorists during the Emergency, one a Special Branch sergeant the other a CID officer.[117] Old scores remained to be settled, and the bitterness held against the police could not easily be put aside. The British had been very well aware of both the immediate and the longer-term dangers of having policemen armed and deployed like soldiers, especially in urban areas. As a quasi-military force, perceived as the principal arm of state coercion, the police had been placed in the front line of the struggle against EOKA. They had established a degree of control over the situation, but at the cost of their legitimacy in the eyes of the majority of the people as an impartial civil authority. This was, of course, a product of the ethnic question that came to dominate police recruitment and deployment and which was enshrined in the agreements which brought independence.

It is undoubtedly true that the British learned from the cumulative experience of colonial counter-insurgency campaigning in the 1940s and 1950s in Palestine, Malaya and Kenya:[118] but there were few lessons for the police that could reconcile the contradictions between maintaining control against terrorist insurgency and keeping faith with the professed aim of moving the colonial police away from methods of coercion and towards policing by consent. In Cyprus communal politics predominated over any broader sense of the evolution of policing as a system of social control. Any remaining notion of policing by consent was entirely linked to the question of ethnicity.

Notes

1 Cyprus Police Annual Report, 1955, p. 1, Public Records Office, Kew [PRO], CO 69/59; 'Report of political situation, Cyprus', February 1956, PRO CO 926/209; Charles Foley and W. I. Scobie, *The Struggle for Cyprus* (Stanford, 1975), pp. 32–41; Nancy Crawshaw, *The Cyprus Revolt: an account of the struggle for union with Greece* (London, 1978), pp. 105–8; Crawshaw was permitted privileged access to official British documents on the Cyprus Emergency on an 'unattributable basis'. The decision to offer assistance to her arose from the idea that an official history of the Emergency should be written in order to project the 'British view' of events. See Macleod to Foot, 21 December 1959, and related papers in PRO CO 926/1076.

2 Crawshaw, *Cyprus Revolt*, p. 102.

3 John Reddaway, *Burdened with Cyprus: the British connection* (London, 1986), pp. 11–18. Reddaway was a senior official in the administration of Cyprus throughout the Emergency, and served on the Cyprus Intelligence Committee.

4 For example, Doros Alastos, *Cyprus Guerrilla: Grivas, Makarios and the British* (London, 1960); R. R. Denktash, *The Cyprus Triangle* (Nicosia, 1982); Evangelos Averoff-Tossizza, *Lost Opportunities: the Cyprus question, 1950–63* (translated from Greek by Timothy Cullen and Susan Kyriakidis: New York, 1986).

5 For other studies which view Cyprus from a comparative colonial perspective see: David J. Clark, 'The Colonial Police and anti-terrorism: Bengal 1930–36, Palestine 1937–47 and Cyprus 1955–59' (D.Phil, University of Oxford, 1978); and Thomas R. Mockaitis, *British Counterinsurgency, 1919–60* (London, 1990).

6 *Disturbance in Cyprus, October 1931*, Cmd 4045, passim.
7 Clark, 'Colonial Police', pp. 277–8; G. H. Kelling, *Countdown to Rebellion: British policy in Cyprus 1939–55* (Westport, CT, 1990), pp. 8–10; Sir Charles W. Gwynn, *Imperial Policing* (London, 1936), pp. 331–66; Sir Ronald Storrs, *Orientations* (New York, 1937), pp. 534–41.
8 Kelling, *Countdown*, p. 9.
9 Clark, 'Colonial Police', pp. 277, 390–1.
10 See D. M. Anderson and D. Killingray, 'Consent, coercion and colonial control: policing the empire, 1830–1940', in their *Policing the Empire: government, authority and control, 1830–1940* (Manchester, 1991), pp. 1–15.
11 Cyprus Police Commissioner Report, 1956, pp. 2–5, PRO CO 1037/11; Report of Colonial Office Inspector-General of Police, 1950, PRO CO 537/6245.
12 Clark, 'Colonial Police', p. 282.
13 Clark, 'Colonial Police', pp. 281–3; Kelling, *Countdown*, pp. 52–4; T. W. Adams, *AKEL: the Communist Party of Cyprus* (Stanford, 1971), remains the best history of the Left in Cyprus.
14 Kelling, *Countdown*, pp. 67–88.
15 Kelling, *Countdown*, pp. 77–9.
16 House of Commons Debates: vol. 458, col. 363, 17 November 1948; vol. 459, col. 358, 8 December 1948. See Clark, 'Colonial Police', p. 281 for a summary.
17 Clark, 'Colonial Police', p. 283.
18 H. C. Debs., vol. 531, cols. 504–25 for the statement and the debate which followed; Kelling, *Countdown*, pp. 140–2; Crawshaw, *Cyprus Revolt*, pp. 75–9.
19 Clark, 'Colonial Police', pp. 394–7.
20 Foley and Scobie, *Struggle for Cyprus*, pp. 13–22, *Terrorism in Cyprus: the captured documents* (HMSO London, 1956), p. 32; *The Church and Terrorism in Cyprus: a record of the complicity of the Greek-Orthodox Church in Cyprus in political violence* (Nicosia, 1957), p. 29.
21 Cyprus Police Commission Report 1956, p. 5, PRO CO 1037/11.
22 Cyprus Police Annual Report 1954, p. 4, PRO CO 69/57. For more detailed impressions, see the papers of G. H. Robbins [Robbins Papers], MSS. Medit. S, pp. 9–12, Rhodes House Library, Oxford. See also, Y. Yusuf, 'Cyprus: British strategic considerations and the recruitment of Turkish-Cypriot policemen, 1955–58' (MA dissertation, University of London, 1988), p. 20.
23 W. A. Muller, 'Report on Cyprus Police', 22 December 1955, p. 3, Robbins Papers; Cyprus Police Annual Report 1956, p. 5, PRO CO 69/61.
24 Cited in the Report of the Cyprus Police Commission, 1956, pp. 9–11, PRO CO 1037/11.
25 This argument is convincingly advanced by George Kelling from his reading of British policy documents leading up to the Emergency; Kelling, *Countdown*, pp. 148–53.
26 Cyprus Police Commissioner Report 1956, p. 12, PRO CO 1037/11.
27 'Political situation in Cyprus', minute (signature illegible), 25 January 1955, PRO CO 926/209.
28 The decision to begin the campaign came on 29 March, at a meeting between Grivas and Makarios at Kykko monastery. See, *Terrorism in Cyprus*, p. 20.
29 Crawshaw, *Cyprus Revolt*, pp. 114–15; Foley and Scobie, *Struggle for Cyprus*, p. 41. Afxentiou remained a fugitive with a price of £5,000 on his head until killed in the Makheras Valley by the British army in March 1957; Foley, *Island in Revolt*, pp. 140–1.
30 Foley and Scobie, *Struggle for Cyprus*, pp. 40–2.
31 Cyprus Police Annual Report 1955, PRO CO 69/59.
32 For the relations between Makarios and Grivas in the period before the violence of 1955, see especially G. Grivas, *The Memoirs of General George Grivas*, edited by Charles Foley (London, 1964).
33 Grivas, *Memoirs*, pp. 23, 39.
34 Foley and Scobie, *Struggle for Cyprus*, pp. 38, 45.
35 Foley and Scobie, *Struggle for Cyprus*, p. 39.
36 'Report by Stourton', 8 June 1955, p. 7, Robbins Papers. *The Times*, 5 and 7 September 1955.

37 For a discussion of 'fear' in the EOKA campaign in its comparative context, see Mockaitis, *British Counterinsurgency*, pp. 132–8.

38 Foley, *Island in Revolt*, pp. 35–8.

39 For an account of these riots, see J. N. Elderkin, 'In aid of the civil power', *Royal Engineers Journal*, LXX, no. 4 (December 1956), pp. 363–8.

40 Crawshaw, *Cyprus Revolt*, pp. 120–1.

41 Cyprus Police Annual Report 1955, PRO CO 69/59.

42 For a critique of these methods, also applied in Ireland, Malaya and Kenya, see Mockaitis, *British Counterinsurgency*, pp. 66–7, 135–6.

43 H. J. Scott, 'Police Mobile Reserve', *Cyprus Police Magazine*, I, no. 2 (November 1956), p. 12.

44 Harding to Lennox-Boyd, telegram, 17 October 1955, PRO CO 926/351.

45 Emergency Powers (Public Safety and Order) Regulations, 1955.

46 For his own account, see Sir John Harding: 'Terrorism in Cyprus I: ruthless leadership and the Church's blessing'; 'Terrorism in Cyprus II: fighting a stranglehold of fear'; 'Terrorism in Cyprus III: violence could still put the clock back', *Daily Telegraph*, 7, 8 and 9 January 1958.

47 'Notes on the State of the Force for HE, Governor', G. H. Robbins, 3 October 1955, Robbins Papers. A summary of the various official visits is to be found in the Cyprus Police Annual Report 1956, pp. 1–2, PRO CO 69/61.

48 Mockaitis, *British Counterinsurgency*, pp. 180–9.

49 'Notes for discussion with General Templar', no date, Robbins Papers; Clark, 'Colonial Police', p. 299.

50 Harding, 'Terrorism in Cyprus II'; W. R. Muller, 'Report on Cyprus police', 22 December 1955, p. 1, Robbins Papers. For a summary of those changes, the more important of which will be discussed below, see Cyprus Police Annual Report 1955, PRO CO 69/59.

51 The following paragraph is drawn from the Report of the Cyprus Police Commission, 1956, PRO CO 1037/11, and additional commentaries in two related files, PRO CO 1037/10 and CO 1037/55. The Commission was requested by Harding in February 1956. It is evident that Harding already had a clear view of the sort of reforms he wished to see. He also expressed his desire to replace Robbins, who he felt lacked 'the inspiration and drive' needed for the job, and pushed for the inclusion of White, then Chief Constable of Warwickshire, as one of the Commissioners. White ultimately replaced Robbins as Chief of Police. The suggestion that Young might serve on the Commission, whose Kenya and Malaya experience might have been thought to fit him well for the task, was rejected by Harding on the somewhat ambiguous grounds that his presence would 'generate local suspicion'; Harding to Lennox-Boyd, 14 February 1956, PRO CO 1037/11.

52 For an explicit public statement of this, see Cyprus Police Annual Report 1956, p. 20, PRO CO 69/61.

53 Cyprus Police Annual Report 1950, PRO CO 69/49.

54 Clark, 'Colonial Police', p. 401.

55 Cyprus Police Commission Report, p. 34, PRO CO 1037/11.

56 Harding, 'Terrorism in Cyprus II'.

57 Clark, 'Colonial Policing', p. 319.

58 Figures calculated from Cyprus Police Annual Reports.

59 Cyprus Police Annual Report 1955, p. 8, PRO CO 69/59.

60 Cyprus Police Annual Report 1958, p. 11, PRO CO 69/65; Clark, 'Colonial Police', pp. 357–60 for a general discussion of recruitment.

61 Cyprus Police Annual Report 1953, p. 22, PRO CO 69/55; Cyprus Police Annual Report 1955, pp. 31–2, PRO CO 69/59.

62 Clark, 'Colonial Police', p. 352.

63 Clark, 'Colonial Police', p. 351.

64 'Progress Report on Cyprus Police, 13 March 1956', Robbins Papers. In May 1957 the Auxiliary Police numbered 1,399 men, only 46 of whom were Greek Cypriots: Cyprus Police Annual Report 1957, p. 9, PRO CO 69/63.

65 Cyprus Police Commission Report, p. 39, PRO CO 1037/11.

66 *The Times*, 30 January 1956, p. 7. Yusuf, 'Turkish-Cypriot policemen', p. 18.

67 Cyprus Police Annual Report 1956, p. 8, PRO CO 69/61.

68 Yusuf, 'Turkish-Cypriot policemen', pp. 17–18.

69 *Terrorism in Cyprus*, pp. 60–1.

70 Crawshaw, *Cyprus Revolt*, pp. 406–8.

71 Yusuf, 'Turkish-Cypriot policemen', pp. 30–1. For full details of these and other cases see 'Communal incidents in Cyprus, PRO CO 926/422 and 'Political situation reports, Cyprus, 1954–56', especially reports from John Weston (DC Famagusta) for 1956, PRO CO 926/209.

72 Foot to Lennox-Boyd, series of telegrams, 18–22 July 1958, PRO CO 926/1015.

73 Weston (DC Famagusta) to Reddaway, 2 July 1956, Intelligence Report, PRO CO 926/209, reported the widespread Turkish belief that the British condoned their attacks on EOKA. See also Clark, 'Colonial Police', p. 336. TMT became more aggressive in its policies during 1958, and was responsible for the murder of two policemen. Cyprus Police Annual Report 1958, p. 14, PRO CO 69/65.

74 Yusuf, 'Turkish-Cypriot policemen', p. 23; 'Communal incidents in Cyprus, 1954–56', minute by Goldsworthy, 15 June 1956, PRO CO 926/422.

75 Cyprus Police Annual Report 1958, p. 17, PRO CO 69/65; Clark, 'Colonial Police', pp. 324, 328, 339.

76 Yusuf, 'Turkish-Cypriot policemen', p. 24; 'Methods used in controlling Rioters', PRO CO 926/900, provides papers relating to allegations concerning one incident in 1957.

77 *Allegations of Brutality in Cyprus* (Nicosia, 1957). In June 1958 a Special Investigation Group was established to look into all allegations of misconduct by the security services. The group investigated 325 cases between June and December 1958. Cyprus Police Annual Report 1958, p. 23, PRO CO 69/65. See also Clark, 'Colonial Police', pp. 362–4.

78 Weston to Reddaway, 2 July 1956, PRO CO 926/209.

79 Clark, 'Colonial Police', p. 403.

80 Further Colonial Police with Palestine and Kenya experience had been brought in by February 1957. Clark, 'Colonial Police', p. 358.

81 'Governor's Report to Chiefs of Staff', 5 June 1956, PRO CO 926/384.

82 Minute by Muller, 13 October 1955, PRO CO 1037/55.

83 Harding to Lennox-Boyd, 6 October 1955, PRO CO 1037/55.

84 Minute by Stourton, 1 June 1956, PRO CO 1037/53; Cyprus Police Commission Report 1956, para. 219.

85 Minute by Witney, 23 November 1955, and related papers, PRO CO 1037/55.

86 Witney, 'Note on Report of Cyprus Police Commission', 26 May 1956, PRO CO 1037/10.

87 Cyprus Police Commission Report, 1956, para. 221. For further papers see 'Reinforcements for the UK Police Unit in Cyprus, 1954–56', PRO CO 1037/53.

88 Robertson (Police Adviser) to Edmonds (Treasury), May 1956, PRO CO 1037/53.

89 Clark, 'Colonial Police', pp. 316, 358–60.

90 'Reinforcement of UK Police Unit, 1954–56', various papers, February to May 1956, PRO CO 1037/53.

91 Minute by Robertson, 1 June 1956, PRO CO 1037/53, reporting conversation with Lockley, Officer Commanding the UK Police Unit. See Clark, 'Colonial Police', pp. 362–4, for a general discussion of police discipline during the Emergency.

92 These figures calculated from the Cyprus Police Annual Reports for 1954–58.

93 Cyprus Police Annual Report 1959, p. 7.

94 Cyprus Police Annual Report 1954, p. 18, PRO CO 69/57. For criticism of Special Branch, see the Cyprus Police Commission Report 1956, PRO CO 1037/11.

95 Foley and Scobie, *Struggle for Cyprus*, pp. 32–3.

96 Crawshaw, *Cyprus Revolt*, p. 141; Clark, 'Colonial Police', p. 404; Harding, 'Terrorism in Cyprus I'.

97 'Notes on the state of the Force for HE Governor', 3 October 1955, p. 1, Robbins Papers.

98 'Informal report of Cyprus visit', Director Military Intelligence, 26 October 1955, PRO WO 216/889.

99 Grivas, *Memoirs*, pp. 66–7. The British made a similar estimate by June 1956: 'Governor's Report to Chiefs of Staff on security situation in Cyprus: minutes of meeting', 5 June 1956, PRO CO 926/384.

100 Crawshaw, *Cyprus Revolt*, pp. 101–13; Clark, 'Colonial Police', pp. 293–6.

101 Some documents were discovered at Lysi, others in Nicosia. *Terrorism in Cyprus*, *passim*; Crawshaw, *Cyprus Revolt*, pp. 198–200; Foley, *Island in Revolt*, pp. 97, 139–40; Foley and Scobie, *Struggle for Cyprus*, pp. 102–3.

102 Deputy Governor to Secretary of State, 6 December 1956, and subsequent papers, PRO CO 926/454. Foley and Scobie, *Struggle for Cyprus*, pp. 114–18, 120.

103 Clark, 'Colonial Police', p. 322.

104 Cyprus Police Annual Report 1955, p. 4, PRO CO 69/59. John Reddaway represented the Governor on the Intelligence Committee: see 'The Nature of EOKA, 1954–56', PRO CO 926/454, for minutes of some meetings of this committee.

105 Cyprus Police Annual Report 1955, p. 26, PRO CO 69/59.

106 Cyprus Police Annual Report 1958, pp. 5–8.

107 'Governor's Report to Chiefs of Staff', 5 June 1956, PRO CO 926/384.

108 Clark, 'Colonial Police', pp. 330–1. Mockiatis, *British Counterinsurgency*, pp. 135–6, 188–9.

109 R. Holland, *European Decolonisation: an introductory survey, 1918–81* (London, 1985), pp. 250–9.

110 Quoted in R. Stephens, *Cyprus: a place of arms* (London, 1966), p. 166.

111 Crawshaw, *Cyprus Revolt*, pp. 340–5; Foley and Scobie, *Struggle for Cyprus*, pp. 152–7.

112 For Grivas' own attitude, *Memoirs*, p. 192. On arms handed in, see Foley, *Island in Revolt*, p. 235.

113 Cyprus Police Annual Report 1959, PRO CO 69/67, pp. 2–3, 11.

114 Cyprus Police Annual Report 1959, pp. 2–3, 14.

115 Cyprus Police Annual Police 1959, p. 12. All Cypriots surely felt the irony and political poignancy of the appointment of Polycarpus Georgadjis, the EOKA leader in Nicosia and the man responsible for organising EOKA informers within the Cyprus Police, as Minister of the Interior in the government of independent Cyprus: his ministry was responsible for the police and prison services.

116 Cyprus Police Annual Report 1959, pp. 4, 7.

117 Cyprus Police Annual Report 1959, p. 15.

118 Mockaitis, *British Counterinsurgency*, presents strong evidence for the 'learning curve' of British experience, but the thrust of his argument is toward the military response. For a more equivocal comment on policing directly relevant to Cyprus, see Minute by A. M. MacDonald (Intelligence Adviser), 4 January 1959, PRO CO 926/1076.

INDEX

Note: Page references in italics indicate tables and illustrations.